GLOBAL PERSPECTIVES ON THE NEW TESTAMENT

GLOBAL PERSPECTIVES
ON THE NEW TESTAMENT

EDITORS

Mark Roncace
Wingate University

Joseph Weaver
Wingate University

Boston   Columbus   Indianapolis   New York   San Francisco   Upper Saddle River
Amsterdam   Cape Town   Dubai   London   Madrid   Milan   Munich   Paris   Montréal   Toronto
Delhi   Mexico City   São Paulo   Sydney   Hong Kong   Seoul   Singapore   Taipei   Tokyo

Editor in Chief: Ashley Dodge
Publisher: Nancy Roberts
Editorial Assistant: Molly White
Director of Marketing: Brandy Dawson
Executive Marketing Manager: Kelly May
Marketing Coordinator: Jessica Warren
Managing Editor: Denise Forlow
Program Manager: Mayda Bosco
Senior Operations Supervisor: Mary Fischer
Operations Specialist: Eileen Corallo
Art Director: Jayne Conte
Cover photo: Shutterstock, Inc.
Cover design: Bruce Kenselaar
Director of Digital Media: Brian Hyland
Digital Media Project Manager: Tina Gagliostro
Full-Service Project Management and Composition: Integra Software Services, Pvt. Ltd.
Printer/Binder: RRD/Harrisonburg
Cover Printer: RRD/Harrisonburg
Text Font: 11/13, Times LT Std

Credits and acknowledgments borrowed from other sources and reproduced, with permission, in this textbook appear on appropriate page within text (or on page 223).

Many of the designations by manufacturers and seller to distinguish their products are claimed as trademarks. Where those designations appear in this book, and the publisher was aware of a trademark claim, the designations have been printed in initial caps or all caps.

Library of Congress Cataloging-in-Publication Data
CIP information not available at time of publication.

10 9 8 7 6 5 4 3 2 1

ISBN 10: 0-205-90920-5
ISBN 13: 978-0-205-90920-9

BRIEF CONTENTS

CONTENTS

PREFACE

This book is a lot like the Bible itself in that it is a diverse collection of writings emanating from a variety of geographic, social, cultural, political, economic, and religious contexts. But wait—that first sentence has already indicated a great deal about us (the editors) and about our views of the Bible. Maybe we've already revealed more about us—our background, education, life experiences, and so on—than about the Bible itself. To us, the Bible—and specifically the New Testament—is indeed an eclectic anthology, much like this book. However, if someone else were to have written that first sentence, they might have started by introducing the Bible as the infallible Word of God, a book that provides moral and ethical guidelines for everyday life and God's plan of salvation. Another person might have opened with the claim that the Bible is one of the most toxic texts ever produced and that its continuing influence in our world is one of the great mysteries and tragedies of our day. Incidentally, neither of these two potential perspectives is incompatible with our statement that the Bible is an eclectic anthology.

The point is this: It's all about perspective. People are different. They approach the Bible with their own various ideas, beliefs, and assumptions, which means there are a myriad of possible ways to write that first sentence. Nobody can say anything without saying something about themselves.

But you may have already known that. Most people living in our postmodern world— or whatever we are supposed to call it now (that's also a matter of perspective)—realize that there is no neutral, objective perspective from which to assess things, no position that is unencumbered by a specific life setting. Everyone comes from somewhere. Everyone is born in a certain time and place to certain parents and has had certain experiences that shape how we see the world. All those "certainties," to which many more could be added, make up who you are; they define your specific context and perspective. They also mean that you can be certain that your interpretation of a given biblical text is not the only way that it can be interpreted. While the idea of varied perspectives is hardly new, you may not be aware of the extent and nature of some of those different readings. Hence this book.

FORMAT OF THE BOOK

Herein we have gathered four essays around 22 New Testament texts. Our intention is for you to read the given portion of the New Testament and then to consider what four people from various contexts and backgrounds have written about it. In doing so, you will see the biblical text in a new light; you will learn something about the various interpreters and their particular location; and you will discover something about yourself. Put differently, when we encounter views that are different from our own, we have the wonderfully enriching experience of learning about (1) the New Testament and (2) other interpreters and the places from which they come, which in turn (3) helps us see our own lives and views in a new way. We are thus engaging the New Testament, each other, and ourselves. It's a dynamic, interactive triangle.

But all three corners of the triangle must be present. The importance of your corner bears emphasizing: You must read the New Testament for yourself. This is absolutely indispensable. You must read carefully and develop your own insights and analyses. This will not only help you "hear" the biblical voice (filtered through your own context, of course), but it will also enable you to appreciate the four different perspectives. We instructed the authors of the essays not to summarize the New Testament passage; there is no sense in using valuable space on something that you can do for yourself. So, you must uphold your end of the deal: You must read the Bible! Yes, you are reading a translation of the Bible and a translation is already an interpretation; but, still, it's crucial that you experience the text on your own.

To encourage you to do this, we have not included any of our own introductory material to each biblical passage, as it would inevitably reflect our own perspective, which would defeat the book's purpose of including as many different points of view as possible. Furthermore, you should read the essays with a Bible in hand; many times the authors include only the biblical reference (not the full quotation), which you would do well to look up in order to help you interact thoughtfully with the essay.

To facilitate further your engagement with all three corners of the triangle, we have included four questions at the end of each set of essays (one question for each essay). Use the questions to prompt your critical interaction with the various essays. If the question could occasionally be answered "yes" or "no," don't simply leave it at that. Assume that "Why or why not?" or "Explain your answer" follows—we just thought it unnecessary to write it out for you. Yes, our questions inevitably reveal our own interests and ideas, so please feel free to add your own questions and to question our questions. In fact, if you don't, you probably aren't thinking hard enough.

There are a mere 88 essays in this book; this, needless to say, is a pittance of the possible number. A book titled *Global Perspectives on the New Testament* should not be a book at all, but rather a multivolume encyclopedia. But if that were the case, you would have had a much harder time buying it and carrying it around. Think for a moment about how this book barely scratches the proverbial surface of global perspectives on the New Testament. If there are approximately 7 billion people in the world and if only 1 in every 1,000 has something to say about the Bible, then our 86 authors represent only about 0.000012 percent of perspectives on the Bible. We make this point—odd as it may seem—because we hope this collection of essays encourages you to seek out many more interpretations of the New Testament, whether they be from scholarly books and commentaries or friends and family over lunch. These essays are intended to start conversations, not end them. It's a big world, and this book is terribly small. We are hoping you will create the rest of the encyclopedia.

We have done our best to assemble a wide range of views. Nevertheless, the book should probably be titled *Global* Perspectives* on the New Testament**. With the first asterisk we call attention to the fact that as English speakers we could only accept essays written in English. We also solicited submissions via e-mail. As such, by requiring contributors to write in our native language and to have Internet access, we have by necessity precluded a majority of the world's population. Furthermore, we live and work in the United States. Most of our personal and professional connections are here; therefore, there are far more contributors from the United States than any other single country. Because of this, we feel as though we should iterate that we mean "global" in more than simply the geographic sense. There is religious, ethnic, ideological, political, and socioeconomic diversity in the essays, and those elements, of course, are not bound by particular geographic location. We also assembled contributors from various walks of life; this book is much more "global" than a typical collection of professional academic papers.

The second asterisk shows that, while limiting our fingerprints as much as possible, the essays were proofread and minimally edited. We made the decision to standardize spelling and punctuation, and even to capitalize the word "Bible." Beyond that, we did little else. We did not standardize, for example, the style of referring to eras (B.C.E., C.E., B.C., A.D.); we did not change inclusive or non-inclusive language or capitalization for pronouns referring to deity. The third asterisk denotes that the term "New" in "New Testament" reflects a Christian perspective in so far as it implies that there is something "Old" in need of fulfillment. Furthermore, although we did not begin with a prescribed list of 22 New Testament texts for which to solicit essays, we did, of course, ultimately determine which texts the book would address.

Let's mention one more asterisk-worthy matter. You will notice that each set of essays opens with a page featuring a map locating each of the four authors in that set. But where on the map should we put each author's dot? Where the author was born? Where they have spent most of their life? Where they went to school? Where they were when they wrote the essay? Where they reside now? The place about which they write? It's not that easy. We live in a transient world. We have decided to put the dot in the place, or places, about which they are writing. Or if geographic location or context is not central to their essay, then the dot is located in the place of their primary current residence. Hence all the dots should have an asterisk to that effect too.

In short, this is only one of many possible ways to assemble a book called *Global Perspectives on the New Testament*. Despite its limitations and the inherent difficulty of producing a book of this nature, we are confident that you will find these perspectives to be enlightening and engaging. There are many additional introductory and hermeneutical issues that we could explore at the outset, but in the interest of space, let us limit ourselves to two final thoughts. First, the New Testament is the sacred literature of the Christian tradition, but the influence and impact of the New Testament—and the Bible as a whole—have extended beyond Christianity. People who are not Christian read or are familiar with the New Testament. In our effort to offer as many global perspectives as possible, we have included views by those who do not treat the Bible as Scripture. We fully understand that some people with a faith commitment to the text may feel that those outside the tradition do not have anything to offer. We respectfully disagree, and both of us—for the record—are in the Christian tradition.

Our world is too big and complex to ignore thoughtful and intelligent readers simply because they approach the text without a set of traditional religious lenses—or because they come from a tradition other than Christianity. We sincerely appreciate all of the authors of these essays for allowing their work to be published in a book that includes approaches with which they may strongly disagree.

Second, if the essays are eclectic, then so too are the biblical texts that they interpret. Much of this has to do with the nature of the New Testament—it's not a tidy collection, and some parts have garnered more attention than others. As a result, sometimes the essays in a chapter are in direct dialogue over the same specific text or topic, while other times they address different portions of the passage. Hopefully, every set of essays will draw you into the discussion.

The Bible has a sort of "unevenness" to it, and so do the various sets of essays that follow, which in turn reflects the complex nature of the world in which we live. And thus, we end this short Introduction where it began: If the perspectives herein feel somewhat scattered—all over the place—then we say, "Yes, exactly, and so is both our global world and the New Testament." Hence a book with our title will inevitably be a bit messy. And yes, this view again reflects our particular perspective as white, Western-educated, middle-class, heterosexual men in the Christian tradition. From where we stand, the following essays offer fresh, compelling readings of the New Testament from a variety of perspectives. Tell us what you think from where you stand.

STUDENT AND TEACHER RESOURCES

This text is available in a variety of formats—digital and print. To learn more about our programs, pricing options, and customization, visit www.pearsonhighered.com.

MySearchLab with eText

A passcode-protected website that provides engaging experiences that personalize learning, MySearchLab contains an eText that is just like the printed text. Students can highlight and add notes to the eText online or download it to an iPad. MySearchLab also provides a wide range of writing, grammar, and research tools plus access to a variety of academic journals, census data, Associated Press news feeds, and discipline-specific readings to help hone writing and research skills.

Instructor's Resource Manual and Test Bank (0-205-92700-9)

This valuable resource provides chapter outlines, lecture topics, and suggested media resources. In addition, test questions in short essay formats are available for each chapter.

MyTest (0-205-95461-8)

This computerized software allows instructors to create their own personalized exams, to edit any or all of the existing test questions, and to add new questions. Other special features of this program include the random generation of test questions, the creation of alternative versions of the same test, scrambling question sequences, and test previews before printing.

ACKNOWLEDGMENTS

As the editors, not the authors, of this book, the list of people we gratefully acknowledge can be found in the Table of Contents. Indeed, the 86 contributors deserve more thanks than we can offer. Their timely and insightful work made this project a reality. We offer our sincerest gratitude to each and every one of them.

We also express appreciation to our wonderful colleagues at Wingate University for designing and implementing a new core curriculum, which was the impetus for this textbook. Without their vision and support, this book never would have happened. We are so grateful to the reviewers who took the time to assess this text prior to its publication: Wayne Brouwer, Hope College; Steven Godby, Broward College-South Campus; Warren Johnson, East Texas Baptist University; and Jeff Tillman, Wayland Baptist University. We also thank Maggie Barbieri for expert editorial guidance and Nancy Roberts for her willingness to take on such an unwieldy project.

Mark Roncace

Joseph Weaver

CHAPTER 1

BIRTH OF JESUS

Matthew 1–2; Luke 1–2

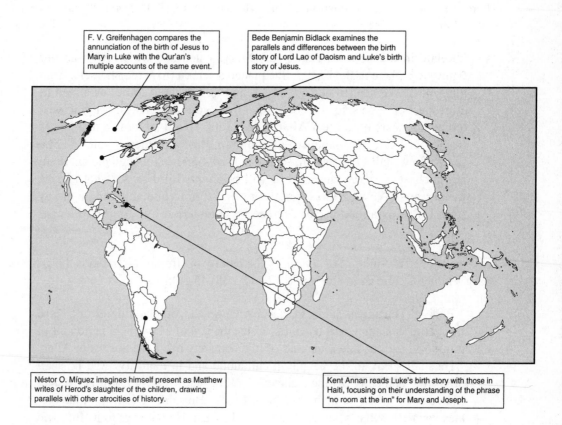

F. V. Greifenhagen compares the annunciation of the birth of Jesus to Mary in Luke with the Qur'an's multiple accounts of the same event.

Bede Benjamin Bidlack examines the parallels and differences between the birth story of Lord Lao of Daoism and Luke's birth story of Jesus.

Néstor O. Míguez imagines himself present as Matthew writes of Herod's slaughter of the children, drawing parallels with other atrocities of history.

Kent Annan reads Luke's birth story with those in Haiti, focusing on their understanding of the phrase "no room at the inn" for Mary and Joseph.

READINGS

The Annunciation to Mary in the Qur'an
F. Volker Greifenhagen

Comparing the Birth Stories of Lord Lao and Jesus
Bede Benjamin Bidlack

Herod's Slaughter of the Children and Other Atrocities
Néstor O. Míguez

Reading Luke's Christmas Story with Those in Haiti
Kent Annan

THE ANNUNCIATION TO MARY IN THE QUR'AN

F. Volker Greifenhagen (Canada)

The annunciation by a divinely sent messenger to Mary of the birth of a special son is narrated not only in Luke's gospel (1:26–38) but also in the Muslim scripture, the Qur'an, originating with the prophet Muhammad in the seventh century C.E. in Arabia. There the story is told not just once, but twice. In Surah 19 *Maryam* ("Mary") 16–21 we read thus:

> [16]Relate in the book (the story of) Mary, when she withdrew from her family to a place in the East. [17]She placed a screen (to screen herself) from them; then We sent to her our angel, and he appeared to her as a man in all respects. [18]She said, "I seek refuge from you to (Allah) most gracious; (come not near) if you fear Allah." [19]He said, "No, I am only a messenger from your Lord (to announce) to you the gift of a righteous son." [20] She said, "How shall I have a son, seeing that no man has touched me and I am not unchaste?" [21]He said, "So (it will be); your Lord says, 'That is easy for me, and (We wish) to appoint him as a sign to humanity and a mercy from Us'; it is a matter (so) decreed." (Translation by 'Abdullah Yusuf 'Ali, 2001)

It is again found in Surah 3 *Ali 'Imran* ("The Family of 'Imran"—'Imran is the name of Mary's father according to Qur'an 66:12 and 3:35) 45–49:

> [45]Behold! The angels said, "O Mary! Allah gives you glad tidings of a word from Him; his name will be Christ Jesus, the son of Mary, held in honour in this world and the hereafter, and of (the company of) those nearest to Allah. [46]He shall speak to the people in childhood and in maturity. And he shall be of (the company of) the righteous." [47]She said, "O my Lord! How shall I have a son when no man has touched me?" He said, "Even so: Allah creates what He wills; when He has decreed a plan, He but says to it 'Be,' and it is! [48]And Allah will teach him the book and the wisdom, the law and the gospel. [49]And (appoint him) a messenger to the children of Israel, (with this message): 'I have come to you with a sign from your Lord, in that I make for you out of clay, as it were, the figure of a bird, and breath into it, and it becomes a bird by Allah's leave. And I heal those born blind, and the lepers, and I quicken the dead, by Allah's leave. And I declare to you what you eat, and what you store in your houses. Surely therein is a sign for you if you did believe.' " (Translation by 'Abdullah Yusuf 'Ali, 2001)

Furthermore, the Qur'an alludes to the annunciation in two other verses. Surah 21 *al-Anbiya* ("The Prophets") 91: "And (remember) her who guarded her chastity: We breathed in to her of Our Spirit, and We made her and her son a Sign for all peoples."

And Surah 66 *al-Tahrim* ("Prohibition") 12: "And Mary, the daughter of 'Imran, who guarded her chastity; and We breathed into (her body) of Our Spirit; and she testified to the truth of the words of her Lord and of his Revelations, and was one of the devout (servants)." (Translation by 'Abdullah Yusuf 'Ali, 2001.)

The qur'anic versions of the annunciation to Mary accord with Luke's story in many respects. An angel announces that she will bear a son, to which she responds with bewilderment since she is a virgin. Her virginity, however, is no obstacle, for God is able to create a child within her without a human father. The Qur'an unpacks the angel's more terse assertion in Luke's gospel that "nothing will be impossible with God" (1:37) by having the messenger explain that when God decides anything, God merely needs to say "Be!" and it is—it is thus easy for God to do what is impossible for mortals. God's Spirit is involved in the miraculous conception in both the biblical and qur'anic accounts, and in both versions the child will be named Jesus. Mary devoutly accepts the message in both Luke and the Qur'an, although her assent in the Qur'an is not explicitly verbalized as it is in Luke. Finally, like the account in Luke, both of the fuller qur'anic accounts of the annunciation are preceded by the story of the annunciation to Zechariah, who, as in the biblical version, distrusts the announcement and is struck mute.

There are also differences. The Qur'an is not interested in details such as the town where Mary lives, and it omits entirely the sign of Elizabeth's pregnancy and any mention of Joseph. The qur'anic versions especially highlight the chastity of Mary by depicting her as withdrawing alone from her family and screening herself from them (19:16–17), a motif that leads to a heightened sense of Mary's alarm when she is approached in her seclusion by the messenger, whom the Qur'an describes as appearing like a human man in all respects. Mary, fearing molestation, needs to warn him off by seeking refuge with God. In an atmosphere charged with sexual danger, more explicit than the confusion or perplexity she experiences in the Lukan account, Mary displays proper propriety. Finally, one of the titles to be given to her son in the Qur'an is "son of Mary," a name that stands out as unusual in a patriarchal context in which descent was reckoned from one's father, and thus it serves to emphasize even further Mary's virginal status. (The title "Jesus son of Mary" appears in Mark 6:3, but seems there to be used as a slur against him.)

But the biggest differences lie in the description of the son that will be born to Mary. In the qur'anic accounts, he is not named "son of God"; nor is his career portrayed as that of a king, although he is called Christ or Messiah. Rather, the Qur'an emphasizes his qualities of righteousness and honor, and describes his career in terms of learning the holy scriptures and being sent as messenger to the children of Israel with miraculous powers of healing, animation of dead matter, and foreknowledge. This depiction accords with the prophetic paradigm applied by the Qur'an to all those that it names prophets; namely, that they are righteous folk who function primarily to bring a message from God to a specific people, encapsulated in a book, and confirmed by miracles.

Interestingly, some Muslim commentators have discussed whether Mary herself functions as a prophet in that she receives a "word" from God (3:45). While this "word" is usually glossed as a mere reference to God's command "Be!" by which

Jesus is miraculously conceived, it bears an uncanny resemblance to the divine *logos* or word which is used of Jesus in the Gospel of John (1:1–18). Rather than some willful misunderstanding, the Qur'an has here redirected emphasis on Jesus as God's word, and on his miraculous conception, away from indications or proofs of his divine status to demonstrations of the divine creative power of God. Even Jesus' miracles, the Qur'an insists, are performed by God's permission (3:49).

In shifting the focus in this manner, the Qur'an gets behind the postbiblical Christian doctrinal ideology of Christ's status as God. Luke, for instance, depicts Jesus mainly as subordinate to God (see especially the early Christian preaching described in Acts, such as 2:22–24; 3:13, 17–26; 4:27–28), joined to God by the Spirit but not identical with God. Overall, the Qur'an attempts to steer a middle course between what it sees as the excessive claims made about Jesus by Christians, on the one hand, and the rejection of Jesus and his significance by Jews, on the other. The Qur'an rejects the interpretation, found in Jewish literature, of the story of Jesus' birth from a virgin as a cover-up of fornication but it does not go as far as Christians in deifying Jesus even though Jesus clearly has a preeminent status among the prophets in the Qur'an. The Qur'an's versions of the annunciation to Mary, with their insistence on her chastity and virginity equally and her submission to God's will, as also her son's submission, can trigger a reading of Luke's account of the annunciation uncoupled from later theological overlays.

F. V. Greifenhagen is Associate Professor of Religious Studies at Luther College, University of Regina, Canada.

COMPARING THE BIRTH STORIES OF LORD LAO AND JESUS

Bede Benjamin Bidlack (United States)

Laozi was a philosopher of ancient China and is traditionally considered the author of *Daode jing* and the founder of Daoism (Taoism). Over time he became revered as a deity; indeed by the second century A.D. he was worshipped as Lord Lao. In Daoist beliefs, Lord Lao comes down when the ways of humankind fall into grave error, wander from the Dao—the Ultimate Reality in the Daoist worldview—and need instruction on how to get back into harmony with the Dao. He appears to the ruler or to a person who later becomes a religious leader as a result of the encounter.

In sixth-century China, Daoists and Buddhists were competing for royal favor and met in a series of court debates. The question concerned who was prior: Laozi or Buddha. The tradition with the older religious founder was considered the superior religion. To prove the superiority of Daoism over Buddhism, Daoists looked to the *Scripture of the*

Conversion of the Barbarians (*Huahu Jing*). The *Scripture* was written from a tradition of transformations of Lord Lao when he descended into the world on a regular basis to provide guidance to rulers and to reveal sacred scriptures.

The central story of the *Scripture* tells of how Lord Lao traveled West, transmitted the *Daode jing*, then continued to convert the Indians to Buddhism, which Daoists understood as a diluted form of Daoism. A later version of the story escalated the polemical character of the text: Laozi and his companion Yin Xi journeyed to the West; there was an exchange of banquets with the barbarian kings; Laozi and Yin Xi underwent ordeals; after emerging from the ordeals, they punished the barbarians for their unbelief; they tried to civilize the barbarians with Buddhist precepts; Laozi left to convert other lands, while Yin Xi remained and was known as the Buddha. In these narratives, Lord Lao was the creator of the universe, a supporter of rulers, the source of scriptures, and the personification of the Dao. The *Scripture* describes the arrival of Lord Lao this way:

> In those days, in the reign of Tanjia of Yin with the year star in *geng-shen*…the Highest Venerable Lord came down from the eternal realm of the Dao. He harnessed a cloud of three energies and strode on the essence of the sun. Following the rays of the nine luminaries, he entered into the mouth of the Jade Maiden of Mystery and Wonder. Taking refuge in her womb, he became a man.
>
> In the year *gengshen*, on the fifteenth day of the second month, he was born in Bo. Nine dragons sprinkled water over him to rinse and wash his body then they transformed into nine springs.
>
> At that time, the Venerable Lord had white hair. He was able to walk upon birth. A lotus flower sprouted under each step he took. After nine steps, he pointed to heaven with his left hand, to the earth with his right hand and announced to the people…"I shall reveal the highest law of the Dao. I shall save all things moving and growing, the entire host of living beings."

While the birthing of Lord Lao contains many parallels with that of Jesus, four differences are apparent at the outset. First, Dao is not equivalent to God, as it is impersonal and not above the universe, but it *is* the universe. This is a monistic worldview. Therefore, Lord Lao, the embodiment of the Dao, is the universe as well. Second, Lord Lao is not the son of the Dao, as Jesus is the Son of the Father. Lord Lao is a particular divine person who is accessible to the world. Third, this is one of many of Lord Lao's appearances, but Jesus comes only once. Fourth, Laozi's body itself is different from any person's body, although it is very real and of flesh and bone. His body is the representation of the Dao accompanied by mythical markings—such as white hair at birth or bone protrusions on the forehead —that are rich symbols and points of meditation. The marks are similar to those attributed to the body of the Buddha in Mahayana Buddhism.

The interaction with Buddhism in the court debates and elsewhere resulted in a free exchange between Buddhism and Daoism. The birth narrative shows close links to the stories of Buddha's birth. By adopting the birth story and other elements of

Buddhism, Daoism claims itself as a universal religion and Lord Lao as the seat of all creation and the source of all teachings, particularly of Buddhism. But what about the similarities with Jesus?

The birth of Laozi is situated in history, even to the date and location, as is Jesus' birth in Luke. In contrast to Jesus' annunciation, Lord Lao's conception is told with a spectacle of light and energies, but he ends up, like Jesus, in the womb of a woman of cosmic importance (Luke 1:26–27), where he became man. His birth is accompanied by dragons, which not only serve to represent nature—as do the presumed animals in Jesus' stable (2:7)—but also angels, insofar as they are beings that travel between heaven and earth (2:9, 13). Immediately at birth, Lord Lao is able to walk and talk—an image analogous to Jesus' advanced wisdom at a young age (2:46–47). Finally, he is identified as the savior of the world (2:11).

Authors of both Luke and the *Scripture* tell of events and characteristics of the descended deity to express that the child will be different from ordinary people and will do something great. The experience of the divine coming into our world is too fantastic for common words. The event is beyond our normal experience, so special words or literary devices are necessary to tell it. The images draw attention to the special identity of these people. Noticeably, both are identified as saviors. But what does it mean for Lord Lao to be a savior and is that the same role that Jesus has?

Salvation as the end of earthly struggles was such a radical departure from Chinese thought that an outside influence cannot be ruled out. Up until that time, dynasties were empowered by a Heavenly Mandate that bestowed on the sovereign, and therefore the entire kingdom, the power to provide prosperity, security, and integrity. A dynasty rose by receiving *de,* "virtue" or "power," from Heaven. Upon wandering from the Dao, the Heavenly Mandate and its *de* would be rescinded by Heaven, causing the downfall of the kingdom. It would be given to the next dynasty, which would follow the next predictable fate of rise and fall.

In texts like the *Scripture*, Lord Lao brings salvation to the kingdom, which was the cosmos to the ancient peoples of China. "Salvation" does not mean redemption from sin, but harmonization with Dao. Lord Lao harmonizes by making several appearances to rulers at times when they have wandered from the Dao. Upon following his divine teachings, the kingdom regains harmony with the Dao and is on the right track for reaching the final age, the Age of Great Peace. In this way, Lord Lao saves little by little until the Age of Great Peace blooms and a perfect harmony with the Dao endures on earth forever.

The *Scripture's* focus is not on the final age, but on the claim of the conversion of the barbarians, as its title states, thereby establishing Daoism as the superior religion over Buddhism. In the court debates, Lord Lao's dramatic birth, acceptance of disciples, and movement to the West were primarily for the purpose of converting those beyond China's borders.

Bede Benjamin Bidlack is Assistant Professor in the Department of Theology at St. Anselm College, United States.

HEROD'S SLAUGHTER OF THE CHILDREN AND OTHER ATROCITIES

Néstor O. Míguez (Argentina)

The Feast of the Holy Innocents was established in the Christian calendar in memory of the slaughter of the children of Bethlehem, which was ordered by Herod upon hearing of the birth of the one who would be Messiah, as we read in Matthew 2. In the story, Joseph receives a warning in a dream and flees with Jesus and Mary, but the remaining children in the village are murdered.

Matthew did not allow the memory of the homicidal Herod to be erased. Herod repaired the temple but destroyed the people. He obtained the throne, backed by the (Roman) Empire, and ends up killing the children of his own people to avoid losing his own unjust power. Soldiers against children, weapons against weeping: terror as the king's method. He who fears losing his throne cannot help but see threats at every turn. But what of the mothers of the innocent who refuse to be comforted.

From my Argentina, I stand alongside Matthew as he writes his gospel. I sit at his worktable and say to him: "For centuries, the commentators will debate if your account is historical dear Matthew, if it squares with the facts, or how theologically to justify the death of the innocent to save the life of the savior. Go ahead and include these details, brother. History will prove them true. I can tell you, from my sad experience that the facts align with your account. Time and again the unjust allies of the Empire—the powers that be—perpetuate their power by killing the innocent. They call it 'preemptive war' or 'collateral damage.' Sad copies of Herod."

I go on, "What is more, Matthew, I know those mothers who refuse to be comforted. They have names: Azucena Villaflor, Adela Antokoletz, Nora Cortinas, Hebe de Bonafini, Estela Carlotto. Some have suffered the same fate as their children; some have died. Others live on, refusing to be consoled, refusing to lower their hands—ceaselessly marching in circles in front of Herod's home, in the town square of uprisings and deaths, the square of the people and of treasons, demanding on behalf of their children. Their white headscarves are an emblem of pain turned to struggle—those mothers who refuse to be comforted because their pain is a part of their struggle. They are the untiring grandmothers who trace the footprints of horror because they know that there they may find, hidden away, the heirs of their dreams."

I carry myself away with my own words, forgetting Matthew and going on: I see those beloved faces—some known, some unknown—equally lovable in their expression of terror. I, like Matthew as he writes, am a witness of the facts even as I speak. "Cry out, mothers of pain and of hope. Do not cease to cry out throughout the centuries, you mothers of Rama and Bethlehem. Alongside the mothers of Iraq and Gaza, and again of Bethlehem. With the mothers of Auschwitz or of Armenia, and the mothers of all the genocides of humanity's senseless history. Weep and cry with the mothers of all our indigenous peoples of America, decimated in their own lands by the homicidal zeal of the conquistador in search of gold and power. Cry with the mothers of Soweto, of Hiroshima, with the millions of mothers of the holocausts of the innocent that pride, ambition, and prejudice sow in our history. With the mothers of Biafra and Haiti, seeing their children die from imposed hunger, from calculated misery. Join your worn voices with the mothers of children born with deformities due to senseless pollution of lands and waters, or in the hells let loose by the napalm of Vietnam. Join together with millions upon millions of those voices that have witnessed the crushing of the heads of children by the homicidal hordes that the empires and their allies, stocked with arms and money, have unleashed time and again on defenseless peoples. May your cries of terror resound forever, without ceding to the offers of comfort from those who purchase consciences. Do not listen to the sweet words with which those preachers of undignified reconciliation wish to soften you. May you never cease in your determined lament, that unceremonious demand for life, the endless marches around the town squares; may the demand for justice that rises from the bottom of the centuries and remains to this day never be silenced, so that the Empire may never sleep without feeling, even if it covers its ears, that its massacres have not been forgotten."

Matthew looks at me, astonished. The names are strange, the situations familiar. "Write, dear Matthew, brother. Write. Your words call out to thousands throughout time. History will sadly corroborate your story, your gospel encouragingly faithful. Keep writing this mirror of the human soul, keep going and don't stop until the necessary resurrection," I say to him, as if the Spirit had not already told him.

Néstor O. Míguez is Professor of New Testament Studies at ISEDET, Buenos Aires, Argentina.

READING LUKE'S CHRISTMAS STORY WITH THOSE IN HAITI
Kent Annan (Haiti)

It was Christmas Eve in Haiti seven years ago. My wife, Shelly, and I were living there and had gathered on our porch under the palm trees and starry sky with a dozen friends and neighbors. We'd shared a meal of rice and beans and all the fixings. The plates had been cleared away.

Dusk settled, conversation continued, and someone suggested reading the Christmas story. We got our Creole Bible, lit a kerosene lamp, and one of our neighbors, a young man with a strong clear voice, read aloud the narrative of Jesus' birth from the gospel of Luke. The story was read a couple of times and then Shelly or I (can't remember who) asked what stood out to people.

We were informally using *lectio divina*, an ancient approach to reflecting on Scripture that we had adapted and were using as part of a Christian education program with churches and schools in Haiti.

After hearing the story a couple of times, everyone was invited to share their thoughts on what they heard. And everyone did, from young (seven years old) to not-so-young (a couple in their late sixties) to in between.

There were comments about Christ entering the world as a child, comments about Joseph and Mary's faithfulness, and then the discussion began to focus on the phrase: "There was no room for Mary at the inn." Except in the Creole version this read, "There was no *place* for Mary at the inn," a slight variation that seems inconsequential.

At least it did to me. When I heard the verse read that night I understood, as I always had, that literally the inn had no rooms left—a full house, a first-century version of a flickering neon "No Vacancy" sign.

But our friends on the porch understood it a little differently. To them, "No *place* for her in the inn" didn't so much mean that there wasn't a vacancy, but that there was no place for someone *like* Mary in the inn. There was no place for someone who had just ridden in on a donkey. There was no place for someone dressed in peasant clothes. No place for someone who came from the nowheresville of Nazareth. No place when you don't have money, because, let's be honest, if you have enough money you can always find a place.

One neighbor who is a farmer said, "If Mary and Joseph would have been wearing nice clothes and had lots of money, there would have been a place for them. They would never have made her give birth with the animals."

"Yes," someone else said, "they would have treated them differently if they had money."

"And that is just how it is for us too," said the farmer, speaking again. "If we tried to go to one of the good hospitals in Port-au-Prince, there would be no place for us. If we tried to go to one of the hotels in the city, they would see our clothes and shoes, and they would know we're peasants. There wouldn't be a place for us either."

The conversation paused, a silence acknowledging the truth of his words.

"But isn't it amazing," spoke up another friend, "that our Lord chose to come to this earth through a woman who had no place, who was given no place. And even more amazing, God came to earth with good news to tell us: *that we do have a place*! He came to tell us, 'You have a place here as a child of God. And you have a place after this. In fact, right now my Father is preparing another place for you too.' "

There was another pause, but this time it was a silence of peace and of hope.

It was a holy moment I'll remember for the rest of my Christmases. It permanently changed how I hear that phrase in Jesus' birth story. So what happened?

We listened with people who were, in many ways, different from us. Our economic, racial, educational, national, and cultural backgrounds are very different from the friends we were sitting with. Some of these neighbors had no formal education and lived close to the edge of survival. Something happens—or at least can happen—when we listen together. The hermeneutic imagination expands. I then hear not only as myself, but also have a chance to hear through the ears/experience of the person sitting next to me. This can happen in another country or in a small group in your neighborhood. For example, I hear with increased intensity and specificity if listening to a Psalm of lament while sitting next to a woman whose husband just died. If we also listen to each other's reflections on the Bible, this possibility opens up even more.

We listened in another language. Our experience reflected what Frederick Buechner wrote in *Wishful Thinking*, "If you have even as much as a nodding acquaintance with a foreign language, try reading the Bible in that. Then you stand a chance of hearing what the Bible is actually saying instead of what you assume it must be saying because it is the Bible."

We listened to Scripture. There are so many differences, but we were brought together by a common story: the story of Jesus. That's the reason we were gathered on that eve. That's what led us to open a book that everyone, despite our differences, holds dear.

We listened in a way that ensured everyone present could participate. Some literate and some not. I don't think anyone there had finished high school, and at least a few were illiterate and probably had never spent a day in school. But we didn't think about education levels when it was happening. We had been (and continue to be) carefully developing how to approach Christian education in a country where about 50 percent of people are illiterate, so there is pedagogical strategy behind using *lectio divina*, which can be done by listening even if you can't read. But as it happened, we were just there with friends, thinking about Jesus' birth, and finding a way to share a meaningful moment together.

We listened to each other. Really listened.

We listened for God. This feels like an outrageous move of faith sometimes, but also the reason to go to the Bible. Since my faith wavers at times, I'm glad we can listen for God together, lean on each other. Maybe I'll hear something of God, but if not, maybe someone else will hear a whisper and let the rest of us know.

It's not that you couldn't get this insight sitting in your church or reading alone at home. But that didn't happen for me. It happened with these friends on that porch in Haiti.

The night was meaningful, hopeful, and peaceful, but the undercurrents of what is radical and gritty about faith were also right there in the midst of the story and the interpretation. In the shared reading. In the shared lives. In the work for justice that was—and is—ahead.

Kent Annan (M.Div., Princeton Theological Seminary) is author of After Shock *and* Following Jesus through the Eye of the Needle; *he is codirector of Haiti Partners.*

QUESTIONS

1. How do the biblical details, in contrast to the sparse nature of the Qur'an, influence one's reading experience?

2. Bidlack states that one of the purposes of the *Scripture* was to convert those outside China's borders. What was Matthew's and Luke's purpose in composing their birth narrative (they may be different)?

3. Imagine Matthew's response to Míguez. What is your response to Míguez's imagined conversation?

4. What other elements in Luke's story—besides Mary and Joseph having "no place"—might resonate with Annan's group?

CHAPTER 2

SERMON ON THE MOUNT

Matthew 5–7

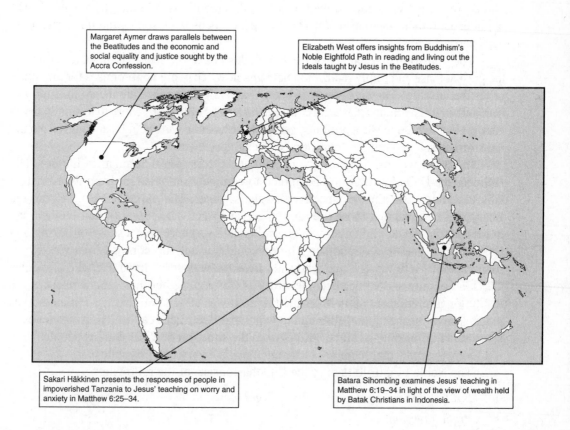

Margaret Aymer draws parallels between the Beatitudes and the economic and social equality and justice sought by the Accra Confession.

Elizabeth West offers insights from Buddhism's Noble Eightfold Path in reading and living out the ideals taught by Jesus in the Beatitudes.

Sakari Häkkinen presents the responses of people in impoverished Tanzania to Jesus' teaching on worry and anxiety in Matthew 6:25–34.

Batara Sihombing examines Jesus' teaching in Matthew 6:19–34 in light of the view of wealth held by Batak Christians in Indonesia.

READINGS

Buddhism's Noble Eightfold Path and Jesus' Beatitudes
Elizabeth West

The Beatitudes and the Accra Confession
Margaret Aymer

The Sermon on the Mount and Wealthy Christians in Indonesia
Batara Sihombing

Reading Matthew 6 with Those in Tanzania
Sakari Häkkinen

BUDDHISM'S NOBLE EIGHTFOLD PATH AND JESUS' BEATITUDES

Elizabeth West (United Kingdom)

The Beatitudes can be usefully revisited with Buddhist insights. The eight simple statements of Jesus known as the Beatitudes contain the very essence of his teaching. Most Christians think they know them well. However, their richness can be lost because our minds are loaded with conditioned beliefs and perceptions. We may have been taught to understand them in a particular way that prevents us from seeing them in other, perhaps deeper, ways.

The transformative power of the Beatitudes lies in the fact that they are written in the present tense and imply realization here and now. They are not promises for the future or for the afterlife! They are states of being that as Christians we are meant to enter into here and now. The Beatitudes are a course in how to be "blessed." More than simply being happy, "blessed" suggests a profound sense of unshakable well-being that comes from the transformed self and not the acquisition of wealth or power.

In 1994 I was privileged to be present at the John Main Seminar in London. His Holiness the Dalai Lama, who had agreed to comment on passages from the Christian Gospels from a Buddhist perspective, led the seminar. The moment when he read the Beatitudes was one that those present will never forget. The power of that moment lay in the fact that he so embodied what he was reading. There was a sense of having *met* Christ. That a member of another religion could be such an icon of Christ was a profound lesson. Here we saw one who truly lives the way Jesus lived. He who embodies Christ's teaching and values becomes truly as Christ, whether they are members of the institutional religion set up in his name or not. It was clear to all that His Holiness lives in this state of unshakable well-being to which the Beatitudes call us. His joy radiates to all around him in spite of all he suffers from the situation of Tibet and his people. Here is a living example that happiness here and now is a very real possibility.

The Noble Eightfold Path of the Buddha consists of the following:

Balanced view (or Right seeing or Right view);

Right intention;

Right speech (or Positive speech);

Right action (or Wholesome action);

Right livelihood (or Harmless livelihood);

Right effort;

Right mindfulness (or Awareness);

Right samadhi *(a difficult word to translate—possibly meditation/contemplation)*

The Eightfold Path of Buddhism is also a list of means to happiness. In fact it is the expansion of the Four Noble Truths, which is the truth that tells us how to end suffering. "Suffering" is not a very accurate translation of the Sanskrit word *dukkha*; a closer translation would be unsatisfactoriness. *Dukkha* is a state of dissatisfaction which our minds create around the situations of our lives. This then is the Buddha's list for achieving the cessation of suffering which is the opposite of happiness. The list clearly shows that my suffering is self-created and that my happiness and that of others are inseparable. What I do to be happy must also make others happy or at least not increase their suffering. We cannot be happy at the expense of others. This is a mistake people often make.

The term *right* in the Noble Eightfold Path implies an approach that will lead to freedom. It means to be true, on course, being in such a way that will enable us to be happy. One meaning of the Greek word for sin is "to miss the mark." Such an interpretation enables us to see sin as something that destroys happiness, both for ourselves and others.

The Buddha also stressed that we cause our own suffering and that nothing outside ourselves can make us suffer. Sin brings its own consequences rather than it being the punishment of God. This is something we Christians need to ponder deeply to free ourselves from the fear that the old teaching on sin tended to engender. The fear of hell enhances the fear of death, and fear is the greatest block of all to living in the fullness of life that Jesus came to bring us. This fullness of life is enshrined in the teaching of the Beatitudes. All the Buddha's teaching is focused on the attainment of those mental states that eliminate suffering for ourselves and the ways in which we cause suffering to others.

His Holiness the Dalai Lama points out repeatedly that the one thing all human beings have in common is the desire to be happy and to avoid suffering. Whether a religious person, a businessperson, a politician, or a criminal, each still has the desire for happiness as a basic motivation; the difference lies in the way one expects to find that happiness.

Some people do not think they deserve to be happy and it is reflected in a number of ways. Some feel that they are too unworthy and sinful for happiness, that they should be punished and suffer instead. The sad thing is that this can be a deeply held yet unconscious view that prevents happiness from being present. Others feel that it is wrong to be happy when there is so much suffering in the world. Yet if one is not happy it only adds to the suffering in the world! If we are unhappy how can we help and heal others? Thus it is very important to seek to heal any sense we may have that we do not deserve to be happy.

"Blessed are the poor in spirit for theirs is the kingdom of heaven." This short sentence sums up one of the truths that is at the very heart of the Buddha's teaching. He pointed out that one of the main reasons we suffer is because we fight life, clinging to what we want and pushing away what we do not like. If we can free ourselves from craving after "worldly things," this is the first key to true happiness. It is not about whether or not we have them, it is about our attitude toward them.

"Blessed are the pure in heart; they shall see God." Purity of heart follows from poverty of Spirit. Perhaps this is the Beatitude we as Christians are inclined to take least seriously. Yet the Buddha taught that it is possible, if very difficult, to eliminate suffering in this life and live in harmony with all that is. Enlightenment can be seen as being full of the light of the Divine Presence—that ultimate mystery which cannot be grasped in words, but which is the birthright of every human being. The Buddha refused to speak about "God" because words can never contain that mystery; he chose rather to give people the means by which to attain that state in which they would no longer need words.

Blessed are the gentle (meek), merciful, and the peacemakers. From the Buddha's teaching, it is clear that we cannot truly be any of these things until we have at least a small measure of poverty of spirit and purity of heart. The Buddha spoke of Four Immeasurable Qualities or Divine Abidings: Loving-Kindness, Compassion, Empathetic Joy, and Equanimity. These qualities grow out of letting go of ourselves and turning toward the Truth, the Divine. We cannot love and care for others until we glimpse who we truly are.

How do we do this? How do we reach purity of heart? The answer is contained in the Buddha's teaching on Meditation and Wisdom, which helps us to control our minds so that we can become aware of the true nature of reality. Teachings on Contemplation have largely been pushed aside and forgotten in Christianity, but today there is a hunger in the world as never before to discover who we really are and to find true happiness. The Eight Beatitudes sum up this path. The Buddha's teaching and the meditations he taught can help us do just that, whatever our spiritual background may be. The Buddha and most of his followers today are not interested in converting people to their "religion," but rather in offering all the ways they can to help humankind grow in happiness and well-being and so bring about in the world those qualities Jesus laid out in the Beatitudes.

Elizabeth West (M.A., World Religions) was a Catholic nun for 30 years, teaching in the United Kingdom and Africa; she founded the Buddhist Christian Vedanta Network for those who find themselves practicing the teachings of more than one faith.

THE BEATITUDES AND THE ACCRA CONFESSION

Margaret Aymer (United States)

In 2004, the World Alliance of Reformed Churches, a global organization of Protestant churches, convened in Accra, Ghana. From that meeting came a confession called "Covenanting for Justice in the Economy and the Earth," known today simply as the Accra Confession. In the Accra Confession, the churches said, in part (Accra 19):

> We reject the current world economic order imposed by global neoliberal capitalism and any other economic system, including absolute planned economies, which defy God's covenant by excluding the poor, the vulnerable, and the whole of creation from the fullness of life. We reject any claim of economic, political, and military empire which subverts God's sovereignty over life and acts contrary to God's just rule.

This and other portions of the confession were considered scandalous by rich Christians in Europe and the United States of America. However, the confession was not saying anything that Jesus had not already said in the Beatitudes millennia ago.

The Beatitudes occur in Matthew and Luke and, although different, are complementary. Jesus' first four beatitudes in Matthew hold up as honorable the "poor in spirit," the "mourners," the "meek," and those who "hunger and thirst for righteousness" or justice (5:3–6). These four groups of people are really one group, the group that the Accra Confession calls "the poor, the vulnerable and the whole of creation." In Jesus' day, poverty and poverty of spirit were not considered inevitable. It was caused by persons who had taken too much of the limited goods of society for themselves, leaving others poor. This is why Zacchaeus is hated (Luke 19); he has grown rich on the backs of his fellow citizens. It is also the reason why the rich man, who could not see poor Lazarus at his front door, is condemned (Luke 16).

What Jesus only implies in Matthew, he states outright in Luke. Not only are those who are "poor," "mourners," "hungry," and "persecuted" honorable, but those who are "rich," "laughing," "stuffed," and "well-spoken of" are shameful (6:24–26). Jesus does not sidestep the issue. He points squarely at those who have profited on the backs of the poor and says, "Shame on you."

The Beatitudes reveal that the Accra Confession is not saying something new, but something very old: that the concern of heaven is with those who are powerless on earth, and that it is the business for people of faith to be thus concerned also. It goes further, however, to charge that those who would have the concern of heaven today are those facing the underside of neoliberal economic globalization.

The Accra Confession is not only a condemnation of the policies that cause poverty and want, however. It is also a pledge as people of faith to stand with those who have been harmed. It reads (Accra 26):

> We believe that God calls us to stand with those who are victims of injustice.
> We know what the Lord requires of us: to do justice, love kindness, and walk
> in God's way (Micah 6:8). We are called to stand against any form of injustice in the economy and the destruction of the environment, "so that justice
> may roll down like waters, and righteousness like an ever-flowing stream."

This too is an echo of the Beatitudes. For, if the first verse of Jesus' Beatitudes in Matthew excoriates those under an unjust economic system, the second verse honors those who work for justice. Jesus upholds "the merciful," "those with integrity," "the peacemakers," and "those who are persecuted for the sake of righteousness" and justice as being equally the concern of heaven. The call to the disciples is to stand with "those who are victims of injustice" as people of mercy, integrity, and peace.

However such a stand does not come without a cost. As the Accra Confession affirms, "We believe in obedience to Jesus Christ, that the church is called to confess, witness, and act, even though the authorities and human law might forbid them, and punishment and suffering be the consequence (Acts 4:18ff). Jesus is Lord."

And, once more an echo is heard from the mountain on which Jesus preaches the Beatitudes in Matthew. "Blessed are you when people revile you and persecute you, and say all manner of evil against you falsely for my sake" (5:11). There are, both in contemporary and ancient times, consequences to standing with those who suffer and against those who profit. The consequences may be financial, social, or, in the case of Jesus himself, mortal danger. Nevertheless, there are consequences.

Despite the parallels between the Beatitudes and the Accra Confession, the Beatitudes are rarely seen as a radical text; and they are certainly not the source of condemnation that the Accra Confession has been. Perhaps what makes some people uncomfortable with the Accra is that it dares to ask this question: Who are the blessed poor today?

Note: In 2010, the World Alliance for Reformed Churches joined with other global Protestant bodies to become the World Communion of Reformed Churches (WCRC). The WCRC has also adopted the Accra Confession.

Margaret Aymer is Associate Professor of New Testament at the Interdenominational Theological Center in Atlanta, Georgia, United States.

THE SERMON ON THE MOUNT AND WEALTHY CHRISTIANS IN INDONESIA

Batara Sihombing (Indonesia)

Corruption is a well-known phenomenon in Indonesia. Indonesia is declared by the international economic institutions as one of the most corrupt countries in the world and the champion of corruption in Asia. It has faced economic crisis since 1998 when Suharto was forced to step down. Many factories have closed, the price of goods has risen steadily, and the rate of crime is high. It is publicly acknowledged that the well-known *KKN—Korupsi, Kolusi, Nepotisme* (Corruption, Collusion, Nepotism)—is the reason behind the crisis. Greed seems to have played an important role in making Indonesia morally and economically bankrupt.

In fighting this corruption the Indonesian government has established a *Komisi Pemberantasan Korupsi* (Corruption Eradication Commission). As a result, during the present time, we often hear that many high-ranking government officials—ministers, generals, governors, mayors, legislators, diplomats, and so on—have been imprisoned due to their corruption. But there is no easy way to eradicate greediness for wealth. People tend to have the bad eyes ("greedy") instead of good eyes ("generous") in dealing with money (Matt. 6:22–23). They are not aware that the eye of a greedy person is never satisfied with his or her share. The lover of money will never be satisfied with money. People store up treasures on earth instead of in heaven (6:19–20). So, it is under-standable that their hearts focus on earthly materials (6:21).

When we look at the position of Indonesian Christians, particularly the Batak Christians (6 million) to which I belong, we find that they too have contributed to Indonesia's moral bankruptcy. The Batak place much importance on wealth. Their three highest values are *hamoraon* ("riches"), *hagabeon* ("fecundity"), and *hasanga-pon* ("honor"). Every adult Batak knows these ideals.

The traditional Batak orients their life to these three objectives with a high com-petitive element. The reason for such orientation is that the Batak people entered mod-ern Indonesia only at the beginning of the last century. Thus, their values originate from their old religion. These ideals bring about covetousness toward all sorts of positions that can give prestige and toward material possessions. Many Bataks abandon their vil-lages in the Batakland and move to new places in order to attain riches, honor, and fecundity.

Further, the Batak desire for wealth can be seen from their *umpasa*, that is, the pro-verbial prayers to God, the giver of wealth. The use of *umpasa* is very popular among the Batak especially in cultural functions. There are more than 47 *umpasa* which express a strong wish to be wealthy. Although several Batak proverbial requests also point out that wealth should be obtained in appropriate ways, their main goal is to be wealthy no matter what it takes and to attain the praises and admiration of family and friends. For example, every Christmas and New Year many Batak families return to their villages or their parents' home. In this homecoming visit, many of them come with new cars and bring many kinds of presents for their families who are delighted to receive such gifts and to admire their success. Conversely, those who are less (or even not at all) success-ful are looked down upon by villagers. This is the major reason why many unsuccessful persons, especially the young people, do not return even though they have not seen their parents for years. Being unsuccessful and poor is shameful.

However, people hardly question the means of obtaining these riches. Many are young professionals, government officials, or businessmen. Their salary alone would not enable them to enjoy such wealth. So, where do they get their riches? The answer is, most likely, by corruption. It is not difficult to imagine that in a community which highly values the rich, people will employ whatever means necessary to accrue wealth. But, as Jesus reminds us, one who has an evil eye or greedy eye will become evil (6:22–23). Besides, love of money will bring about evil things in life (6:24). Jesus encourages people to have wealth in an honest and just way, "to strive first for the kingdom of God and his righteousness, and all these things will be given to you as well" (6:34).

It is clear that the Batak face the danger of mammon, the idolatry of materialism. Satan has used mammon as a means of challenging God's plan for the Batak people. In this case, unchecked greed has brought about the bankruptcy of the Indonesian econ-omy, a high rate of unemployment and poor people, and increased crime. Jesus says, "You cannot serve God and mammon" (6:24).

Batak and Indonesian Christians should faithfully serve God. They should store up treasures in heaven by sharing what they have with those who are in need (6:19–21), and they should avoid taking the treasures that do not belong to them. They should be generous givers because God is also generous to them (6:22–23). In so doing, they walk in the way of righteousness (6:33–34), and do not need to be anxious (6:25, 31, 34) because God will provide for their needs (6:32–33).

Batara Sihombing is a Pastor of Huria Kristen Indonesia *(HKI) Church; he also teaches Biblical Studies at the Divinity School of Silliman University, Dumaguete, Philippines.*

READING MATTHEW 6 WITH THOSE IN TANZANIA
Sakari Häkkinen (Tanzania)

The village of Kinywang'anga is one of the poorest in the Iringa district in the middle of Tanzania. It consists of approximately 1,000 inhabitants who all make a living from their own little farms ranging from one to ten acres in size. Almost all of them would be considered peasant farmers. There is one primary school with five teachers. Even though the teachers receive government pay, each also has a small farm with some cattle. In addition, there are two religious leaders in the village, one a Lutheran evangelist and the other an Anglican priest. They also have farms. There are no other professions among the inhabitants of the village and no one goes to work outside of the village.

People from three different tribes—the Hehe, Bena, and Kinga—live in Kinywang'anga. These tribal names are also the names of the languages spoken in the village. There are no cars. There's only one tractor and a few bicycles. Despite the lack of transportation, people make weekly visits to neighboring villages to meet with relatives and friends and sometimes to try to find medical treatment, though health care is a constant challenge. Also, in recent times HIV and AIDS have struck the village more heavily than most parts of the world, making nearly one in every four adults HIV-positive.

People in Kinywang'anga are totally dependent on the products of the earth. If there is no rain, there is no crop and they are in danger of starvation. The last time this happened was in 2000. Other catastrophes might destroy the crop as well. There are no barns or other storehouses in the village which enable them to keep surpluses to use during hard times or to sell as a way of providing additional income. However, the village grows sunflowers, which are pressed for their oil and sometimes sold to people travelling the main road, which is two miles outside the village. In 2008 a water pipe system was built for them, so now they have a place from which to fetch water. There is no electricity in the village.

The villagers live in traditional African clay houses with grass roofs. They are very poorly dressed; many people have no shoes. Approximately 50 percent of the population is comprised of children. According to international standards, the people in Kinywang'anga live in absolute poverty—that is, under $1.25 a day.

I discussed Matthew 6:25–34 with the villagers. The text was not read from a book with leather covers, but rather performed in narrative style. In Tanzania the oral culture and narrative tradition is still alive and well. By telling the stories from memory I tended to get their first reactions, which may have been different had I simply read to them from the Bible. Some of the villagers were non-Christians, so they were not too closely acquainted with the text beforehand. Even the Christians heard the narrative differently compared to the way they had heard it in local church. I had hoped to have a lively discussion of the poverty stories in the Gospels, and I most certainly did. Often the religious authorities (a pastor, an evangelist, or some other religious leader) were present, but I politely asked them not to take part in the discussions since they are professionals and I wanted to hear the voices of ordinary people. They agreed to my request, but I usually visited their home afterwards so that they did not feel left out. I also asked the people gathered at the meeting place to set aside their understanding of the story if they had already heard it and to listen as if they were hearing it for the first time in their lives. At the meeting there were some 20 people present, from both genders and all ages, and approximately 10 of them took part in the discussion.

In Kinywang'anga people sometimes have no food at all, clothing is meager and they have enjoyed the "pure" water from the pipes for only a couple of years now. In normal years they have enough food, but it is quite simple and not very nutritious. In Kinywang'anga the context for this gospel passage is totally different from that of my own country of Finland as well as most Western countries; instead it is quite close to the conditions of first-century Galilean villages, the original context of Jesus' teaching. It is important to note, however, that the religious and cultural context of the people in Kinywang'anga is not identical with that of the first audience. Key terms in the passage such as "heavenly Father," "Solomon in all his splendor," "Gentiles," "strive first for his kingdom and his righteousness" would have resonated with first-century Jewish listeners differently from the Tanzanian poor, who would be without an important context for understanding the passage.

The meeting took place in an outside area in the shade. During the time of year that we met, the "flowers of the field" were very beautiful and everything was green; the "birds of the air" flew over us and sang (6:26, 28). A lively discussion followed the performance of the text. The discussion was opened by an elderly man who said, "Maybe Jesus spoke these words because he found that the people had very little faith. He wanted to teach them about faith." I suppose that what the man meant by "faith," was *trust in God's care*, but I am not sure. Another man said, "Jesus found people so keen on material things that they forgot the spiritual things and God. They were concerned about food, clothes, and other things, but not God." A woman said that if someone came to say such words to her, she would think that this person is not good. "It would be better if somebody would tell me a better way how I could manage my life in order to get things and not to say 'Do not worry.'" Another said that a person who said such things would be considered "mentally disabled" by the villagers. The Lutheran evangelist interjected, "Some worry is understandable, because we need many things, but one should not worry about things that are beyond one's ability to influence or control, for example, weather. It is, however, good to plan your future." When I asked if they knew anyone who did not worry about tomorrow, they strongly denied knowing such a person. The same elderly man who started the discussion, said, "Jesus knew the people and their problems and needs, so he wanted to give them a change, a new perspective, a new way of thinking." I asked, what would happen if they stopped worrying about daily food and drink and clothing and just trusted in God? Someone said that then life would be very bad. Another said that it is a matter of faith. If the people believed what Jesus said and stopped working they would have thought everything comes automatically, without human involvement, if they just believed. A young woman with a baby said, "The speech of Jesus must have divided the people in two groups: some had faith and thought that 'this is true, why worry,' while the others thought 'this is not possible.' Faith is the main topic of Jesus' speech." One man said that if you trust God, you will have everything you need.

In further discussion over sodas we found a tentative solution for this problematic text. If someone is worried, he or she soon becomes depressed and is not a joy to his or her friends and relatives. So it is better not to worry too much about worldly things that you cannot do anything about, but instead to rejoice with family and friends for all the good we have.

It became clear to me that the *Do Not Worry* passage is difficult to comprehend in a village where people are living in ongoing poverty. The villagers tried to find a spiritual message in the saying, maybe because they found it unreasonable to live a careless life, as Jesus seemed to be advising. They interpreted the saying in the light of the kingdom of God (6:33), which they seemed to have understood as spiritual.

Sakari Häkkinen is the dean of the Lutheran diocese of Kuopio, Finland.

QUESTIONS

1. What practical and philosophical differences, if any, are there between the Beatitudes and the Noble Eightfold Path? Is the idea that "nothing outside ourselves can make us suffer" consistent with the biblical text?

2. Aymer treats the Beatitudes in Matthew and Luke 6 as complementary. What differences might be noted between the two versions, and which one, overall, is more in line with the Accra Confession?

3. How might Batak Christians respond to Sihombing's criticisms? How might they argue that the Beatitudes support their actions and desires?

4. Assess Häkkinen's interview techniques and questions. How would you have approached the opportunity to discuss the Sermon on the Mount with people in Tanzania?

CHAPTER 3

PARABLES OF JESUS (PART I)

Luke 10:25–37; Matthew 13:24–30; Matthew 25:1–13

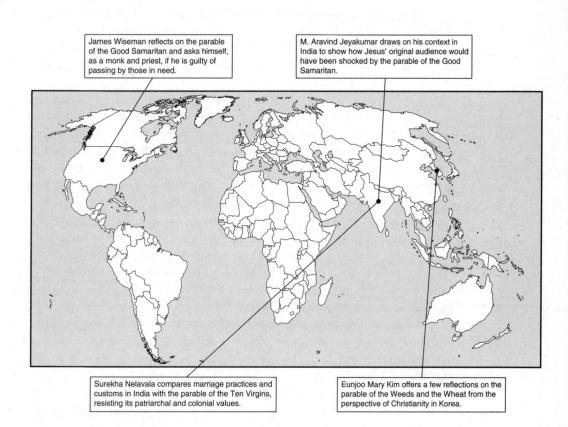

James Wiseman reflects on the parable of the Good Samaritan and asks himself, as a monk and priest, if he is guilty of passing by those in need.

M. Aravind Jeyakumar draws on his context in India to show how Jesus' original audience would have been shocked by the parable of the Good Samaritan.

Surekha Nelavala compares marriage practices and customs in India with the parable of the Ten Virgins, resisting its patriarchal and colonial values.

Eunjoo Mary Kim offers a few reflections on the parable of the Weeds and the Wheat from the perspective of Christianity in Korea.

READINGS

The Parable of the Good Samaritan and Those in Need
James Wiseman

An Indian Reading of the Good Samaritan
M. Aravind Jeyakumar

The Weeds and Wheat in Korean Christianity
Eunjoo Mary Kim

Marriage Practices in India and the Parable of the Ten Virgins
Surekha Nelavala

THE PARABLE OF THE GOOD SAMARITAN AND THOSE IN NEED

James Wiseman (United States)

As a monk, I have taken a vow of poverty. Although in the technical sense that vow means that I own no possessions, the fact that my monastic community provides everything I really need for my work (including the assurance of three meals a day and a room that is well heated in winter and air-conditioned in summer) means that I am in fact a member of the white middle class in what is generally considered the most powerful country in the world. It is within this context that I reflect daily on passages from the Bible, including some that are definitely challenging and even discomforting.

Being an ordained priest as well as a monk, I am particularly challenged by Jesus' parable of the Good Samaritan, for I have to ask myself to what extent I, like the priest and Levite in the parable, pass by "on the opposite side" instead of actively coming to the aid of someone in need. I will never forget the day a few years ago when a religious sister who had dedicated her life to helping the homeless took me and a few other ministers to visit a site under one of the freeway bridges here in Washington. What we saw were the living quarters of about 20 homeless men, each of whom had staked out his own spot with an array of cardboard boxes. Each man's bed was just a blanket or two spread on the ground, or at best a dilapidated mattress salvaged from some alleyway or dump. Our visit took place on a pleasant summer day, but as I write this, we are in the midst of a headline-making cold spell, complete with snow and a fierce northwest wind. What must life under that bridge be like tonight? What is my responsibility toward the people who are presumably still living there? I can, with impeccable logic, tell myself that my obligations toward all of my students at the university prevent my doing all that that sister was doing to befriend and aid the homeless, but do my academic responsibilities absolve me completely? Might I, like that priest and Levite, really be passing by on the opposite side and thereby be running the risk of ultimately ending up on another opposite side—with the goats rather than the sheep—as described in the Last Judgment scene in Matthew 25?

Or, to take a less dramatic example, what does the parable of the Good Samaritan tell me about how to treat the many people begging for money on the downtown streets of my city, their numbers larger than ever in this time of widespread unemployment? True, I cannot give generously to everyone who asks (and actually have very little pocket money myself), but I will always remember something that another religious sister once wrote—that the worst pain experienced by any beggar is to be totally ignored, to have passersby avert their eyes so as not even to see him or her, to reduce the beggar to the status of a nonentity, a nobody. Is not the parable warning me to avoid walking literally "on the opposite side" of the sidewalk, calling me instead to look the beggar in the face and give, if not a monetary donation, then at least a pleasant word? Here, too, all sorts of "logical escapes" are possible, such as the sensible reminder not to encourage the panhandling that in many areas is illegal anyway, but I dare not forget that Jesus was not particularly interested in enforcing man-made laws when other higher values were at stake.

Jesus was also insistent that his followers avoid too many words, whether when praying or on other occasions, and that they turn instead to doing what is required of them in particular circumstances. In this parable, it is important to notice that Jesus doesn't directly answer the lawyer's question about a certain fact ("Who *is* my neighbor?") but talks about *behavior*, about how to *act* toward people whom we are inclined to avoid. In asking his questions about what is required to inherit eternal life, the lawyer was interested in boundaries, ones defined perhaps by "being in the Abrahamic covenant" or "being recognized by the religious elite as righteous." What he got instead was a story that brought home the effacing of any and all boundaries for love and compassion. Jesus was saying that none of his followers dare circumscribe their concern by placing anyone outside the scope of their concern, regardless of the other's religion, race, or nationality. Note that in the parable there isn't even mention of the nationality of the man who had fallen in with robbers. We might well assume he was a Jew, but for the Good Samaritan race didn't matter. He simply came to the aid of a person in need, no questions asked.

As often in the Gospel accounts of Jesus' interaction with others, he concludes with a question of his own: "Which of these three, in your opinion, was neighbor to the victim of the robbers?" Receiving the only possible reply—that it was the one who treated him with mercy—Jesus concludes with the words, "Go and do likewise." What does this mean for me? Or for you?

James Wiseman is a Benedictine monk at St. Anselm's Abbey in Washington, D.C., and a professor of theology and religious studies at Catholic University of America, United States.

AN INDIAN READING OF THE GOOD SAMARITAN

M. Aravind Jeyakumar (India)

Through centuries the parable of the Good Samaritan has been interpreted variously. The allegorical reading of this parable, for example, posits the traveler as "sinner," the priest and the Levite as the religions of the world, and the Samaritan as Jesus. Many readers limit their interpretations to the message of "love your neighbor" and give to charity and philanthropies. However, without underestimating the importance of acts of kindness emphasized in this parable, the sociocultural background of the text should not be overlooked.

Jews and Samaritans were both descendants of the tribe of Joseph. They had the same heritage and lineage. There was no great religious or ethnic difference between the Jews and the Samaritans prior to the exile. However, after the exile, the Samaritans intermixed with non-Hebraic races. Because of this racial mix, the Jews categorized them as "out-castes"; they were thought of as Gentiles, foreigners. Thus, the Samaritans were marginalized. In the parable, then, the different characters represent different levels on the social hierarchy that existed in the time of Jesus. The priests and the Levites were considered to be pure-blooded and so they occupied the top position. The common people were next, and at the bottom were the Samaritans.

There are many marginalized people in India today, people with no worth, value, power, or social standing. More than that, they have no identity whatsoever and are treated worse than animals; they are destitute and dehumanized. It is in this context that the parable of the Good Samaritan speak so powerfully. The priest and the Levite pass by the stranded and injured traveler. As "high-caste" people, they want nothing to do with a polluted man lying in a ditch on the side of the road. They treat him as a nonperson. But then the lowly Samaritan comes along and does the right thing. He acts benevolently and helps the beaten traveler. He treats him as a human being.

The original Jewish audience of this parable would no doubt have been utterly shocked. The highly respected and upper-class holy men—the priest and Levite—are the ones whose behavior is denounced. It is not right, Jesus says, to pass by on the other side in order to protect one's social class and standing. Rather, it is the Samaritan who is presented as the one with human values. It is the lowly Samaritan who identifies with the oppressed, transcends the traditional barriers of culture and creed (to help a Jew) by identifying with the needy, and renounces ritual purity when ethical action and mercy require it. With this parable, Jesus opened the eyes of his Jewish audience to see a marginalized Samaritan as the role model of compassion and life-giving actions.

In India, the marginalized could never be seen as a role model—religiously, socially, or otherwise—because the hierarchical social structures strip them of their basic humanity. Outcastes are inherently wicked and evil and worthless—simply by virtue of their marginal status. They could never be seen as good, loving people. It is this conventional thinking, which existed in the time of Jesus just as it does today India, that Jesus is forcing his audience to rethink.

The oppressive structures that exist across the globe and that divide humans in status were created by humankind only. It is very difficult to eradicate such structures since religious and sociocultural factors uphold them. But Jesus' parable of the Good Samarian—and many other of his teachings as well—challenge those structures. Jesus was a rebel. Jesus aimed at a society without discrimination. In this sense, Christianity can have a major role in making the world a better place.

M. Aravind Jeyakumar (B.D., M.Th., Gurukul Lutheran Theological College and Research Institute, Chennai, South India) is Lecturer in the Department of Biblical Studies at Leonard Theological College, Jabalpur, Madhya Pradesh, India.

THE WEEDS AND WHEAT IN
KOREAN CHRISTIANITY

Eunjoo Mary Kim (Korea)

Here I offer a few reflections on the parable of the "Weeds and the Wheat" found in Matthew 13:24–30 from the perspective of Christianity in Korea. Christianity was introduced to Korea in two different historical epochs. The first time was during the high peak of the Yi dynasty in the eighteenth century. Some government officials and liberal Confucian scholars who visited China as delegates or envoys of the dynasty met Roman Catholic missionaries and obtained Christian literature written in Chinese. They were fascinated by its new teaching about God, humanity, and the way of life, and wanted to spread the good news of Christianity to their families, villagers, and the larger community. However, it was not good news to the authorities of the dynasty, governed by Neo-Confucian principles and systems based on the hierarchical order of classism and sexism and the polytheistic religious practices and cultural tradition. For them, Christian believers who followed the religious and moral teaching of Christianity that emphasized monotheism and egalitarian love were "weeds," dangerous and harmful to their grain field. In order to protect the "wheat" growing in their traditional cultural and religious soil, they hastily made every effort to pull the weeds out of the field before they quickly spread all over their grain field. As a result, Christianity was banned in Korea, and tens of thousands of early Christians in Korea were persecuted and martyred.

The second tide of Christianity in Korea was led by Protestant Christians during the late nineteenth century. Since the 1870s, the Yi dynasty had been on a downward path and Korean society was in chaos politically, socially, economically, and religiously. Neo-Confucianism, which had provided the moral and religious foundation for the society, was no longer the stronghold of the people's morality and the social system and order. The corruption of the government and religious leaders; the military threats of Japan, China, Russia, and other foreign countries; and severe drought, plagues, and dire poverty had caused local and national revolts. The suffering masses felt discontent and despair with the existing social order and the conventional cultural and religious teaching. They yearned for a new religious and moral guidance that was able to restore their social stability and personal and communal well-being.

The government's persecution of Catholicism continued until the early 1870s. In the following decade, however, the government officially opened a door to Christianity and welcomed Christian missionaries by making a Treaty of Amity with the United States in 1882 and with other Western countries shortly thereafter. Immediately, Protestant Christian missionaries from the United States and other Western countries entered Korea, and many Koreans and their political leaders welcomed it as a new leading spirit, alternative to the traditional Confucian and Buddhist formalities and the rigid literati mentality.

Indeed, Christianity has contributed to transforming the Korean soil. The "good seed" grew and multiplied its fruits in the Korean soil, overcoming turbulent hardships in particular seasons with the Koreans: During the period of the Japanese annexation of Korea (1910–1945), many Christian believers fought against Japanese imperialism and militarism. They were involved in the independence movement, even at the cost of their lives, and their churches played a major role in providing the oppressed colonized people with a spiritual home, in spite of horrible persecution executed by the Japanese authority. During and after the Korean War (1950–1953), churches in South Korea made unparalleled relief efforts and encouraged the people with a hopeful message for their future. During the 1960s and the 1970s, when rapid social changes, spurred by the processes of industrialization, modernization, and urbanization, generated culture shock and feelings of anxiety and displacement among the people, the Christian church embraced those weary people. Moreover, Korean theologians and ministers who were influenced by Korean liberation theology (*Minjung* Theology) actively participated in both the labor movement and the democratic movement and struggled with and for the oppressed against military dictatorship during the 1980s.

The public's favorable view of Christianity based on its positive social and political impacts and the zeal of Christian leaders for evangelism have contributed to a conspicuous increase in the membership of the church. Today, about one-third of South Korea's 45 million people identify themselves as Christian. They dominate Korean ethos and culture as the majority group in the multireligious and pluralistic Korean society.

Obviously, the Korean field is full of Christians. But, it is questionable whether it is a field of wheat or of weeds. It must not be overlooked that many Christians and their churches are consciously or unconsciously creating and exacerbating numerous complex problems and issues within and beyond the church, such as denominationalism, sexism, consumerism, and Christian triumphalism. In many cases, for example, the message that is proclaimed behind the pulpit is no longer the gospel of Jesus Christ, who suffered and died on the cross, but the gospel of prosperity and positive thinking, co-opted by popular human wishes and worldly desires. Many Korean missionaries dispatched to Asia, Africa, South America, and other continents are agents of Christian triumphalism who think their mission is to conquer the world with their denominational doctrines and dogmas, which is *the* gospel for them. The more critically we reflect on contemporary churches in Korea through the biblical lens, the more we find in them characteristics of weeds that are unfruitful rather than those of wheat that bear grain.

In the parable in Matthew 13:24–30, the servants urgently report to the householder about weeds growing in his field and request of him permission to get rid of the weeds. However, the householder does not permit his servants to pull out the weeds from the wheat immediately, for he is worried that his servants might uproot wheat plants along with the weeds by mistake in this early season. Instead, he orders them to allow both the weeds and the wheat to grow together in his grain field until harvest time. When the time comes, everything will be clear by its fruit: Without grains, it is obviously a weed that must be thrown to be burned, and with ripened grains, it is obviously wheat that must be stored in the householder's barn.

Ironically, Matthew describes this mixed, ambiguous field of the householder as the kingdom of heaven here and now, in which God is present and rules with patience and compassion. In this kingdom, it is uncertain who is to be burned and who is to be stored in the barn, for God's measuring stick in the harvest time will be different from ours (cf. Isaiah 55:8–9). As H. Richard Niebuhr has suggested, the self we loved might not be the self God loves, the neighbors we did not prize might be God's treasures, the truth we ignored might be the truth God maintains, the justice which we sought because it was our own might not be the justice that God's love desires, and the righteousness God demands and gives might not be our righteousness but be greater and different.

What, then, if non-Christians, whom Christians believe to be weeds unless they are converted to Christianity, turn out to be wheat in God's coming reign? What if heretics and minority Christian groups, whom mainstream Christians label as weeds, turn out to be wheat in God's sight? Or, what if those who confidently believe that they are good Christians turn out to be weeds without fruit in the harvest time?

It is grace that the kingdom of heaven is different from our kingdom on earth, in which we hastily sort out the bad from the good and throw them to be burned. It is gracious that God does not weed us now but patiently waits until we bear the good fruit of the Spirit—love, joy, peace, patience, kindness, generosity, faithfulness, gentleness, and self-control (Galatians 5:22–23)—a hundredfold, 60, or 30 times.

Eunjoo Mary Kim is Associate Professor of Homiletics at the Iliff School of Theology, Denver, Colorado, United States.

MARRIAGE PRACTICES IN INDIA AND THE PARABLE OF THE TEN VIRGINS
Surekha Nelavala (India)

Jesus explains his teachings using parables, which is an effective communication method that uses known subjects in order to introduce new or unknown concepts. For instance, to explain the nature of the kingdom of God, an unknown concept, Jesus uses many parables with which the people can easily associate and resonate. Therefore, the parables rely on the day-to-day life of his social context in order to make the unknown contexts far more comprehensible. Therefore, on the one hand, Jesus' parables help to simplify the complex subjects of his teachings, and on the other hand, they are the resources for understanding the social context of the ancient Palestinian society, its values, culture, and norms.

The parable of the bridegroom and the ten virgins in Matthew 25:1–13 is one such parable used to explain the nature of the kingdom of God, while also revealing social customs and norms. In this parable, Jesus uses a wedding setting as a metaphor, in which the roles of the bridegroom and the virgins, along with their privileges and stereotypes, bear many similarities to the wedding and marriage context of India. Thus my questions and interpretation of the text come mainly from my own social location and a perspective informed by Indian culture, values, challenges, and observations. My interpretive approach to the parable is from an Indian feminist perspective. First, as an Indian contextual reader, I try to emphasize the social context presented in the parable, while comparing and contrasting it with the specific Indian context. Second, as a feminist reader, I use the feminist lens to understand and interpret the parable while being mindful of the significant impact that the text has on the common people.

In my encounter with the text, this parable leaves me uncomfortable regarding the way in which it could read in an Indian context where the bridegroom, or potential bridegroom, is always in demand, and assumes a higher status. It also makes me uneasy because of the dichotomization of the ten virgins, some as wise and some as foolish, judging by whether or not they found favor with the bridegroom. This parable demonstrates the patriarchal nature of the context that it is portraying. The parable characterizes one bridegroom against the ten virgins, although most scholars conveniently interpret them as bridesmaids instead of potential brides. In the parable there are 10 women fighting for one man, and whoever is able to find favor with the bridegroom will, in fact, make it to heaven.

A similar story plays out in many ways in the lives of Indian women. As an Indian woman, when I read this text, I am deeply affected by the fact that male privilege and female discrimination are widely prevalent as accepted norms in current Indian society. In the arranged marriages, which are predominant in Indian society, the men are always in demand, and the women are regarded as fortunate if they are somehow favored by men for marriage. As the wise virgins in the parable are equipped with extra oil, the wise virgins of India and their families must be equipped with dowry and wedding-related expenses. These kinds of stereotypes are not unique to the marriage setting in patriarchal cultures but rather apply to almost all spheres of life. For instance, a woman is considered a good cook only if she can satisfy her husband's taste, which is not necessarily a reflection of her culinary skills, although it is considered a vital qualification for a wife. Similarly, a virgin is considered worthwhile only when she is liked by the groom's family and the groom. In an arranged marriage system, the potential bridegroom and his family visit the bride's family to assess and judge the bride's beauty and familial qualifications, such as her cooking, cleaning, and working skills. A young girl is presented to the potential groom's family at her best, sometimes with added exaggeration. In addition, the real wisdom and preparedness of the virgin is tested by discussing the dowry with her parents. Whoever can afford the anticipated dowry is highly regarded as the wise family of virgins, and others are often criticized as foolish if they cannot marry off their daughters when qualified grooms approach them.

In the parable, the description of the wise virgins is that they are the flawless ones, the ideal virgins who are always eager, ready, and at the service of the man. In this parable, the virgins wait so long that they eventually fall asleep. The wise virgins are extra careful and equipped enough to meet the bridegroom at his arrival, but the foolish virgins do not have what they need. The wise virgins do not take any chances when it is a matter of impressing their potential bridegroom, whereas the foolish virgins take it easy. This parable reinforces the status quo of male privilege and female discrimination. The delay of the bridegroom communicates his privilege while the virgins eagerly wait for him. The same privilege is not a possibility for the virgins. The five virgins who do not meet the bridegroom at his arrival are forever denied their opportunity to be potential brides to the qualified groom.

What made the so-called foolish virgins unprepared and unequipped? Do they not understand that they do not share the same privilege of delayed arrival as the bridegroom? However, after the bridegroom arrives, he does not wait for the other five virgins who went out to fetch some more oil. The man of the parable enjoys his full privileges to take his time and delay his arrival, while the women wait for him at the expense of their sleep and lamp oil. Once he is ready, he responds harshly when the five virgins return, saying that he does not know them. The bridegroom metes out the severe punishment of abandonment for the late women, and he provides no explanation for his delay. This parable offers a clear example of male privilege and female marginalization.

Jesus' words offer no challenge to the status quo, but rather use it as an example to explain the kingdom of God. As an Indian reader, for whom this parable is not just a metaphor but a real experience, my interpretive stance is not only to learn about and understand the kingdom of God but also to feel genuine fear about the status of males and females in the kingdom of God. If God perpetuates equality, justice, and liberation, how should this parable be interpreted as it simply reinforces male privilege? As an Indian feminist reader, I challenge both the metaphor and also the concept of the kingdom of God that contains patriarchal and colonial values of power and privilege rather than justice and liberation that are the true values of God's household.

Surekha Nelavala is a Mission Developer at Global Peace Lutheran Church in Frederick, Maryland, United States.

QUESTIONS

1. How does Wiseman's context, which he explains in the first paragraph, shape his reading of the biblical text? How do you think he himself would ultimately answer his final question? How would you answer it?

2. Who are the Samaritans in your social and cultural context whose benevolent actions would come as a "shock"?

3. What would Kim say about the status—wheat or weeds—of "liberal Confucian scholars" or those who banned Christianity in Korea? Is there any basis for exclusion or condemnation of any group or individual?

4. How does Indian society, as described by Nelavala, compare to your particular cultural context in terms of gender discrimination in marriage practices. How could your context be brought to bear on the parable?

CHAPTER 4

PARABLES OF JESUS (PART II)

Matthew 20:1–16; Matthew 25:14–30; Matthew 13:33
and Luke 13:20–21; Matthew 13:1–23

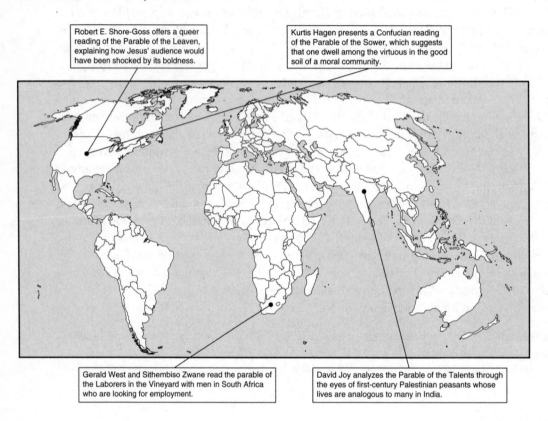

Robert E. Shore-Goss offers a queer reading of the Parable of the Leaven, explaining how Jesus' audience would have been shocked by its boldness.

Kurtis Hagen presents a Confucian reading of the Parable of the Sower, which suggests that one dwell among the virtuous in the good soil of a moral community.

Gerald West and Sithembiso Zwane read the parable of the Laborers in the Vineyard with men in South Africa who are looking for employment.

David Joy analyzes the Parable of the Talents through the eyes of first-century Palestinian peasants whose lives are analogous to many in India.

READINGS

The Laborers in the Vineyard and the Unemployed in South Africa
Gerald West and Sithembiso Zwane

Reading the Parable of the Talents with Those in India
David Joy

A Queer Reading of the Parable of the Leaven
Robert E. Shore-Goss

A Confucian Perspective on the Parable of the Sower
Kurtis Hagen

THE LABORERS IN THE VINEYARD AND THE
UNEMPLOYED IN SOUTH AFRICA

Gerald West and Sithembiso Zwane (South Africa)

Every day groups of men, some South Africans and others from the southern African region, sit on the side of the street in downtown Pietermaritzburg, South Africa, waiting for work—a scene repeated in nearly every city in our country. Some have the tools of their trade with them, such as shovels and trowels, while others hold only their meager lunch in their hands. They are our day-laborers. Most of them have some trade or work experience, but others have few formal skills, offering nothing more than their willingness to work. All of them are the flotsam of capitalism's relentless pursuit of profit, whether in the guise of the racial capitalism of apartheid or the more recent globalized form of neoliberal capitalism. They are among the products of systemic forms of economic exploitation going back more than three centuries.

The Theology and Economic Justice Programme of the Ujamaa Centre for Community Development and Research, in the School of Religion and Theology at the University of KwaZulu-Natal, has noticed these men and has begun to work with them. On a regular basis we have "hired" them for the day to spend time with us reflecting on the role that biblical and theological resources play in their lives. To demonstrate our commitment to socioeconomic justice, we compensate them for a full day's work and we also use our networks among a range of faith-based and nongovernmental organizations to assist these men in finding more permanent employment. At first apprehensive about the ideo-theological "work" we offer them, the men now eagerly embrace this opportunity to "do theology." They are contributing to a project called Contextual Bible Study, in which the resources of socially engaged biblical scholars and these casual workers are shared in order to construct a worker's theology. Among the texts we have read together is Matthew 20:1–16. We have approached this parable in a number of different ways, offering both "capitalist" and "socialist" readings of the text.

Initially this text was used to explore a socialist vision of society. In this collaborative reading, we would focus on the recognition the parable gives to the reality of day-laborers and the equitable payment to each according to their need. However, our longing for such a socialist vision was not enough to silence the features of the biblical text that stood over against such a reading. For while we overtly take up the Bible as a resource for economic survival, liberation, and life, and while we discern a prophetic socioeconomic trajectory weaving its way through the literary and sociohistorical contexts of the Bible, we are committed to respect the detail of particular biblical texts, recognizing that just as socioeconomic contestation is central to our own South African context it is also central to the sociohistorical sites of production of biblical texts.

In this case we were regularly troubled in our readings by the class identity of the "landowner," and his autocratic manner in hiring, paying, and dealing with the complaints of the day-laborers. We were also worried about his payment of the minimum wage and his delegation of the task of payment to "his manager." Most of all we were disturbed by the landowner's capitalist sounding rhetorical question, "Am I not allowed

to do what I choose with what belongs to me?" The detail of this text aroused our hermeneutic of suspicion, and we wondered if this parable *should* be read in a liberative manner. Clearly it *could* be read as supporting aspects of socialism, but only if we ignored
some of its detail. Was there a way, responsible to the detail of the text, to read this text
within our socialist ideo-theological orientation?

Our determination to read this text economically was frustrated by the refusal
of much of biblical scholarship to even engage with this dimension of the text. We
were drawn therefore to William Herzog's reading of this parable, identifying with
his notion of Jesus as "pedagogue of the oppressed," and his location of this parable
within the realities of the conflictual interface between "agrarian societies and traditional aristocratic empires" (*Parables as Subversive Speech: Jesus as Pedagogue
of the Oppressed* [Louisville: Westminster/John Knox, 1994], 85). Read from such
a perspective the contours of the parable are clearer. The owner of the vineyard is
likely an absentee landowner, a member of the economic urban elite, employing a
manager to handle the daily affairs of the vineyard, and engaged in a form of agri-
culture that produced a crop that can be converted into a luxury item (wine), mon-
etized, and exported. Unable to calculate how many laborers he will need, such is
the extent of his landholdings, the owner must make a number of trips to the agora
to hire workers. Regular assessment of the number of workers he needs also enables
the landowner to keep his workers to the minimum necessary to harvest the crop
within the designated time period. Furthermore, by hiring small numbers of laborers
during the day the landowner exercises his unilateral power, negotiating only with
those hired at the beginning of the day for the minimum daily wage, but leaving
the wage for those hired later in the day indeterminate (vv. 4, 7). For in a context
of chronic systemic unemployment and underemployment, the day-laborer is in no
position to insist on a just wage. Far from being generous, then, the householder is
taking advantage of an unemployed workforce to meet his harvesting needs by offering them work without a wage agreement. By telling a story in which the landowner
is actively involved in the economic process, Jesus foregrounds the socioeconomic
contestation of his time, making the usually invisible absentee landlord visible and
so setting up a direct encounter between the elites and the expendables.

The arbitrary power of the landowner is evident in the payment process. His power
is signaled in the delegation of his manager to make the payments, but is fully manifest
in his deliberate flaunting of protocol by refusing to pay the first-hired laborers first; by
making the first-hired wait until last he flaunts his power and shames them. The dignity
of those who have worked all day demands a response, and so they risk a protest (vv.
11–12), speaking back to power, invoking the principle of equal pay for equal work.
Singling out their spokesperson (v. 13), the landowner condescendingly reminds the
resisting workers of their contractual agreement, knowing full well that the day-laborers
were never in a position to negotiate anything other than the minimum wage, and then
goes on to dismiss their complaints, reiterating his right to do what he pleases with his
power (v. 14), and concluding by blasphemously asserting that the land which has sys-
temically been coerced from the very peasant farmers who are now day-laborers belongs
to him (v. 15). At this point the systemic violence beneath this text becomes palpable.

The Contextual Bible Study we have constructed to explore both the "socialist" and "capitalist" interpretive possibilities of this text generates considerable excitement and discussion. Most participants are unfamiliar with multiple ways of reading the same text, and most are unfamiliar with an overtly socioeconomic reading of the Bible. The discussions within each group are usually animated and intense, for we as participants have much at stake in our reading, particularly those who yearn for decent work but whom our economic system consumes as casual workers.

Gerald West and Sithembiso Zwane are coordinators at the Ujamaa Centre in the School of Religion and Theology at University of KwaZulu-Natal, Pietermaritzburg, South Africa.

READING THE PARABLE OF THE TALENTS WITH THOSE IN INDIA

David Joy (India)

The parable of the Talents in Matthew 25:14–30 has spawned volumes of interpretations from various viewpoints. Unfortunately, the parable has been misused to subjugate the weak, the vulnerable, the less privileged, and the voiceless. For example, in India migrants and the lower caste are inevitably branded as people with less talent and worth; and the parable has been interpreted as support for their continued oppression. Likewise, the parable has been used to promote capitalism which typically leads to the suffering of those who cannot produce capital, "for whoever does not have, even what he has will be taken from him" (25:29). Thus, there is a significant need to launch a fresh reading. This article is an attempt to read the parable through the eyes of the peasants of first-century Palestine, whose lives in many ways are analogous to a large portion of the population of India. I believe that such a reading will bring out the liberative meaning of the parable and the Gospel truth which it contains.

Many parables of Jesus reflect the fact that Palestine was occupied by Roman forces during that time. Thus, the sayings, parables, and miracles of Jesus need to be studied against the context of Roman colonialism. Such an approach is particularly relevant in today's world where millions of people become migrants and homeless due to liberal economic (capitalist) policies. Our so-called subaltern-cultural reading is concerned with the location, condition, and mind-set of the ordinary people in Jesus' audience and their everyday world. In this particular parable, it pays special attention to the third servant. Why is he afraid of the master? Why is he treated so harshly? What reaction is the audience supposed to have to the servant and the master?

To answer these questions we must pay attention to the social, cultural, and economic context of first-century Palestine, as a number of modern commentators have done quite well. This parable, for instance, assumes a context in which a household had compliant slaves who would make every effort to benefit materially and socially their master in order to exemplify faithful discipleship (i.e., the first two servants). The text offers no critique of this socioeconomic structure or of the particular activities of the obedient slaves, which may very well involve accumulating wealth at the expense of others (v. 24). The audience, then, is supposed to supply the critique. Namely, they are to recognize that the "specific socioeconomic commitment of the master and the activities of the first two slaves are not to be imitated" (Warren Carter, *Matthew and the Margins: A Sociopolitical Religious Reading*, [Bangalore: TPI, 2007], 488).

This reading is supported by several factors in the text. First, the third servant claims that the master has acquired his wealth through dishonest means ("harvesting where you did not sow and gathering where you did not plant," v. 24). Remarkably, the master himself affirms the truth of this (v. 26). Surely, the audience is not meant to approve of this unethical behavior. Second, the master's response to the servant seems obviously cruel and unfair, not to mention exaggerated and absurd. The "worthless" servant has his one talent confiscated and given to the servant with 10 before being expelled from the house—which again is hardly a response to be admired. In sum, though this parable might smack of capitalism, it is more clearly a critique of it, which Jesus presumes the audience will actively supply.

The parable, then, is one which presents the vulnerability of the oppressed class in Palestine. More specifically, it calls attention to the world of retainers—people who are part of the system of social dependency for survival—in the household of a powerful elite. The audience's sympathy for the wounded psyche of the fearful and helpless servant can translate into a motivation to work on behalf of the homeless, migrants, and all dispossessed people in India, or any other economic context which exploits a segment of the population. Perhaps it can also inspire the disenfranchised to stand up and demand dignity. In the name of social and political power too many people have been denied the basic necessities of life for too long. In this parable, Jesus challenges such political and economic systems by affirming that everyone ought to have a rightful place in God's just world.

David Joy is a Presbyter of the Church of South India, South Kerala Diocese, and a Professor of New Testament at the United Theological College, Bangalore, India; he has authored a number of books.

A QUEER READING OF THE PARABLE OF THE LEAVEN

Robert E. Shore-Goss (United States)

Jesus' parable of the leaven appears in Matthew 13:33 and Luke 13:20–21. The text stresses the action of the woman who has concealed the leaven in three measures of flour until the flour is entirely leavened. Typically, clergy and churches have understood the point of the parable as proclaiming that a small amount of leaven will pervade a large amount of flour, nearly 50 pounds. It is interpreted in the same ecclesial interpretation of the parable of the mustard seed: Small beginnings of God's reign will produce large consequences. The action of the woman hiding the leaven in the dough is preached as a positive action.

Generally, queer Christians do not read the scripture from the lens of hetero-sexuality. We read the scriptures as gay, lesbian, bisexual, transgendered, or inter-sexual folks with our own life contexts and our own particular histories within a given community. Queering the text is a reading strategy of the queer community to read and appropriate the texts for themselves. In other words, it is a reading strategy that disrupts the traditional heterosexist interpretations of the scripture. We read the scriptures as outsiders of many churches, for we have been marginalized by many Christians because of our sexual-orientation differences and gender variances. Our reading of this parable of the leaven is comprehended from the social context of queer folks as outsiders. We understand ourselves as leaven within many Christian churches.

As outsiders, we recognize the subordinate status of the woman who conceals the leaven in the dough. Jesus understands that women will have a role in the implementa-tion of the reign of God. First, that is problematic for many first-century C.E. Jewish holiness groups who find women more susceptible to pollution and impurity than men. Women in the Jewish tradition of the day, as in other Mediterranean cultures, were associated with the unclean, the religiously impure, through her monthly menstrual cycle. Men were more structurally aligned with religious purity and holiness. Could the kingdom come about or result through women and other devalued peoples who are marginal, often unseen, and expendable?

Second, the word "hidden" is perhaps better rendered "concealed" and has a nega-tive sense in the metaphorical language of the parable. The obvious question that many clergy fail to ask about this parable is this: What if the woman was caught for conceal-ing the leaven in the huge amount of dough? Would she be punished for her subversive action? Why is the fact that she stealthily placed the leaven in the dough stressed in the parable? The baker will be surprised to see the dough rise. Was this bread of leaven used for the Passover feast?

Many closeted LGBT Christians have acted stealthily, concealing their true lives from family, friends, church, and society. I concealed my life as a gay Jesuit priest for several years. The Catholic hierarchy labeled homosexuals as "intrinsically evil, objec-tively disordered." Homosexuals were impure and polluted in their erotic desires and lives, just as women were in first-century Judaism.

While closeted, I was able to subvert institutional pastoral practice and to release gay and lesbian Catholics burdened from guilt in their struggles to be good Catholic Christians and to be themselves. For example, I remember a lesbian Catholic who lived with a female lover for over 20 years being denied absolution in confession unless she left her lover—all this as she was undergoing surgery with a great deal of risk. I was able to do even more as an out gay priest after I was released from the Jesuits because I was gay and in love. There are many stories of LGBT folks who hid the leaven in different churches and social organizations to make them more humane and compassionate to the lives of queer folks.

Another significant metaphor is the leaven. Leaven in the ancient Mediterranean world was understood as "unclean, impure, or corrupt." In Hebrew Scriptures, there is an identification of leavened bread with the ordinary days of the year, and unleavened bread with the high holy days. Leaven becomes a metaphor for corruption, the impure, and the ordinary. One creates leaven by taking a piece of bread and storing it in a damp, dark place until mold forms as the bread rots and decays. Thus, leaven became a natural symbol for putrefaction, impurity, decay, and corruption, and by extension, leaven became associated with moral impurity and corruptions (Hosea 7:4). Likewise, in the New Testament leaven is equated with corrupt teaching (Mark 8:15) or associated with sexual immorality (1 Corinthians 5:8).

So the three elements "woman," "conceals," and "leaven" form a trinity of paradoxical images in the parable of the leaven that few religious figures would employ to speak about the reign of God. God's reign, Jesus affirms, is like moral corruption. But it is contextually different from the leaven or teachings of the Pharisees and Herod. The three images denote an agency that expands and transforms the three measure of dough into leavened bread. Jesus' audience would have been shocked or silenced by the boldness of the parable. Jesus in his teachings on compassion and his table fellowship with suspect or stigmatized men and women transgressed Jewish holiness/purity codes. In fact, the assembly, who delivers Jesus before Pilate, levels the following charge: "We found this man perverting the nation..." (Luke 23:2). This sums up Jesus' ministry of God's reign that perverted various notions of purity and pollution.

The language of purity/pollution has been reinscribed today in the strong moral rhetoric of contemporary religious conservatives and fundamentalists. Same-sex sexuality is characterized as disgusting, an abomination, sinful, perverted, intrinsically evil, and a threat to family and Western society. Employing rhetorical purity strategies of saving and protecting our children from homosexual marriage, they depict same-sex marriage as a contagion eroding "American traditional family values." Indeed, "queer" and "leaven" are functionally synonymous in many contemporary Christian purity maps. Queer folks blur the boundaries of contemporary Christian maps of sexual purity with the infusion of arguments for same-sex marriage or marriage equality, the creation of LGBT families of choice, and the right to gender transition. Like the woman in Jesus' parable, queer Christians insert their leaven of marriage equality and the right to family into the dough of Christian churches.

Imagine when the baker mixes up the 50 pounds of dough with the leaven mold and the dough rises. His reaction might well be similar to the Christian right's reaction upon discovering the spread of marriage rights of same-sex couples in several U.S. states and among several Christian denominations.

Queer readers would describe this insertion of leaven into the three measure of dough a "queeruption" of heterosexist thought. For Jesus says the leaven—those queer folks and all morally throwaway people—will be instrumental to bring in the reign of God. There will be a shock how the three measures of dough will surprisingly arise, and it is already too late, for God's reign will already be expanded through queer leaven. A queer reading of Jesus' parable of the leaven recaptures its original shock value and brings new leaven into contemporary Christian purity codes.

Robert E. Shore-Goss (Ph.D., Comparative Religion and Theology, Harvard University) is the gay Pastor of the MCC Church in the Valley; he is author of Jesus ACTED UP: A Gay and Lesbian Manifesto *and* Queering Christ: Beyond Jesus ACTED UP.

A CONFUCIAN PERSPECTIVE ON THE PARABLE OF THE SOWER
Kurtis Hagen (United States)

Here I will offer a Confucian interpretation of the parable of the Sower found in Matthew 13:1–23. Let me begin by discussing Mencius, the second great Confucian thinker of China's classical period, who told a parable reminiscent of the one in Matthew 13. According to Mencius' parable, barley seeds grow similarly when they are sown during the same season, in similar conditions, and are similarly cultivated. However, he points out, "There will be differences, due to differences in the quality of the soil and the distribution of rainfall, as well as in human efforts" (*Mencius* 6A7). That is, the seeds are basically similar, but outcomes may still vary if the conditions vary. We should also consider the compatible metaphor for which Mencius is most famous: People are born with "sprouts" of benevolence, appropriateness, ritual propriety, and wisdom (*Mencius* 2A6, 6A6). So, to "bear fruit," from this perspective, would involve fully developing these "spouts," and ultimately contributing to the increased harmony of the world: "If one were able to fully develop them, that would suffice to nurture and protect all within the four seas" (*Mencius* 2A6). On the other hand, if someone does not become virtuous and caring, it is not because he or she was a "bad seed," Mencius suggests, but because the development of his or her sprouts was thwarted by environmental conditions (*Mencius* 6A8).

In the parable of the Sower, placement is critical: where each seed falls determines its outcome. And yet, could *we* each be somehow responsible for whether or not we are "sown on good soil" and "bear fruit"? From a Confucian perspective, at least, our placement is neither merely a matter of chance nor of predetermined fate. For our "fate," as it is understood in Confucianism, is influenced by our own choices. As Mencius put it, "A person who understands 'fate' (*ming*) does not stand beneath a wall that is about to collapse" (*Mencius* 7A2). Indeed, our responsibility for our own placement is a theme repeatedly emphasized in the Confucian tradition. Confucius, for example, said, "It is the presence of benevolence (*ren*) that make a neighborhood admirable. If one chooses not to dwell among benevolent people, whereby can one achieve wisdom?" (*Analects* 4.1) Similarly, Xunzi, the third great Confucian thinker of the classical period, writes thus:

> If one finds good friends to associate with, then one can witness faithful service, living up to one's words, respect, and deference being put into practice. In their moral character they will make daily progress with respect to benevolence and appropriateness, without even realizing it, for it is proximity that makes it so. On the other hand, if they dwell with the morally inept, then they will hear of deceit, slander, cheating, and fakery, and will witness debasement, wonton depravity, and corruption in action. Without even noticing, they will be doing terrible violence to their moral character, for it is proximity that makes it so. (*Xunzi*, Book 23, "Innate Dispositions are Detestable")

From the Confucian perspective, then, the parable of the Sower evokes the value of having morally cultivated associates. It is a lesson about carefully choosing one's neighbors, friends, and general social environment. Associating with the virtuous will be fruitful. It will help one develop into a virtuous person oneself—a model of exemplary conduct. One will then be a good neighbor and friend of others, and thus not only bear fruit oneself, but many times over, as Jesus' words "some a hundredfold, some sixty, some thirty" seem to likewise suggest. Similarly, Mencius remarks, "Some are exceeded others by twice, five-fold, or even countless times, because they are unable to make the most of their potential" (*Mencius* 6A6). This multiplying effect is possible because, as Confucius says, "The moral power of the exemplary person is the wind; that of the petty person is the grass. When the wind blows over the grass, it will surely bend" (*Analects* 12.19). The message a Confucian draws from the parable of the Sower, then, is practical and sensible: Hearing of the proper path, but not understanding it, one will fail to fulfill one's potential to grow fully as a person, and to contribute to others. Hearing of the proper path, rejoicing in it, but not dwelling among the virtuous, one will ultimately fail as well. But if one hears of it, and commits to it, in the good soil of a moral community, one will both fulfill oneself, and have a significant transformative influence on others. So, choose your neighbors and associates wisely.

Kurtis Hagen is Assistant Professor in the Department of Philosophy at State University of New York, Plattsburgh, New York, United States.

QUESTIONS

1. Based on your own careful assessment of the biblical text, which is the better reading of the parable—the socialist or capitalist one? How do you suspect that your own economic context and views influence your response?

2. Assess Joy's interpretation of the parable of the Talents. How does it compare to your own reading?

3. How do the citations of other biblical texts help to support Goss's argument?

4. Based on Hagen's Confucian interpretation, how might one revise or improve Jesus' parable?

CHAPTER 5

TEACHINGS OF JESUS (PART I)

Luke 4:18–19; Matthew 15:4–9; Mark 12:38–44; Mark 7:24–30
and Matthew 15:21–28

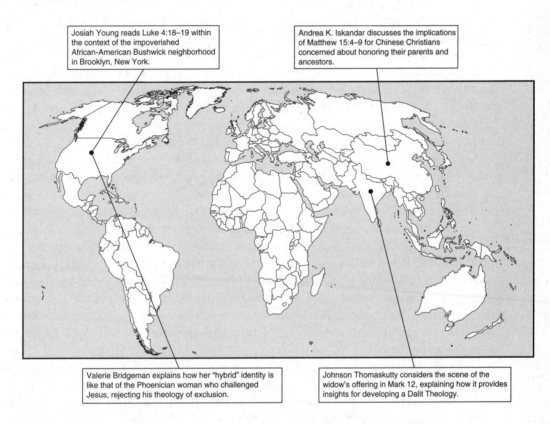

Josiah Young reads Luke 4:18–19 within the context of the impoverished African-American Bushwick neighborhood in Brooklyn, New York.

Andrea K. Iskandar discusses the implications of Matthew 15:4–9 for Chinese Christians concerned about honoring their parents and ancestors.

Valerie Bridgeman explains how her "hybrid" identity is like that of the Phoenician woman who challenged Jesus, rejecting his theology of exclusion.

Johnson Thomaskutty considers the scene of the widow's offering in Mark 12, explaining how it provides insights for developing a Dalit Theology.

READINGS

Luke 4 and the African-American Bushwick Neighborhood
Josiah Young

Honoring Your Parents and Ancestors
Andrea K. Iskandar

The Widow's Offering and Dalit Theology
Johnson Thomaskutty

Personal Reflections on the "Hybrid" Identity of the Phoenician Woman
Valerie Bridgeman

LUKE 4 AND THE AFRICAN-AMERICAN BUSHWICK NEIGHBORHOOD

Josiah Young (United States)

I grew up in Bushwick, a neighborhood in Brooklyn, New York. Life there in the 1960s was fatal for many African-Americans, especially underclass males. They died young from substance abuse and homicide. The hostility of the public school system and the aggression of law enforcement agencies toward them did not help. Neither did their dysfunctional households. The escalation of crime coincident with the hard drugs that flooded the "community" seemed to suck them in like a black hole. Unfortunately, places like Bushwick continue to exist today. Black males are among the most uneducated and unemployed caste in America. The black residents of Bushwick and other ghettos still suffer from crime, segregation, poor schools, and early death. Regentrification policies add to their misery by displacing them, forcing them to move to other depressed areas or rendering them homeless.

Perhaps Luke 4:18–19 is pertinent to these sad circumstances, for it depicts Jesus of Nazareth as bringing "good news to the poor." By the time one reads Luke 4, one knows Jesus is the Christ, the "Son of the Most High," from the time his mother conceived him by the Holy Spirit's power. He has triumphed over the "devil" in the aftermath of his baptism and anointing with the Spirit of God. So none is surprised when the Christ, reading from Isaiah in Luke 4:18–19, says "the Spirit of the Lord is upon" him and has anointed him to make the blind see and set the oppressed free. He proclaims "the year of the Lord's favor," which alludes to the Jubilee year, in which the Hebrew elite were to release their Hebrews slaves. None is surprised that he fulfills the prophecy as he heals and feeds the poor. And after the Romans put him to death, the Christ rises bodily from the dead. He is exactly who he said he was—God's anointed.

Many Bushwick folk brave the dangerous streets on Sunday morning just to hear the powerful words of the Gospel; for the words do provide hope for the oppressed. They long for "the year of the Lord's favor" and trust that it is coming, for Christ's sake. Their hope motivates them to challenge their adversity and work for the betterment of humankind. But the Jubilee was the year the Hebrews set their Hebrew slaves free and kept their *non*-Hebrew slaves ("the aliens") "as a possession" for their children (Leviticus 25:44–46). No Jubilee for them. Luke's parables that feature master–slave relationships make me wonder whether he had the Hebrew or the "alien" slaves in mind (cf. 12:41–48). Is there good news for Bushwick's African-Americans, of whom Luke never heard? Are they like the "aliens" without Jubilee rights?

I think that the Gospel of Jesus Christ is broader in scope than the Jubilee that is only for some. It must be broader than that if it is to be taken seriously. Otherwise, the Gospel would lose much of its power to instill hope in the oppressed and in anyone else who hopes that the Kingdom of God is for all creation. I, then, cannot confine the Gospel to slave codes far more ancient than Luke's gospel. The narratives of the risen

Christ break through such antiquated practices precisely because they promise that a new creation is coming and has already come in the glorified Christ. May it come for the rest of us soon (and very soon).

Josiah Young is Professor of Systematic Theology at Wesley Theological Seminary, Washington, D.C., United States.

HONORING YOUR PARENTS AND ANCESTORS
Andrea K. Iskandar (China)

"I have 2 siblings. Both of them are now Christians and I'm the only one left. If I convert to Christianity as well, who will take care of our parents and ancestors? Who will take care of their altar and keep on praying for them? Please don't ask me to dishonor my parents and ancestors." Such an empathic statement is not uncommon among Chinese people when they're challenged to accept Jesus as their savior. In this context, Matthew 15:4–9 is an important and encouraging passage to consider.

Chinese people are known for the high respect they give to their parents and ancestors. Upon a person's death, an expensive festival is due. The deceased's children and relatives will prepare a set of "living provision" to ensure the deceased's well-being in the afterworld. Depending on the family's wealth, the provision may include a large mansion, a villa and its furniture, fancy cars, a couple of maids and servants—all of which are beautifully made of colorful and expensive papers—as well as a large amount of afterlife bills. These are all meant to sustain (or even increase!) the deceased's lifestyle and well-being in the afterlife compared to the one he or she had while alive. At the end of the burial or cremation ceremony, the deceased's children and relatives will burn all of them as a way of sending these provisions to the afterlife. It is believed these crafts made of fancy papers will be transferred into real stuff in the afterlife, so a burnt Jaguar paper craft would turn to an actual Jaguar as a means of transportation in the next world. The process of respecting the deceased doesn't end there. After the body is buried or cremated, an altar will be kept in the family's houses for generations with the deceased's photograph hung above it so his or her descendants will continue praying and burning some afterlife bills that function much like monthly stipends for the deceased to sustain his or her lifestyle and well-being in the afterlife until reincarnation.

Apart from the expensive paper accessories to be burned, a number of food offerings are also involved. From the mourning days prior to the burial or cremation ceremony, and continuing for many years afterwards, there are highly exquisite and expensive foods involved in the offering. All these actions constitute "honoring the parents and ancestors." Furthermore, this culture knows no such thing as "empty nesters." Grown-up adults in most cases still live with their parents until they get married, and as both parents and children grow old, parents will live near to or in the same house with their children. Grandparents are highly involved in rearing their grandchildren and married children are responsible for taking care of their aged parents. Although retirement houses are available, letting one's parents stay in a retirement facility may be deemed as a sign of disrespect and neglect, a gesture of unwillingness to hold responsibility toward parents.

It thus becomes a serious barrier for many people of Chinese descent to convert to Christianity, fearing that no one else will take care of their parents' and ancestors' well-being in the afterworld. Converting to Christianity is understood as neglecting the care of one's parents and breaking away from one's family. Christian converts are often labeled by their parents as disrespectful children who are not concerned about their parents and ancestors—indeed, this is a very serious accusation which would be akin to having your parents spit on your face for abandoning them and dishonoring the family's name.

Then the following questions arise: "Can I follow Jesus and yet still honor my parents and ancestors? But then again, how can I honor my parents and ancestors while I neglect my service to their altar? Which one should come first: God or my parents? Can I make peace between the first and fifth commandments—how do I worship God alone and still adhere to ancestral traditions?"

A part of the issue that is rarely mentioned, however, is that this respect to parents and ancestors has often been overvalued at the expense of the actual respect shown to parents while they are still alive. It's not strange to find children who devotedly pre-pare the food offering on the parents' altar, but during their parents' life they would often be involved in arguments and fights, not to mention never taking their parents to a restaurant to enjoy the kind of fancy food now offered to their parents' soul in the afterworld. As for the parents, when they accuse their children of disrespectful behav-ior, they are often worried more about their children's devotion to them after their death (for it involves their well-being in the afterworld) and less about these children's actual devotion to them in the current life.

Matthew 15:4–9 helps to clarify the stand of the Church in face of such accusa-tion that "you cannot convert to Christianity without being disrespectful to your parents and ancestors." It helps the Chinese families and parents realize that the Bible actually puts a high emphasis on respecting parents. Believers are not expected to give to God at the expense of taking care of their parents. Instead, provision for parents' well-being is to be put ahead of offerings given to God. One cannot honor God without honoring parents.

Jesus speaks in terms of tangible (financial) gifts to parents while they are still alive. Applying Jesus' teaching in today's context, we might conclude that if one has enough money to treat one's parents to a fancy meal, then one ought to do that instead of offering them exquisite food after their death.

Of course, it is evident in this passage that Jesus expects his followers to be respect-ful of parents not just in terms of material provision but also in terms of relationships. He expects people to have a right heart, a proper attitude (vv. 8–9). Children should not quarrel or speak disrespectful words to their parents. Such honor and respect, we might say, surpasses the demands of the Chinese cultural tradition. In sum, Matthew 15:4–9 provides a comforting and corrective passage to people of Chinese descent who worry about the well-being of their parents as a result of their conversion to Christianity.

Andrea K. Iskandar (M.Div., Cipanas Theological Seminary, Indonesia) is Chairman of the Board of Youth Ministry at Gereja Kristus Ketapang, Jakarta, Indonesia.

THE WIDOW'S OFFERING AND DALIT THEOLOGY
Johnson Thomaskutty (India)

The Dalits, the majority community of India, are politically powerless, socially untouchable, economically poor, and religiously voiceless. Even today casteism is practiced in several parts of the country, by which the interests of the elite are protected. Dalit women of India are victims of patriarchal and androcentric customs as well as natural and accidental catastrophes. They are still victims of a cruel and oppressive socioreligious order. The customs of the society traumatized the feelings of women, especially Dalit women, in the past and even now it hurts their identity. Many of them are homeless, jobless, starving, sick, oppressed, exploited, persecuted, robbed, raped, hungry, and dying.

Today, the Dalits are eagerly waiting for a paradigm message of transformation and equality to overcome the dehumanizing structures. Mark 12:38–44 is just such a text which provides powerful insights for developing a Dalit Theology. In this passage Jesus targets his criticism primarily toward the scribes due to their neglect and exploitation of the widows, the helpless people. In the story, Jesus is seated upon a bench watching the people bringing their contributions to the Temple treasury. Jesus' position beside the Temple allows him to observe a succession of rich contributors who come and deposit their coins. Many of those donating large sums were wealthy landowners who lived in or near Jerusalem; others were Jewish businessmen and merchants who had journeyed to Jerusalem for the Passover holiday. In contrast to the rich who contributed large sums, the woman tossed in two tiny coins. The coin referred to here (lepton/mite) was the smallest in circulation in Palestine. The widow's two coins were all that she had—it was the sum total of her possessions, which constituted a day's wage, a puny amount.

Jesus was in sharp conflict with the Judaism of his time and the crucifixion was the end result. The theme of Mark's Gospel—the Son of Man came not to be served, but to serve and give his life as a ransom for many—connects well with the story of the needy-poor-widow-woman. Jesus raises the status of the woman before the rich; that is the climax of this rhetorical irony. In Mark's Gospel, one of the primary teachings of Jesus is about discipleship: the one who "acts," rather than the one who speaks. In 8:34 Jesus says, "whoever desires to come after me let that one deny self, and take up his/her own cross, and follow me." Here, it is obvious that discipleship requires complete denial, that is, total surrender to Jesus Christ. The widow in 12:41–44 represents and reaffirms such a model of discipleship, as she rendered her whole livelihood.

The story of the poor widow was told not merely for preaching purpose, but to turn the human acumen toward the moral and spiritual responsibility for a transformed life. Jesus' people-oriented approach for transformation provides us a frame for molding a theology of liberation and emancipation here and now. The first and the foremost task in our mission for and of Dalits is to give them hope that they are "new people" and no more "no people." That is what we comprehend from the story of the needy-poor-widow-woman. In India, poverty is not simply an economic problem. This problem is produced and perpetuated by a system of exploitative structures which makes the rich richer and the poor poorer. It is similar to the scribal-and-widow woman tension within the Markan story.

The widow in Mark 12 is a victim of an imbalanced society in which she was oppressed as poor, subjugated as a woman, and dehumanized as a widow; she was indeed suffering from triple-oppression. A Dalit Christian woman is a woman, a Dalit, and a Christian. There is in India a tradition defining what each of these identities involve which is so strong that a Dalit Christian woman can be described as thrice handicapped or thrice alienated on the basis of her gender, her caste, and her membership in a minority religious community (i.e., Christianity in India). The Women's Movement in India has emphasized that Dalit women are the dust of dust in Indian society—the thrice oppressed, brutalized, and abused not only by the upper castes/classes but by Dalit men too.

While the rabbis walked around in long robes, the widows ended up with tiny coins; while the rabbis were greeted with respect, the widows were considered a public disgrace; while one people group was comfortable with their best seats, the other was without a place to lay their heads; and while one constructed their own splendorous mansions including the Temple, the other had their houses devoured. These caricatures go well with the context of lower caste–higher caste or poor–elite disparity in the Indian scenario. The presentation of the Markan widow over against the giant men can be taken as a symbolic expression of a social reality. The life-situation of the widow in the narratives of Mark provides paradigmatic rhetoric for us to apply to the life-situation of India.

Dalit women who are victims of patriarchal constraints within the Dalit-fold itself are emerging as a volatile force to challenge the status quo. They are the targets of sexual abuse by upper castes in a context of caste/class clashes, of state-sponsored violence in various forms, and of domestic violence in the hands of their own men. The widow of Mark 12 is a living testimony for all the widows, oppressed women, and all the Dalit people in India and elsewhere around the globe. She must not be looked at merely as a historical monument; instead we must place her into the real-life situation of all the oppressed and exploited classes as a directive force for transforming the dehumanizing structures that are prevalent in the contemporary global scenario.

Not only in this story but throughout all the Gospels, Jesus stood firm for the causes of the marginalized and identified completely with them. Just as Jesus sided with the vulnerable as a prophet of social transformation, so too in the present-day situation the church should raise its prophetic voice on behalf of the Dalits, especially the Dalit women of India.

Johnson Thomaskutty is Assistant Professor of New Testament and Greek Language at Union Biblical Seminary, Pune, Maharashtra, India.

PERSONAL REFLECTIONS ON THE "HYBRID" IDENTITY OF THE PHOENICIAN WOMAN
Valerie Bridgeman (United States)

I am a hybrid woman, born in the rural countryside of the Deep South of the United States, but with a city sensibility. I love the cacophonic sounds of many languages clashing in the air—sounds I've only heard in a big city. I love foods and music from a variety of cultures perhaps because I am the embodiment of a clash of cultures—England slave-owning great-great-great grandfather, Cherokee great-great grandmother, the Africans somewhere in my ancestry. Thus I am mixed, perhaps like the Phoenician woman from Syria (Mark 7:24–30 and Matthew 15:21–28).

I grew up on my maternal parents' farm. My mother's mother, Callie, was part Cherokee and African, a "root worker" who somehow kept us well with the potions and teas she concocted. Healing was her profession. She knew the gift of the land. Perhaps like Jesus. And she always fascinated me. Callie was a woman of few words, but she had sharp eyes and missed very little. She could tell when someone was sick or emotionally distraught. She was fierce. I admired, loved, and feared her at the same time. I remember her performing the esoteric act of "talking fire" out of our bodies should we get burned. And it worked. Healing is a part of my Native American/African heritage.

I also am an African American mother of sons. My daughters are my goddaughters and my granddaughter. Like most mothers, I worry about my children, especially when they are in any kind of distress—physically, economically, spiritually, or socially. My children learned this phrase when they were growing up: "My mama is like a she-bear with her cubs." I inherited my fierce protectiveness of my children from the maternal lineage from which I derive. I have learned that not every mother feels this fiercely, but I do. I always did. And I was never good at hearing "no" when it came to my children. Once, when my son got into a conflict at school, the principal insisted that he would have to be expelled, even though it was not his fault. There was a "no tolerance" policy that was unbendable, he said. That principal told me I had no choice besides the one he offered. I rejoined, "I always have choices, even if it means worrying you until I get what I want." And I did win that battle of wills. I fought for my son despite what seemed insurmountable "rules." That is the spirit of the Syrophoenician woman who approached Jesus. And the spirit of my mother and grandmother, and I imagine, their mothers before them.

And I am a biblical scholar, a preacher, and an artist. All these contexts are really one context. I am an African American mother-scholar-preacher-artist who engages texts with an eye toward liberation and healing. I always want to know how a text may help us live fully and freely in light of God's love for all humanity. For me, the salvation that Christians speak of is not salvation without the ability to live an abundant life.

Jesus' encounter with this woman strikes me for several reasons. The first issue is that he is in her country. He is the foreigner, not her. He goes away, on "vacation," to get away from his daily work of teaching, healing, leading. He is, it seems, a welcomed and honored guest among people who do not share his heritage or his religious history. They accept him. And they want to hear from him. Difference is a gift, another one of my truly held beliefs. And she, this Syrophoenician woman, is "at home" in her land. She approaches Jesus with deference and respect. If one were not paying close attention, Jesus' answer might make you think she is the one out of place, the foreigner. If one only had his reply, one would believe that she was out of order. But she approaches him like many before her.

She is fierce, and will not be put off by Jesus' seeming disinterest in her plight. She will not be insulted. She will not be demeaned. She has a sick child and will suffer whatever indignities she must for her child's survival. As an African American woman, the ability to allow insults to bypass you in order to get justice is a necessary trait. And make no mistake; the encounter is in fact very insulting. There is no way to soften the derogatory sound of "dog" rolling off even Jesus' tongue. The statement simply is pejorative. But she refuses to be deterred. It is her tenacity that is compelling in the text. It is her insistence that her daughter—and by default, all the Phoenician daughters and sons from Syria—deserve the same care and healing as the "house of Israel." She becomes the testimony that the ministry of Jesus is not limited to "his kind."

As an African American woman who remembers the harsh realities of segregation, I know the insult of feeling "less than" because of someone else's presumed superiority and priority. My mother, Bernice, was a proud woman who taught us that we were just as good as anyone else in the world. She taught us that we deserved to be treated with dignity and respect. And while she taught her children that, the world did not always oblige us her lessons. Sometimes, we suffered indignities and disrespect because we were African American. Sometimes, white people seemed to question whether we should even breathe the same air as they did. So this text is a confrontation of cultures, of prejudices, xenophobia, and of expectations. It prods me every time I read it or preach from it. These cultures are not in isolation. How could they be, if Jesus could walk easily into a "foreign" territory? There wasn't that much physical distance. And, it wasn't as if Jesus didn't know what it was to be an outsider, since he would have known that Joseph fled to Egypt when he was born in order to protect him—a stranger in a strange land. Despite the presumed differences, it seems Jesus and this woman were more alike than they were different.

I have preached about the need for health care for all from this text; I've preached that in a culture wealthy with bread, no one should have to settle with crumbs from a full table. I've preached a mother's love can be fierce and that she rejected Jesus' theology of exclusion. She challenged him. That seems daunting in a Christianity that has been taught not to question anything, certainly not Jesus! She is the heroine in this story; she exemplifies God's grace to all humanity and she demands it from the savior of the world. In this story, healing from demonic oppression is just the final moment of redemption. Redemption begins when she challenges Jesus to be the savior of the whole world, and offer the feast of God to more than just his kind. That is good news.

Valerie Bridgeman is Associate Professor at Lancaster Theological Seminary, United States; she is an ordained preacher and published poet.

QUESTIONS

1. How are the residents of Bushwick like and unlike the "aliens" for whom there is no Jubilee?
2. How would Matthew 15:4–9 be appropriated in your cultural context in comparison to Iskandar's interpretation of it?
3. According to Thomaskutty, in what sense is the widow to be emulated? And in what sense is Jesus to be emulated?
4. How does Bridgeman's personal background and identity shape her reading of the biblical text? What elements of your background and identity might yield interesting insights on the story of the Syrophoenician woman?

CHAPTER 6

TEACHINGS OF JESUS (PART II)

Luke 20:20–26, Matthew 22:15–22, and Mark 12:13–17; Matthew 3:10; Matthew 7:16–20; Matthew 12:33; Luke 13:6–9; Luke 18:18–30

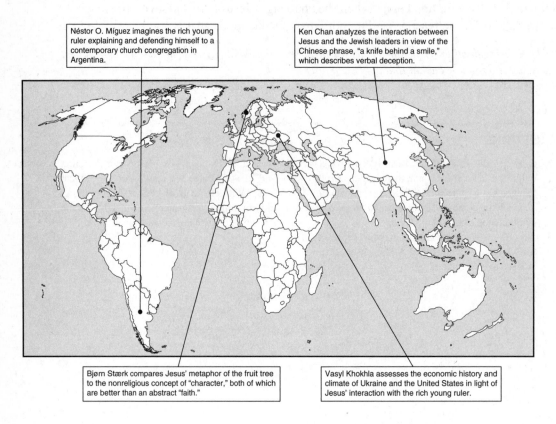

Néstor O. Míguez imagines the rich young ruler explaining and defending himself to a contemporary church congregation in Argentina.

Ken Chan analyzes the interaction between Jesus and the Jewish leaders in view of the Chinese phrase, "a knife behind a smile," which describes verbal deception.

Bjørn Stærk compares Jesus' metaphor of the fruit tree to the nonreligious concept of "character," both of which are better than an abstract "faith."

Vasyl Khokhla assesses the economic history and climate of Ukraine and the United States in light of Jesus' interaction with the rich young ruler.

READINGS

"A Knife Behind a Smile" in the Interaction Between Jesus and Jewish Leaders
Ken Chan

The Metaphor of the Fruit Tree and the Concept of Character
Bjørn Stærk

Ukraine, the United States, and the Rich Young Ruler
Vasyl Khokhla

The Rich Young Ruler in a Church in Argentina
Néstor O. Míguez

"A Knife Behind a Smile" in the Interaction Between Jesus and Jewish Leaders

Ken Chan (China)

The religious leaders did not like Jesus. They felt threatened by him because he was gaining a popular following for his reputation as a miracle worker. Jesus also interpreted scripture (the Old Testament) differently from them. This was uncomforting. They could lose their power over the Jews. They might be out of a job soon.

Their response was to get rid of Jesus, and they needed an excuse. So, in Luke 20:20–26 (as well as in Matt. 22:15–22 and Mark 12:13–17) we read that they watched Jesus carefully, and then they sent out spies to catch Jesus in his words. The spies pretended to be "righteous" people (20:20), and they started off by flattering him: "Teacher, we know that you speak and teach rightly" (20:21). This was a lie. They came to Jesus precisely because they did not believe he "teaches rightly." They hoped to catch Jesus off guard by tricking him with the question: "Is it proper for us to give tax to Caesar, or is it not?" (20:22). The text is ringing with alarm bells, telling the reader that here is a trap.

The Chinese have a phrase to describe this type of verbal deception. We call it "a knife behind a smile." Cantonese (a dialect of Chinese spoken in the southern part of China, including Hong Kong) calls it "a deadly snake behind a smile." For example, it may appear strange that a Chinese who meets you for the first time would treat you like you were the king—strange, until you later find out that the information that was gathered about you had been used to your disadvantage. This is the reason that many Chinese guard information about themselves tightly. When they are asked a question about themselves, they often try to divert the topic of conversation, or fall silent, or ask you a question instead, so as to avoid having to answer the question you had first asked them.

Jesus responded to this trap graciously. He knew what they were up to (20:23), but he did not get angry or yell back. Like a classical Chinese gentleman, he dealt with the problem while remaining calm. The first thing he did was to ask for a denarius coin (20:24). He turned this situation into an object lesson: He taught the crowd how to resolve the apparent conflict between loyalty to the State and to God. Like a good Rabbi, he began by asking a question: "Of whose image and inscription does it have?" For him, paying tax to the Roman government does not equate with denying the authority of God. Jesus was loyal to the absolute claim of God, and yet he recognized the temporal authority of the State in matters such as taxation. Jesus put each thing in its place when he said, "Give the things of Caesar to Caesar, and the things of God to God" (20:25). His statement sounds great to a Chinese because it fits the Rule of the Median as taught by Confucius. The best way forward should address all concerns.

While the religious leaders spent considerable time plotting against Jesus, Jesus was able to respond immediately. This shows that Jesus knew what he believed in. The urgency of the situation revealed the core of himself—a man who knew the will of God and how to apply it in daily life. Jesus gave a good answer. He also acted within his culture by responding indirectly. He busted the fallacious premise that was hidden in the question. But his aim was not to defend himself and save his skin; rather, his desire was to teach the truth on this occasion.

The spies were dumbfounded, since "they were not strong enough to seize upon his words before the people" (20:26). They even had a tinge of admiration at his superb answer. At the end, all they could do was to be silent. This was an unexpected reversal of events. Jesus was supposed to lose face and credibility before the people, but the spies ended up in those shoes. Their silence was their way of minimizing their embarrassment when they had failed to trap Jesus. The irony through it all is that Jesus was not even concerned about whether he would lose face. Jesus knew he was in good standing with God, and he had nothing to be afraid of.

The nonliteral use of words, questions, and facial expressions in the Chinese culture is not always meant for ill, but miscommunication frequently occurs because of it. Often, a Chinese person will come up to you and apologize about something for no apparent reason. It is because that person was reading your facial expression and thought that you were displeased about something. For that person, making a preemptive apology is the best way to clarify any possible misunderstanding before it blows out of proportion and destroys the relationship.

This, in turn, makes it hard to ask a real question. Since a question is often used as (and interpreted as) a verbal criticism, many Chinese simply do not ask questions in public even if they have a burning question. For fear of being misinterpreted, they will (a) leave the question dangling, (b) get the information from a third party, or (c) deduce the answer based on what they already know.

Another cultural norm that blocks communication is that Chinese are expected to agree with one another no matter what. Conformity to the norm is also strongly encouraged in a typical Chinese Christian church. The desire for uniformity makes problem-solving difficult when divergent opinions genuinely exist within the church. It is a generally accepted principle that conflicts can only be resolved by analyzing the alternative positions and rationally weighing their pros and cons. Yet, it is hard to have a real discussion in a Chinese church, since harmony is emphasized. A so-called discussion is often only a beautiful veneer on the outside of a stew of garbled emotions. Such communities would even deny that there is a problem, until the pent-up feelings erupt, and the community splits.

This passage helps me, as a Chinese, to reexamine the distance between my words and feelings, what I actually think and what I say. And when someone with malicious intent comes my way, my job is to (a) see through the trap, (b) be calm, (c) examine my conscience, (d) get rid of the fear of man, (e) speak and teach God's truth in a culturally acceptable way, and (f) apply the Rule of the Median.

Ken Chan (Ph.D., Biblical Studies) is a linguist translator with SIL International serving in East Asia.

THE METAPHOR OF THE FRUIT TREE AND THE CONCEPT OF CHARACTER

Bjørn Stærk (Norway)

In the Christian faith that I grew up in, it is your faith that saves you, not good deeds; but your actions are a reflection of your faith, a demonstration of the role Jesus has in your life. The idea is that only God can see what is in your heart, and in the end that's all that really matters, but everything you do in your daily life, all your actions and choices and habits, reflect what is in your heart. Your actions are not only a demonstration of your relationship with Jesus but a demonstration to nonbelievers of the power and goodness of your religion.

This is a powerful idea. A less religious word for a similar concept is "character." Your actions reflect what's inside of you, your essence as a person. It is your character that makes you good or bad, but your actions display that good or bad character to the world.

Nonbelievers often overemphasize the role of good deeds in Christianity. There's a reason for this. Good deeds are something we can understand and respect, unlike faith, a concept even Christians can find difficult to comprehend. You can only fully understand faith by having it, but anyone can understand good deeds. Anyone can look at what you do and say, "Yes, this is a person who does good things. There must be something good on the inside that causes this."

All of this can be summed up in that perfect metaphor of the tree interwoven throughout Jesus' teaching (e.g., Matt. 3:10; 7:16–20; 12:33; Luke 13:6–9). Just as good trees produce good fruit and bad trees bad fruit, so it is with people. This is an idea that is relevant far beyond Christianity itself.

As an atheist, I am not very interested in faith. I think faith is a morally questionable ideal. But I like the metaphor of the fruit tree, the idea that your actions can be used to judge your character, and I think it shows us a way for different worldviews to coexist without compromising their integrity.

Think about how people with different interests and abilities find a way to get along in daily life. We're rarely fortunate enough to be able to spend our time with people who are exactly like ourselves. We have to deal with people we like but who aren't perfect, people we don't have much in common with, and some people who are just awful. We do this with the help of social lubricants.

One of these is politeness, maintaining a friendly, somewhat ritualized facade, while hiding your innermost thoughts from strangers. Another is keeping your distance, not forcing yourself into other people's lives. You don't have to like the local shopkeepers, just find ways to deal with them without getting into a fight. So you smile, because it's polite, and you don't tell them about your personal life, because they don't want to know. To get along with other people, we restrict ourselves, but we get something valuable in return, so we accept it.

Now think of groups of people, groups with different worldviews. Some of them are religious worldviews; others could be philosophical or political. In the past, everyone who lived near you thought like you, but today we're surrounded by people of different cultures, different faiths, and different ideologies. Again we need a lubricant, some way to make it easier to deal with groups with alien ideals.

Just as the instinct of individuals, beneath all the layers of social indoctrination, is to demand that everyone should think and behave just like ourselves, so it is with groups and their worldviews. All faiths and ideologies would prefer if the whole world could be organized according to their ideals. It would feel so good. And many worldviews go through phases where they try to do just that; they try to impose their views by force.

Eventually they learn better. Just as a person who tells everyone they meet exactly what they think is wrong about them won't make many friends, a worldview that imposes itself through force will be feared, hated, and resented. It may succeed at forcing itself on people, but at a high cost. Modern Christians still live in the shadow of their authoritarian ancestors. In my own country, Norway, anyone who professes a strong personal faith in God risks being associated with authoritarian Puritanism. People will look at you as if you may at any moment rise up and shout, "That looks fun. Let's MAKE IT ILLEGAL!" It's a prejudice, but the prejudice was caused by earlier generations of Christians who wanted to regulate society according to their ideals and force everyone to live by their standards.

So the dilemma of the believer today is this: You have what you believe is a good faith, a true faith, and you want other people to see that, and adopt it themselves. But they don't always want to listen to you. They laugh at you. They live by what you consider to be deeply immoral ideals. And even if you find a political majority for your views, using power to impose your views will not make anyone adopt your faith; it will just make them bitter.

So you remember the metaphor of the fruit tree, and you say to yourself, "I will act out the ideals I believe in. I will live my life as a testimony to my faith. And I will do this together with my family, and my friends, and my congregation. In this evil world, full of hate and despair and sorrow, our community will be an island of good, of hope. People will look at us and wonder what it is that makes us so content. We're only human, but we are humans who strive toward a wonderful ideal, with the aid of Heaven. Sometimes we will do things that are wrong, and people will notice that. But we will regret our mistakes, and try to make up for them, and we hope people will see that too. And they will at worst respect us, and at best become curious about what it is that we have that makes all this possible."

And that is the tree that bears good fruits, or, more accurately, the tree that is so confident that it is willing, even eager, to be judged by its fruits. Imagine a world where all faiths and all philosophies and ideologies think like this. A world where we promote unpopular ideals by living them in practice, and setting a good example. All of us. As individuals, or as groups.

Not everyone can live out all their ideals, but everyone can do it to some extent. Everyone can think of themselves as ambassadors from a better world. We can see other worldviews not as enemies to fight, but competitors to outshine. This doesn't mean that we necessarily see our actions as the core of our ideals, but that we see actions as our chief way of interacting with those who follow other ideals.

And perhaps we will produce good fruits, and be judged by them. Or perhaps we are wrong and produce rotten fruits, but at least we did our best to make the world a better place, without forcing ourselves on anyone. That's something I think most of us can appreciate, no matter what we believe in.

Bjørn Stærk is a software developer from Norway; he is an atheist and former Christian, and writes a blog at http://max256.bearstrong.net.

UKRAINE, THE UNITED STATES, AND THE RICH YOUNG RULER

Vasyl Khokhla (Ukraine)

After the collapse of the Soviet Union in the early1990s, Ukraine became an independent nation. Although Ukraine was officially proclaimed a democracy in 1991, numerous traces of the Soviet past still remain. A swift shift to democracy and capitalism, or "shock therapy" as some economists term it, drove many people to extreme poverty. The gap between the rich and the poor widened. Life in much of Ukraine remains bleak today. Having grown up in Kalush, Western Ukraine, I have witnessed this firsthand. Now that I am studying at a University in the United States, this is the question I ask myself: Why aren't democracy and capitalism working in Ukraine while they are bulwarks of prosperity and development in the United States?

To my mind, the religious, specifically Christian, heritage of the United States has made a big difference. The teachings of Jesus have had a significant impact. In Jesus' encounter with the wealthy young ruler in Luke 18, we see one of many places where Jesus promotes the distribution of wealth, without rejecting the initial accumulation of it. It is to be noted that Jesus instructs the man to "sell all that he owns and give the money to the poor." The man must essentially sell his business, perhaps much like merger and acquisitions that take place today which often drive the economy. The rich man is to share the proceeds of his successful and sound business with the less fortunate in his community. He is to be socially responsible.

The United States, unlike Ukraine, was founded on Christian values in which the ethics of sharing as advocated by Jesus had an important place. This generated a strong trust among people, which, in turn, facilitated business transactions. Trust became the social capital that laid a foundation for a free and ethical enterprise. While the main aim of capitalism is to generate profit, if Americans were setting up business with the sole goal of becoming rich, I doubt they would thrive. If they were simply pursuing their own gain and not worrying about the needs of others, they would not get very far. However, Americans are known as the most giving nation in the world. This is, I believe, due in part to people taking seriously Jesus' words to share with the poor. American business people usually remember their duty to help the community. Indeed, as Max Weber's classic work, *The Protestant Ethic and the Spirit of Capitalism*, explains, Christian values have influenced the success of capitalism.

Ukraine, on the other hand, is a former Soviet Union country where practices of religion were suppressed. Lenin, one of the founding Soviet leaders, felt that Karl Marx was right when he said, "Religion is the opium for the people." Although some people in communist Ukraine worshipped God despite severe persecution, the attitudes of atheism prevailed. With the collapse of the USSR, people received freedom of religion, which led to the emergence of a myriad of religious organizations, including Protestant ones (the predominant religion in Ukraine is the Orthodox Church). Yet, many people are still nonreligious, a direct result of the atheism that was prevalent among Communists, the major political party in the Soviet Union.

Although Democracy brought hundreds of new political parties to Ukraine, the problem is that the politicians in these new parties of the "democratic era" consist of so-called "repainted" Communists. The very same Communists in the Soviet Union assumed a role of democratically elected representatives in the independent Ukraine. Independent Ukraine has thus experienced much corruption and embezzlement, severely hindering economic growth. Instead of showing concern for the well-being of the people, such politicians stuff their own pockets. They indeed represent the antithesis of the ethics of sharing taught by Jesus in Luke 18. As atheists, they have no fear of God, no religious principles to guide them, and as a result they exploit and manipulate the economic system to their own advantage. This has caused the moral erosion of the nation. People distrust such politicians. The majority of the citizenry feel hopeless. Alcoholism is very prevalent.

In my view, then, what Ukraine needs is for people and politicians to live out the Christian ethic of sharing. In order to share, one must first acquire and accumulate, which the young ruler in Luke 18 had done, without any condemnation from Jesus. As the young man discovered, sharing can be difficult, unnatural even. But it is what Jesus calls people to do—and it is what people in the United States in fact do. In my perspective, the success and efficiency of the American capitalistic system is a result of America's religious heritage and tradition, specifically their willingness to follow Jesus' sharing praxis outlined in Luke 18.

Vasyl Khokhla was born in Kalush in Western Ukraine; he is currently working on a law degree in Ukraine and a finance degree in the United States.

THE RICH YOUNG RULER IN A CHURCH IN ARGENTINA
Néstor O. Míguez (Argentina)

Buenos Aires City, Sunday morning. The regular worship of a middle-class Presbyterian Church, with a gentle charismatic influence. The service was moving along as usual. The songs and prayers came and went without incident. The time came for the reading of the Scriptures. A sister read the passage indicated by the pastor, Luke 18:18–30. The congregation listened to the reading with unction, rising to its feet. A prayer was offered, asking for inspiration for the message. The pastor begins to step up to the pulpit when, suddenly, out of nowhere, a strange figure occupies the pulpit—a man richly dressed, but in a style fitting with the first century. We do not recognize the language, but we suddenly begin to understand. He breaks into speech:

Ah, it is so easy for you! Once again you will preach about me, and I will be mistreated—I know already. I am the bad guy, the one who rejected salvation. For centuries I will be labeled as the one who could not say "Yes," the one who rejected Christ. This isn't fair. I was seeking eternal life and now as it turns out, I have eternal shame.

But I want you to hear the other side of the story. As you know, I am a ranking official in my nation and I want to act justly and do right. The majority of my friends and other government and temple officials mistrusted Jesus. He is a rabble-rouser, they said, he mingles with the wrong crowd, and he has connections to the rebel. A lawyer, an expert in the Law, told me that he had interviewed Jesus personally. He told me how it had happened: He had gone to where Jesus was staying, and the people were asking him all kinds of questions. My friend intended to test Jesus on this topic: "What can I do to inherit eternal life?" he asked. Jesus questioned him on the Law—him of all people, an expert in the Law. My friend answered, "Love the Lord your God…," but knowing something about how Jesus thinks, he added, "Love your neighbor…." Jesus told him that if he kept these commandments, he would live. And because the lawyer insisted, Jesus told him a parable about a Samaritan who had helped someone who had fallen into the hands of bandits. And he exhorted him to go and do likewise. It was an intelligent answer. The lawyer was left perplexed. That story had many elements, but Jesus demonstrated the wisdom of the teachers. I was interested in hearing a bit more.

I wanted to meet Jesus for myself. So when I knew Jesus was nearby, I headed out in his direction. I wanted to have good relations with him, and at the same time, the question of eternal life had been an unsettling one for me. I needed to know more. So I went to him and asked him the same question the lawyer had. I was eager to elaborate on that exchange; I had already prepared a few more questions in case I received the same response.

But his initial response surprised me. I called him "good teacher." I was polite, much more so than is expected of a prince when speaking with a village carpenter—his notoriety as a wise man notwithstanding. I expected a response that was equally polite. "Why do you call me good?" he asked, in front of the crowd. I was disconcerted. "God alone is good," he added. Was there a reproach hidden in those words? Was he indirectly denouncing those in my position, saying that nobody is good—as elevated in status as he may be? My mood became uncertain. His follow-up questions reassured me. They had to do with the commandments that relate to one's neighbor. I could see that his response was heading down the same path as the one he had given the lawyer. I replied that yes, I knew the commandments and had endeavored to keep them since I was a boy.

And it was true. I know we government officials have a bad reputation, but as I told you, I try to be honest in my work. I truly do want to obtain eternal life. I was formed in the faith of my elders and I do not want to lose that heritage. I know of the righteousness that comes by the Law of Moses and I try to live according to it. Jesus' initial response lifted my spirits.

But that sense of reassurance wouldn't last long. "One thing you lack," he told me. What could be lacking? Could there be anything more to being righteous than remaining faithful to God, keeping his Law? As a Pharisee, we keep not only the written law but all of the precepts. We undoubtedly seek that everyone might know the Law and keep it. "One thing you lack." I opened my ears.

And then the phrase that has been my nightmare for centuries was pronounced: "Sell all that you have and give it to the poor, and then come follow me." I didn't know how exactly to respond. You here at this meeting, along with many others, are followers of Jesus, so I ask you: Has he asked you the same thing? How many here have sold everything they have to follow Jesus? Did he not ask everything of you as well? Not something, *everything*. Did he ask everything of you, as he did of me? Did you give it to him? Have you given it to the poor? I don't see many heads nodding. I see that many have golden rings. I saw many cars at the door. I also saw many poor people in the streets, and I know that this enormous city is surrounded by shanty towns where children die in hunger. Have you shared your goods with them? And if so, why is there still so much poverty, and you are at ease in this Church?

If you are Jesus' followers, and still hold your goods, then you have been treated more kindly than I have. Is that fair? Jesus didn't simply ask for something, a part, whatever it may be; he asked for everything. Of course I left very sorrowful, I tell you, very sorrowful, a sorrow that lasts even to this day. You think I don't feel that burden. I have lost eternal life, and it is only by some unexpected miracle that I stand before you today.

As if that were not enough, as I left, I heard Jesus himself saying that it is very hard for a rich man to enter the kingdom of heaven. Ah, but for God nothing is impossible, Jesus says to you, and you are at ease. Well it doesn't put me at ease—he gave me no answer that would be of aid to me.

I arrived at home and told my wife: You can't imagine how she reacted! She was extremely upset. She reacted like anyone else in her situation might: "Who does he think he is? You have responsibilities: You have to look presentable for the temple functions, to receive Roman ambassadors, and I can't accompany you without a decent bracelet or an elegant necklace. You can't get rid of everything. So much depends on you and you have to have what's necessary to fulfill your obligations. You are not to blame for your large inheritance. Of course, a poor carpenter knows nothing of these things...Giving everything to the poor...What do we live on from then on? You sell, you give up everything, and in 15 days neither we nor they have anything. I know you're a conscientious person, that you're concerned, but that doesn't work. There must be another way to be generous. All this has done is embitter you. In any case, why did you go to ask a simple carpenter who knows nothing of government responsibilities?"

Look, the other day I received a man named Zebedee, an older man who had come to ask for my help because his sons had gone after Jesus and had left him alone. The man is a fisherman, and now has to take care of the entire family because his sons listened to Jesus and left with him. Who will watch over Zebedee and his family now? No, nothing is as simple as it seems. Zebedee's wife lost her mind and trails after Jesus, asking him to reserve a special spot for her sons, one to the left, the other at the right hand, when he comes in his Kingdom. So they weren't that generous or disinterested either, leaving everything just to receive more. If we politicians do that, along come our critics and call it cronyism, clientelism; but when Jesus does it they call it grace.

You might say I'm resentful, bitter, that I see everything in a negative light. It's just that I've heard too many dreamers who think that this complicated world can be fixed with a little good will and generosity. You have to understand what it is to be in a place of authority, to understand the tensions one suffers. And Jesus, instead of helping me, made it more difficult.

Others—nearly all others—have decided to follow Jesus, and keep their things as if he never said these words. I stayed on the outside, because, honestly, I can't do what he asked me. But I'm still looking for an answer. Help me find it.

Néstor O. Míguez is Professor of New Testament Studies at ISEDET, Buenos Aires, Argentina.

QUESTIONS

1. How does Chinese culture as described by Chan encourage individuals to act in ways that resemble both Jesus and the "spies"? Why does Chan take his "lesson" from Jesus rather than from the "spies"?

2. Compare and contrast Jesus' metaphor of the fruit tree (note the larger context of the biblical passages) with Stærk's explanation of "character."

3. Assess Khokhla's reading of the biblical text. Was Jesus asking the rich young ruler to be "socially responsible"? Did Jesus accept his accumulation of wealth?

4. What is your response to Míguez's imagined "rich young ruler"? What is Míguez trying to do: inspire you to sell all that you have? Cause you to side with the ruler? Or something else?

CHAPTER 7

MIRACLES OF JESUS

Matthew 9:27–30; Mark 4:35–5:1; Matthew 8:5–13

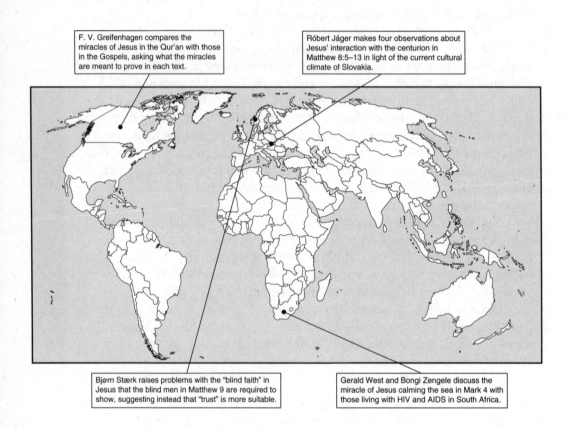

F. V. Greifenhagen compares the miracles of Jesus in the Qur'an with those in the Gospels, asking what the miracles are meant to prove in each text.

Róbert Jáger makes four observations about Jesus' interaction with the centurion in Matthew 8:5–13 in light of the current cultural climate of Slovakia.

Bjørn Stærk raises problems with the "blind faith" in Jesus that the blind men in Matthew 9 are required to show, suggesting instead that "trust" is more suitable.

Gerald West and Bongi Zengele discuss the miracle of Jesus calming the sea in Mark 4 with those living with HIV and AIDS in South Africa.

READINGS

The Trouble with "Blind Faith"
Bjørn Stærk

Reading the "Calming of the Sea" with Those Who Are Suffering
Gerald West and Bongi Zengele

A Comparison of Jesus' Miracles in the Qur'an and the Gospels
F. Volker Greifenhagen

Four Observations about Jesus' Interaction with the Centurion
Róbert Jáger

THE TROUBLE WITH "BLIND FAITH"

Bjørn Stærk (Norway)

In the story in Matthew 9:27–30, Jesus heals two blind men. It is their faith that heals them. Jesus tells them so. He asks them to believe, and says he will heal them according to the strength of their belief. There are many similar stories in the Bible. God does not like to be tested. He does not perform miracles on demand. Faith comes first, genuine faith, and then miracles may—or may not—come later. You don't approach Jesus as some service provider, with a remedy that may or may not work. He sees your heart, so in your heart there must be faith.

Most Christians who have heard these stories throughout the centuries have found themselves living in times of few miracles. The blind remain blind, the mortally ill die. The best of us have perished in wars, slaved in poverty, starved, and/ or suffered. Seeing this, and still believing in a good God who watches over everything and wishes us well, requires a strong faith, stronger than the faith in this story. The two blind men only had to believe for a few seconds before they were healed. Most Christians have to go through their entire lives without a sign like that, and they are still expected to keep their faith. Faith that God has a plan, even when bad things happen. Faith that Jesus really will return, and it may be any day now. Any day.

We often use the term "blind faith" to describe an extreme sort of faith, a faith that doesn't require rational arguments or evidence. But, really, all faith is blind. Faith that isn't blind, that is based on reason or evidence, is called trust. Faith is when you do not have proof, but you choose to believe anyway. We talk of a "leap of faith," meaning that faith is the bridge between what we know and God. Reason may take you part of the way, as it has done for many rationally oriented Christians, but at some point faith takes over.

It is precisely because faith is blind that it has such a romantic appeal. There is something cold about asking for evidence. Imagine if the blind men, when Jesus asked if they believed he could heal them, had responded, "We don't know, but it would be really great if you could try." Cold. Rude. Disconcerting. Compare that with the emotional impact of the simple statement, "Yes, I believe," uttered so often in the Bible, in prayers, and in our stories. Faith is romantic. Faith is beautiful. Faith is inspiring.

But the faith that brings victims of disease to Jesus in the Bible is the same faith that brings people today to faith healers, psychics, homeopaths, and other providers of questionable remedies. It is faith that, for some, creates the bridge from sanity to insanity, peace to violence, pragmaticism to fanaticism. The direction of the leap is different, but the essence of faith is the leap itself.

Faith that isn't blind is called trust. Do an experiment: Take the role faith plays in Christianity, and replace it with trust. In this version of the story, Jesus asks the blind men, "Do you trust that I'm able to heal you?" They say, "Not quite, but some people say you can, and you seem like you mean well, so we're willing to try." He heals them, and asks, "Now do you trust me?" They say, "Yes, now we do." A relationship has been built. It has a concrete basis, and can be built upon further.

Now think of someone who does not live in the age of legends and miracles, perhaps someone who lives today. We can have faith in God, that's easy, but can we "trust" that God oversees the world, and has a plan for everyone and everything? On what basis? The miracles today are few and far between and always tainted with the suspicion of fraud or delusion.

Faith comes beforehand, and is indefinite, absolute. To demand faith is an aggressive, dominant act. Trust comes afterwards, and is built, gradually, over time. Faith is binary, either there or not. Trust has many levels. Trust is not cold and cynical. It is the essence of friendship and love. But it requires some evidence, some reciprocal signals of ability and good intent. We trust our friends because of what we have been through together, and what it has revealed about their character. We do not approach strangers, as Jesus often did, and say, "Become my friend. Trust that I mean you well." "Why should I?" will be their answer.

And that should also have been the answer of the blind men in Matthew 9. It was wrong of Jesus to demand faith from them, and all the other people who approached him for healing, beforehand. It was wrong of him to be angry with people who asked him for proof (e.g., Matthew 16:4; Mark 8:12). It was wrong to build Christianity on faith, when it should have been built on trust.

Humans are both rational and social beings. Faith demands that we restrict our rational abilities, abilities that are part of who we are. Trust allows us to use both our rational and social abilities to their fullest. Faith is a temptation we should learn to avoid. Our ideal, instead, should be trust.

Bjørn Stærk is a software developer from Norway; he's an atheist and former Christian, and writes a blog at http://max256.bearstrong.net.

READING THE "CALMING OF THE SEA" WITH THOSE WHO ARE SUFFERING

Gerald West and Bongi Zengele (South Africa)

The Ujamaa Centre, a community development and research organization, reads the Bible among communities of the poor, marginalized, and working class, with the explicit purpose of participating in God's emancipatory project by working toward social and personal transformation. As part of these Contextual Bible Studies, we have developed a study of Mark 4:35–5:1 with those who are living with HIV and AIDS. Compelling conversations have emerged.

We asked participants the following questions:

QUESTION 1: Retell the story in your own words in "buzz groups" of two. What is the text about?

QUESTION 2: Who is sailing the boat? What is Jesus doing in the boat?

QUESTION 3: When and why do the disciples wake Jesus?

QUESTION 4: What are they afraid of?

QUESTION 5: What are we who are living with HIV and AIDS afraid of?

QUESTION 6: Is Jesus in "the boat" with those living with HIV and AIDS? If he is, is he asleep or awake?

QUESTION 7: If Jesus is still asleep, how do we wake him up?

QUESTION 8: If he is awake or if he were to waken, what would we want him to do?

QUESTION 9: What does this story challenge us to do?

Question 1 opens up space for the group members to share whatever their impressions of this text might be. It is an important question because it establishes that anyone in the group may participate and that any response is acceptable. This question makes it evident, even to new members, that the facilitator is just that, a facilitator and not the "expert" voice.

Questions 2, 3, and 4 return the participants to the biblical text. In this case there is no in-depth probing of the literary features of the text or of the world behind the text. Here the readers simply return to read the text again, giving the text its own voice, and affirming that the text does indeed have a voice. Questions 5, 6, 7, and 8 then shift back again to the readers' reality, in an overtly contextual reading, ending the process with an action plan.

Question 1 generates a host of responses, ranging from answers like faith, fear, anxiety, the power of God, a miracle, to Jesus teaching his disciples. Question 2 often elicits some surprise, as participants notice that it is the disciples who are in control of the boat, not Jesus. They are the ones with expertise in sailing, not Jesus. This detail becomes significant later when they respond to Questions 6, 7, and 8, all of which emphasize the agency of the Bible study participants (all of whom are HIV-positive). Some participants notice that Jesus is asleep "on the cushion," and wonder why Mark has given us this particular detail. Perhaps, some suggest, this is to reassure us that Jesus is only unaware of the danger facing the disciples because he is so comfortable. Jesus is not uncaring. He is exhausted by his teaching and so has fallen asleep, but without the pillow he would probably have woken by himself as the boat became more and more violently shaken by the wind and the waves. Others venture that Jesus is being uncaring, making himself comfortable while the disciples struggle with the task of sailing the boat in increasingly difficult conditions.

Question 3, with its dual focus, reflects on how the disciples only wake Jesus when the situation is no longer in their control, when "the boat was already being swamped"

(v. 37), in the expectation that he might or will be able to help them. Jesus is significant, and at times just his presence is enough, without his active involvement; but at other times he is expected or required to act in a form of participation that exceeds presence.

Question 4 already begins to shift the readers, in most cases, to their own realities, for there is not much in the text to interrogate with regard to this question. Obviously the disciples were afraid of dying (v. 38), but perhaps their fear was heightened by the very presence of Jesus with them. Perhaps they felt some responsibility for him, for he was not, after all, a fisherman, and so would not be familiar with this kind of situation. But more importantly, he was their leader, and so there was the weight of responsibility to protect him. Furthermore, Jesus had given their lives new meaning and so to die now, with him, was a situation worthy of dread. These reflections, however, are intimately linked to the fears of the group's members, who fear not only for their own lives but also for the lives of those for whom they are responsible, particularly their children. They too have discovered a new sense of "life" (*ukuphila*) since their diagnosis as HIV-positive, especially since they joined the group.

The shift to the readers' realities is decisive in Question 5, moving directly from text to participants' contexts. Those living with HIV and AIDS have much to fear. Our government is only gradually rolling out antiretroviral (ARV) treatment, so not everyone who needs ARVs is able to obtain them at the appropriate time. Even when we are able to access ARVs, the stigma associated with taking the medication is as severe as the stigma associated with being HIV-positive. Added to this is the fear of not having sufficient nutritious food to allow the body to cope with the toxic ARV drugs. Then there is the fear that one's body will develop resistance to the particular cocktails available in our country, where we do not yet have second-or third-generation drugs (as Western countries do). But the deepest fear is not living long enough to see one's children go to school or to be reconciled and accepted by one's family.

Question 6 is the question around which the whole Bible study is based. It is derived from the discussions of this text before the Contextual Bible Study itself was developed. In informal reflections around this text Bongi Zengele heard one of the discussants declare, "It is time for Jesus to wake up!" Probing, she discovered that this is what some of them felt when they read this text, though they were not sure they should feel or say such things about Jesus. And so the seed of "an-other" theology was sown! Question 6 opens up formal space, within the safe sacred site of a Bible study, to delve more deeply into this embodied cry: "It is time for Jesus to wake up!"

Question 7 continues to encourage the participants to do theology, invoking our own participation in God's work. Questions 8 and 9 move the study to its conclusion, inviting participants to envisage and plan for transformation. We usually ask participants to work toward concrete "action plans," beginning with an immediate action that can be taken, then planning an action that requires some additional time and resources but which is nevertheless feasible within their context, and finally to imagine a plan of action that might be possible if there were appropriate resources.

What emerges in Contextual Bible Studies such as this, if the group is a sacred and safe space, is that the embodied theologies of the participants find forms of articulation.

Such emergent articulations are what South African theologian James Cochrane calls "incipient theology" (*Circles of Dignity: Community Wisdom and Theological Reflection* [Minneapolis: Fortress, 1999]). Incipient theology is a product of the corporate embodied experience of the group, who draw both on the resources of their own bodies and the biblical text to bring to articulation what is inchoate. So in this case, though this same group of people have affirmed in other Contextual Bible Studies that Jesus stands with them over against stigmatizing society, they are also able to bring to words another part of their lived reality, namely a Jesus who is in some sense asleep. And, as they said, "It is time for Jesus to wake up!" Here is the beginning of a profound theology of both God's presence and absence in the context of HIV and AIDS.

Gerald West and Bongi Zengele are coordinators at the Ujamaa Centre in the School of Religion and Theology at University of KwaZulu-Natal, Pietermaritzburg, South Africa.

A Comparison of Jesus' Miracles in the Qur'an and the Gospels

F. Volker Greifenhagen (Canada)

Miracles are extraordinary events seen as resisting normal human explanation and therefore attributed to divine intervention. The Gospels are replete with accounts of the extraordinary deeds or miracles of Jesus, involving either the healing of humans—by cures, exorcisms, or resuscitations from the dead—or the demonstrating of power over the natural world, such as turning water into wine, calming storms, and miraculously feeding many people.

The Muslim scripture, the Qur'an, originating with the prophet Muhammad in the seventh century C.E. in Arabia, also attributes miracles to Jesus: In Surah 2 *al-Baqarah* ("The Heifer") 87, the Qur'an quotes God as saying, "We gave Jesus, the son of Mary, clear (signs) and strengthened him with the Holy Spirit" (Translation by 'Abdullah Yusuf 'Ali, 2001). In two other passages, the Qur'an more specifically describes various miracles of Jesus.

Surah 3 *al-'Imran* ("The Family of 'Imran") 46, 48-49:

> [46]He shall speak to the people in childhood and in maturity. And he shall be (of the company) of the righteous...[48]And Allah will teach him the Book and Wisdom, the Law and the Gospel, [49]And (appoint him) a messenger to the Children of Israel, (with this message): "I have come to you, with a Sign from your Lord, in that I make for you out of clay, as it were, the figure of a bird, and breathe into it, and it becomes a bird by Allah's leave: And I heal those born blind, and the lepers, and I quicken the dead, by Allah's leave;

and I declare to you what ye eat, and what ye store in your houses. Surely therein is a Sign for you if ye did believe." (Translation by 'Abdullah Yusuf 'Ali, 2001)

Surah 5 *al-Ma'idah* ("The Repast") 110, 112–115:

[110]Then will Allah say: "O Jesus the son of Mary! Recount My favour to thee and to thy mother. Behold! I strengthened thee with the Holy Spirit, so that thou didst speak to the people in childhood and in maturity. Behold! I taught thee the Book and Wisdom, the Law and the Gospel and behold! thou makest out of clay, as it were, the figure of a bird, by My leave, and thou breathest into it and it becometh a bird by My leave, and thou healest those born blind, and the lepers, by My leave. And behold! thou bringest forth the dead by My leave. And behold! I did restrain the Children of Israel from (violence to) thee when thou didst show them the clear Signs, and the unbelievers among them said: 'This is nothing but evident magic.'"…[112]Behold! the disciples, said: "O Jesus the son of Mary! can thy Lord send down to us a table set (with viands) from heaven?" Said Jesus: "Fear Allah, if ye have faith." [113]They said: "We only wish to eat thereof and satisfy our hearts, and to know that thou hast indeed told us the truth; and that we ourselves may be witnesses to the miracle." [114]Said Jesus the son of Mary: "O Allah our Lord! Send us from heaven a table set (with viands), that there may be for us—for the first and the last of us—a solemn festival and a sign from thee; and provide for our sustenance, for thou art the best Sustainer (of our needs)." [115]Allah said: "I will send it down unto you: But if any of you after that resisteth faith, I will punish him with a penalty such as I have not inflicted on any one among all the peoples." (Translation by 'Abdullah Yusuf 'Ali, 2001)

In these two passages, the Qur'an attributes the following seven miracles to Jesus:

1. **Speaking to the people in childhood and maturity (3:46, 5:110).**   The Arabic phrase is understood as meaning "from the cradle as at a mature age," indicating that Jesus miraculously spoke as an infant. The Qur'an elsewhere tells the story of how, when Mary returns to her family with the infant Jesus, they suspect her of unchaste behavior, and Jesus speaks up in her defense (19:27–33). The Qur'an here echoes the Christian Arabic Infancy Gospel, one of the New Testament apocryphal writings, which also depicts Jesus as speaking as an infant from the cradle. Among the biblical Gospels, only Luke narrates the somewhat analogous story of a precocious 12-year-old Jesus astounding the teachers in the Temple with his questions and responses (Luke 2:41–52).
2. **Breathing life into a bird made from clay (3:49, 5:110).**   This miracle, while missing from the canonical Gospels, is narrated in the second- or third-century C.E. Infancy Gospel of Thomas as one of the miracles Jesus performed as a

child—there he fashions twelve sparrows from mud, claps his hands, and they fly off. The qur'anic version is distinct in that Jesus' action evokes the Qur'an's description of God "creating" Adam out of "clay" and then "breathing" life into him (38:71–72).

3. **Healing those born blind (3:49, 5:110).** The Arabic word used here specifically refers to those who have been blind from birth, which intensifies the miraculous nature of these healings. While the Gospels narrate several accounts of Jesus healing various blind persons, only the story in the Gospel of John (9:1–12) specifies that the blind man has been blind from birth.

4. **Healing the lepers (3:49, 5:110).** The Gospels of Matthew, Mark, and Luke describe Jesus as healing lepers.

5. **Resuscitating the dead (3:49, 5:110).** In the Gospels, three specific stories of Jesus raising the dead are found: a widow's son, the daughter of Jairus, and Lazarus.

6. **Declaring what people eat and what they store in their houses (3:49).** These words can be understood as indicating that Jesus had miraculous foreknowledge of what people were eating and storing in their houses. However, it is also possible to interpret these words as portraying rather Jesus' authority to legislate what people can eat and store in their houses, just as Jesus in the Gospels claims the authority to interpret and modify the laws of the Mosaic Torah, and the traditions that have developed around it.

7. **Providing a meal from heaven (5:112–115).** Here the Qur'an describes Jesus' disciples requesting a table set with food from heaven; Jesus subsequently prays for God to provide this miracle. This qur'anic story indirectly echoes the feeding miracles of Jesus in the Gospels; that the table comes from heaven and signifies a "solemn festival" also echoes Jesus' discourse about the bread from heaven in John 6, and the Gospel accounts of the Last Supper and the institution of the Christian Eucharist.

The Qur'an's list of Jesus' miracles includes both healing and nature miracles, overlapping with those found in Christian sources, both canonical and apocryphal. By including miracles from the latter, the Qur'an rehabilitates early Christian traditions that were marginalized because they did not become part of the surviving official Christian biblical canon.

The Qur'an, as usual when it narrates material also found in the Bible, does not provide many details. It neither narrates specific miracle stories of Jesus nor gives the particulars of the persons affected or their circumstances. At the most, the Qur'an tells us that the miracles of Jesus were directed to the "Children of Israel" as "Signs" (3:49–50, 5:110), that the Holy Spirit was involved (5:110), and that disbelievers dismissed these miracles as nothing but magic (5:110). Similarly, "signs" are the favored designation for miracles in John's Gospel (e.g., 2:11, 57), Luke's Gospel especially emphasizes the power of the Spirit behind Jesus' deeds (4:1, 18, etc.), and the early Christians had to defend themselves against the accusation that the miracles of Jesus were mere magic.

What are the miracles of Jesus meant to communicate or prove? This concern, instead of narrative details, seems to be the Qur'an's intent. Miracles play a part in the stories of most of the biblical or Arab prophets mentioned in the Qur'an; they function as one of the "signs" of God meant to convince, or at least refute, disbelievers who reject the message of a prophet. The miracles of Jesus thus function in like fashion to those of previous prophets such Abraham and Moses.

Traditionally Christians, however, have argued that Jesus' miracles are proof of his divinity, as Jesus in John's Gospel seems to suggest: "Even if you don't believe me, believe the miracles. Then you will know and understand that the Father is in me and I am in the Father" (10:38). Yet miracles are not unique to Jesus; they are part of the career of prophets in the Hebrew Bible, and the practice of miracles is continued by the Christians after the death and resurrection of Jesus.

In fact, the portrayal of Jesus in Luke's Gospel and Acts seems to accord more with aspects of the qur'anic depiction of Jesus than with the postbiblical Christian doctrinal ideology of Christ's divinity. Luke presents the miracles of Jesus as proof that God is working through Jesus, not of Jesus' own divine power, as evident especially in the early Christian preaching described in Acts, where, for instance, Peter notes "how God anointed Jesus of Nazareth with the Holy Spirit and with power; how he went about doing good and healing all that were oppressed by the devil, for God was with him" (Acts 10:38). The Qur'an, in its description of Jesus' miracles, likewise repeatedly emphasizes that these extraordinary actions are done "by God's leave." Miracles from this perspective are signs of divine activity, not of divinization.

F. V. Greifenhagen is Associate Professor of Religious Studies at Luther College, University of Regina, Canada.

FOUR OBSERVATIONS ABOUT JESUS' INTERACTION WITH THE CENTURION

Róbert Jáger (Slovakia)

The healing of the centurion's servant in Matthew 8:5–13 is an important and compelling story. A key aspect of this scene is the presence of the centurion—a stranger, an outsider whose faith Jesus admires and underlines as one of the most important attitudes required for the full realization of the eternal destiny of humans (dining with the patriarchs in the Kingdom, v. 11). Jesus was a Jew; the centurion was a Roman. Jesus followed the religious laws; the centurion did not and would have been seen by Jews as a theologically "worthless" person. The centurion is thus both ethnically and religiously an outsider.

The overall interpretation and the focus on certain aspects of a biblical passage are dictated by the individual context of any interpreter, and the case is no different with me. I grew up in a small village in Eastern Slovakia on the border with the Soviet Union in the context of arrogant communist oppression, where human individuals were of no worth. It was a mixed community—Slovaks, Hungarians, Gypsies, and Ruthenians—with a healthy sense of mutuality and Christian solidarity. On the other hand, in school we were forced to accept the official and only legitimate atheist worldview: the leading role of the Communist party, the nation as the owner of all goods, and the total mental obedience to this worldview. Anyone who dared to express something else or publicly practiced his or her faith was exposed to mockery, not to mention political persecution. What was of ultimate importance was the Communist party and its "glorious future," which never came. Thanks to God. Nevertheless, now after 20 years of freedom, a new division is felt in Slovakia: the "orthodox" versus "outsiders." This is true in any aspect of social life—politics, culture, education, and geographical and ethnic relations—in our very tiny country.

When the former Czechoslovakia was split into the Czech Republic and Slovakia in 1993, Slovakia suffered from a tragic lack of constructive efforts for national and economic growth. As a result, there was a pathological search for enemies responsible for all negative elements in the life of the country, which the political elite used (and sometimes still use) to cover up unprecedented thievery of national and financial resources. The new enemy became the Hungarian minority living in Slovakia (about half a million people). The Slovak–Hungarian political tensions within the country and on the international level are well known in Europe. Moreover, today migrants from the East—especially from Russia, Ukraine, Romania, China, Vietnam, and Southeast Asia—are another emerging source of social and political tensions. It is in this context of "orthodox insiders" and "foreign outsiders" that I make the following four observations about the story of Jesus' interaction with the centurion.

First, the centurion's attitude is the example of faith to be followed. He asks for healing not for himself or his family, but rather for a person of lower rank. The centurion must also humble himself by coming to an itinerant Jewish preacher. His faith is attitude in action, demonstrating a strong social and human empathy. Reading through the eyes of my sociocultural context, the strangers coming from the East coincide with the centurion. These migrants take care of each other. They have good, close relationships and a newcomer is never left out. Their mutual support is incomparable with the growing selfish relations of the individuals of my society. For example, the increasing number of older persons left alone in various institutions is alarming. There is no one to take care of them; people are not taking care of their parents and grandparents. The strangers (the migrants from Russia, Belarussia, Ukraine, and so forth) are the ones who help them. Whose faith is better? Those who go regularly to church but forget parents in hospices or those who are close to each other and more significantly take care of the parents and grandparents of strangers? The stranger is pictured as a challenge to Christians of all times.

Second, being Christian and hating any nation or nationality is an absurd contradiction. There are two basic political streams. The nationally (Slovakian) oriented Christians who openly despise those who are not ours (Hungarians, migrants). On the other side, there are the silent Christians who are not standing up fully for the truth and rights of others. In my reading, Jesus' judgment on the sons of the Kingdom in verse 12 points to the false self-esteem of the righteous and orthodox: they have no compassion for the aliens, which will cause them to be cast out. Moreover, such attitude lowers the cultural and moral profile of the nation as such. So besides their eternal fate (thrown into outer darkness), it brings about political and cultural condemnation here and now.

Third, Jesus' immediate positive answer to the centurion's request challenges our attitudes toward aliens. To ignore a stranger on any level of life equals ignoring Jesus himself, who did not despise or disregard strangers and outcasts. Jesus broke the cultural and social boundaries. So should Christians in Slovakia (and elsewhere).

Finally, Jesus' attitude absolutely challenges a kind of "traditional" understanding of faith, that is, ritualism. Unfortunately, the quality of Christian faith is still measured by church attendance, while the social, political, and cultural impacts of faith are seen as something accidental. The opposite ought to be case. This is the first instance where Matthew uses the term "faith." It is significant since the unfolding of the concept of discipleship and faith starts here. To be Jesus' true disciple requires having both the stranger's attitude and Jesus' openness to the stranger.

Róbert Jáger is lecturer and researcher in New Testament Studies in the Faculty of Theology Aloisinianum, University of Trnava; and priest of the Greek Catholic diocese of Kosice, Slovakia.

QUESTIONS

1. Critique Stærk's discussion of the difference between "faith" and "trust." How would you discuss faith and trust in terms of your own life?

2. In addition to the benefits that West and Zengele mention, what are some potential challenges and difficulties, indeed risks, of conducting Contextual Bible Studies?

3. What are some reasons one might give for favoring the biblical version of the miracle narratives over the qur'anic version? And vice versa?

4. How might one challenge Jáger's reading of the biblical text? For instance, is the centurion acting selflessly and humbly?

CHAPTER 8

GOSPEL OF JOHN (PART I)

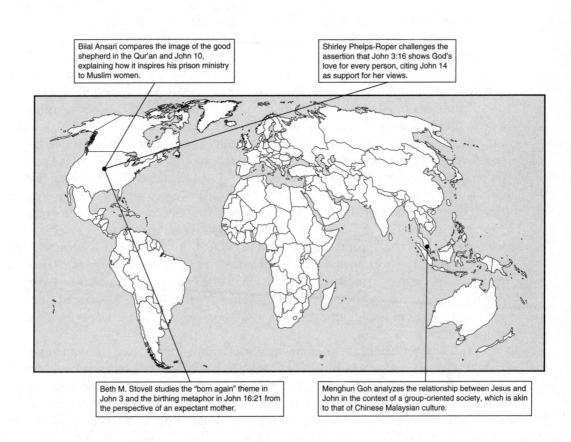

Bilal Ansari compares the image of the good shepherd in the Qur'an and John 10, explaining how it inspires his prison ministry to Muslim women.

Shirley Phelps-Roper challenges the assertion that John 3:16 shows God's love for every person, citing John 14 as support for her views.

Beth M. Stovell studies the "born again" theme in John 3 and the birthing metaphor in John 16:21 from the perspective of an expectant mother.

Menghun Goh analyzes the relationship between Jesus and John in the context of a group-oriented society, which is akin to that of Chinese Malaysian culture.

READINGS

The Good Shepherd as Inspiration for a Prison Minister
Bilal Ansari

Jesus and John the Baptist in the Context of a Group-Oriented Society
Menghun Goh

A Mother's Perspective on Birthing Imagery
Beth M. Stovell

A Reading of John 3:16
Shirley Phelps-Roper

The Good Shepherd as Inspiration
for a Prison Minister

Bilal Ansari (United States)

Shepherding is the sacred, theoretical, and practical metaphor used to explain the ministry of pastoral care in both Hebrew and Christian scriptures. In the Gospel of John, Jesus identifies with the concept of the good shepherd, reminding his audience of the prophetic call and covenant of care, "I am the Good Shepherd; and I know and recognize My own, and My own know and recognize Me" (10:14). The teachings of Islam also employ the good shepherd metaphor, which for me is a call lived out through American prison ministry, specifically pastoral care for Muslim women behind bars.

Jesus describes the good shepherd as one who would risk and lay down his life to care for those in times of crisis and need (10:11). Observing the lack of religious ministry and congregational worship for Muslim women in American prisons, one might conclude that Islam has no parallel for Jesus' concept of the good shepherd and no tradition of pastoral care. Though only men are obligated to attend congregational prayer in Islam, there are religious texts showing clearly that women are not to be prevented from congregational worship. Yet, prison ministry is extended only to Muslim men in American prisons. So why do I uncharacteristically care for the "other" gender behind bars when there is no apparent Islamic obligation to do so? Perhaps it is because I am a convert and my Christian upbringing influences me. Or is it my pledge of allegiance to the constitutional "free exercise of religion clause" that compels me to be the only Muslim male to accept a contract to care for female Muslim inmates? No. In fact, sacred scriptural sources of Islam illustrate a rich tradition of pastoral care which is my motivation and inspiration.

The prophet Muhammad emphatically prohibited the denial of women's free right to congregational worship. As in John 10, Islam does wholeheartedly embrace the prophetic tradition of care as contextualized in the concept of the good shepherd. Jesus' shepherding reference is found in Islam both as a condition of prophetic education and as a means of pastoral formation. Imam Bukhari narrates in his *Sahih of al Bukhari* collection two relevant narratives: one that places the profession of shepherding as a prerequisite of all prophets and the other that illustrates its essential elements. In one narration in volume 7, a person addresses the prophet Muhammad saying, "(O Messenger of God!) Have you ever shepherded sheep?" He said, "There has been no prophet but has shepherded them" (Book 65, Hadith #364). John 10:2 analogously explains this, "He who enters by the door is the shepherd of the sheep." In Islam the doorway is understood as inner piety and outer conformity to the teachings of the Qur'an and Sunna of the prophet Muhammad. The second narrative in volume 1 clearly explains that the entrance door of the good shepherd is spiritual care of the heart: "I heard the Messenger of God as having said this: He who guards against doubtful things keeps his religion and honour blameless, and he who indulges in doubtful things indulges in fact in unlawful things, just as a shepherd who pastures his animals round a preserve will soon pasture them in it" (Book 2, Hadith #49).

It is evident that Jesus' references to the good shepherd in John 10:11 and 14 are echoes of earlier scripture from Prophet David in Psalms 23 and 28:8. Jesus described the courageous ability to care for others in a crisis as a quality of good shepherding and the lack of that care in the shepherd as other than true pastoral care (John 10:12). And comparing how the Hebrew scriptures present the prophet Moses with the qur'anic presentation, we find that the story of Moses in the Qur'an is told more often than any other prophetic narrative, marking the importance of Moses to Islamic thought and practice. The prophet Muhammad—before congregational worship was made law for anyone—was given the Islamic scriptural references of the good shepherd in the story of Moses. In the Qur'an, a chapter called The Narratives (28:22–28) describes at length Moses' crisis, qualities of care, and his formation as a good shepherd just before his prophetic calling. In the Hebrew Bible a comparative description of this narrative is given in Exodus 2:15–21. Both of these narratives relate to John 10:16 in that Moses proactively seeks to care for the women shepherds and their flock, until God made their flock his flock by employing him as shepherd, and this led to Moses hearing God's voice and heeding His call. Islamic scripture showed the way of pastoral care in Islam is through the door of proactively caring for the well-being of women. This is supported and emphasized in qur'anic exegesis as the model of how to become a good shepherd and emphasizes that Moses' pastoral formation and care lasted 10 years before his call from God.

Furthermore, the strong support for women's congregational worship is found in a *sahih* (reliable) hadith. This hadith refers to the very earliest Muslim community after the passing of the prophet Muhammad. It helped preserve women's free exercise of congregational worship when early Islamic law became established. 'Umar Ibn al Khattab, one of the early companions of the prophet Muhammad, became the second caliph of Islam (the second successor to Muhammad) and he essentially functioned as the supreme justice of the Muslim polity. 'Umar's son narrates an example from 'Umar's wife as an empowering example of women's right to congregational worship (and a prime element of the pastoral voice) in Islam. In *The Sahih of Imam Bukhari* (volume 2, book 13, number 23), 'Ibn (son of) 'Umar narrates:

> One of the wives of 'Umar ('Ibn Al-Khattab) used to offer the early dawn and the late evening prayer in congregation in the mosque (at a time when it was completely dark and quite dangerous on the streets). She was asked why she had come out for the prayer as she knew that her husband 'Umar disliked it, and he has great (self-respecting jealousy). She replied, "What prevents him (my husband and supreme justice of Islam) from stopping me from this act?" The other replied, "The statement of the Messenger of God: 'Do not stop God's women from going to God's Mosques' prevents him."

To my mind, in this narrative the prophet Muhammad succinctly conveyed the compassionate pastoral care tradition of the good shepherd to those who followed him just as Moses, David, and Jesus had before him. Muslim women behind bars should be allowed congregational worship and pastoral care. We know good shepherding in Islam and claim it as our own, a continuity that exists in Islamic scripture with the earlier Hebrew Bible and the Gospel of John. The strong pastoral voice in Islam can be witnessed in the foundational texts of Islam itself, but it is only heard by hearts who perceive that voice as the *central* voice and who preserve the good shepherd metaphor as a *normative* model for the spiritual guidance of Muslims, both male and female.

Bilal Ansari is the son of a Christian minister and Muslim imam; he currently serves as an Islamic Faith Leader for the U.S. Department of Justice, Bureau of Prisons, at the Federal Correction Institution in Danbury, Connecticut, a female prison.

JESUS AND JOHN THE BAPTIST IN THE CONTEXT OF A GROUP-ORIENTED SOCIETY

Menghun Goh (Malaysia)

The world of the Gospel of John—indeed the biblical world in general—was a group-oriented society in which acquiring honor and being shamed affected one's social identity and status in the community. To a large extent, a person's worth and credibility were often tied to her or his group membership. If the group, especially the leader(s), had a good reputation, its group members would also have similar honor. The identity of the group and its members were closely intertwined. As such, the notions of honor and shame, whether acquired or inherited, permeate such spheres as economics, culture, sexuality, politics, ethics, and religion. Living in such a world, one would want to accrue, or at least maintain, honor and avoid words and deeds that can bring shame to one's group. One's actions affect not only one's own person but also the public reputation of her or his friends and family for generations. For instance, in John, the Jews insistently claim that they are from the lines of Abraham (8:31–41) and Moses (9:28–29)—this bolsters their honor and credibility. Likewise, Nathanael's reply "can anything good come out of Nazareth" illustrates the concept of group shame (1:46).

This type of group-oriented way of thinking also informs the worldview of many Chinese Malaysians. A Chinese (Confucian) sociocultural value highly regards the teacher figure. A Chinese proverb says, "Even if the person teaches me just one day he will be my father-like figure for life." Thus, when someone shows disrespect toward her or his teacher, it not only shames the person but also her or his family and close associates. The idea is that if the family has taught the person well, she or he will not disregard the teacher. Furthermore, those who remain in close contact with such a person (can only) suggest that they too think and behave similarly; otherwise they would not be associated. It is through this group-oriented lens that I offer a few comments on the relationship between Jesus and John the Baptist as it is presented in the Gospel of John. Indeed, in light of my background and context, it is only natural (and valuable) for me to focus on the identities of Jesus and John as they are linked to their groups via honor and shame.

The first thing that strikes us about the Jesus–John dynamic is that John is continuing to baptize (3:22–4:3), even after John has explained that his understanding of water baptism is to manifest Jesus to Israel (1:31). This is odd. Upon the revelation of Jesus, one might expect John to stop baptizing and work with the Jesus movement. It is therefore ironic that even though John continued to baptize, this Gospel, unlike the Synoptics, does not attribute to him "the Baptist" title. After all, did 1:6–8 not say that God sent John to witness so that he might testify for Jesus and so that all might believe *through* him? This "through" shows the importance of John as a medium or witness for *all* to believe in Jesus.

The significance of "testifying" in the Gospel of John is noteworthy when we find that almost half of the occurrences of witnessing in the New Testament appear in this book (33 of 76 times). Likewise, the content of witnessing occurs 14 times, out of 37 times in the New Testament. If witnessing in the Gospel, which requires firsthand knowledge, is related not only to testifying to facts but also to confessing and proclaiming the truth, then it is puzzling that—although two of John's disciples followed Jesus upon hearing John's witness (1:35–42)—John's other disciples felt envy when they saw "all" people going to Jesus (3:26). In fact, not only does the Gospel say that the disciples confirm John's witness for Jesus in their complaint (3:26), it also has John forcefully say to them that "you yourselves testify for me that I said *I am not the Christ*" (3:28)! Jesus' retort to those who wanted to rejoice in John's light despite John's witness for Jesus is also puzzling (5:33–36; cf. 2:24–25). It appears that even though John's witness about Jesus is true (10:41–42), the Gospel portrays Jesus as not trusting human witness.

Several comments are in order. First, the Gospel reduces John's baptism to witnessing (contra the Synoptics). Such reduction heightens the significance of baptism; without it Jesus would not be revealed to Israel (1:31–34). John 4:1–3 further links baptism with discipleship. Second, if witnessing requires firsthand experience, then how could John witness effectively if he and his movement remained separated from the Jesus movement?

Third, in a collective honor-and-shame society, it is unlikely for one to be honored while the other in the same or related group shamed. For the Gospel, John must be a very honorable figure (cf. 1:19–28; 5:33–35); otherwise it would not have him witness for Jesus. Yet, the Jesus and John movements do not seem to work together. Besides the public tensions in 3:22–26, the attempts to "subordinate" John (1:6–9; 5:33–40; 10:40–42), and the mention of John's disciples following Jesus while John and many other disciples did not (1:39ff) show conflicts between the groups. In a "limited good" worldview, moreover, John's saying in 3:30 that Jesus must increase and he must decrease could give bad press for the Jesus movement. Who would want someone testifying for him to become less while he himself becomes greater? In a group-oriented society, it is more likely that the related individuals and groups either increase together or decrease together. Further, if the Pharisees revered John, it is puzzling that they would criticize and even plot against Jesus to whom John bore witness. Lastly, the conversation in 3:26–28 seems like a double-edged sword that highlights not only the misunderstanding and unwillingness of John's disciples to receive his witness concerning Jesus but also John's competence and authority as a revered *rabbi*.

Given this ambivalent portrayal of John and his disciples from the perspective of *collective* honor-and-shame sociocultural values, the tension between the Jesus and John movements thus also suggests the conflict between Jesus and John. As we cannot easily separate the individual identity from her or his associated groups, our interpretation cannot simply focus on individual figures without considering their social positions in the groups with which they are associated. Now if the text does (re)present the tension between Jesus and John, we cannot help but ask about the role and function of John in the Gospel, especially when John is the figure whom Jesus refers to the most in the four Gospels. This question is noteworthy because if John's witness can bolster the credibility of the Jesus movement, the ambiguity and ambivalence in his words and deeds can also engender unease and suspicion toward the movement. It is therefore not too surprising that the Gospel tells us that while Jesus acknowledges John's witness, he is also troubled by it (5:33ff). In the end, the Gospel tells us that the ultimate witness, and hence honor, comes from God, who honors those who honor God, despite the fact that such honoring may dishonor the social norms and bring shame to oneself (5:36–44). This conception of honor and shame that is not bound by social conventions reminds Chinese Malaysians not to absolutize our framework of honor-and-shame values, especially when it can become hierarchical, and thus, discriminating and stifling to the betterment and transformation of life.

Menghun Goh is writing his dissertation in the Department of New Testament & Early Christianity at Vanderbilt University, United States; he lived in Kuala Lumpur (Malaysia) for 18 years.

A MOTHER'S PERSPECTIVE ON BIRTHING IMAGERY

Beth M. Stovell (United States)

In Nicodemus' encounter with Jesus in John 3, being "born again" or "born from above" by the Spirit is the central theme. While many have discussed the idea of "spiritual rebirth," this passage has not been read in light of the actual experience of childbirth. Here I will offer a reading of John 3 through the eyes of expectant mothers and mothers who have recently given birth, and compare this passage on birth in the Spirit to other passages in the Old and New Testament that discuss birth.

As any mother knows, birthing can be a terrifying and dangerous experience; it brings a woman near to death for the sake of creating a new life. This experience of crisis in birth was even more terrifying in the ancient context, where women frequently died during childbirth, and, even more frequently, babies died in the process. Expectant mothers often felt greater anxiety as the birth approached, not knowing exactly when the birth would take place or whether they or their child would survive. When an expectant mother or a mother who had recently given birth approaches the biblical text, such experiences could not help but come to the forefront of her mind.

Throughout the Bible, God is depicted with maternal and birthing metaphors. In the Old Testament, God's descriptions as mother or as one giving birth are often juxtaposed with traditionally male metaphors such as God as Divine Warrior, God as Father, God as Artisan, and God as Husband. For example, in Isaiah 42 Yahweh is described like a birthing mother calling out and like a warrior yelling a battle cry. The authors of the New Testament also use the metaphors of childbearing and mothering in various ways, including: describing the birthing role of the Spirit (John 3:3–8), of Jesus Christ (1 Peter 1:3, 23; 1 John 2:29; James 1:18), and of God in spiritual transformation (1 John 3:9; 4:7; 5:4; 5:18); predicting the effect of Jesus' death and resurrection on the disciples (Matthew 24:8; Mark 13:8; John 16:21); describing the relationship between the disciples and the Church (1 Thessalonians 2:7); and discussing birth by the flesh versus birth by the Spirit (Galatians 4:29; John 3:6).

These other uses of birthing metaphors provide insight into the use of the birthing metaphors in John 3. Here the Spirit is the giver of a second birth that leads to seeing and entering the kingdom of God. This birth is contrasted with physical birth in two ways: first, through Nicodemus' somewhat humorous question regarding returning to one's mother's womb as an old person, and second, through the differentiation Jesus provides between birth of the Spirit and birth of the flesh. As is typical of John's theology, this differentiation is more than simply a differentiation between spiritual and physical birth. It is describing the believer's need to be born anew through cleansing.

Yet, should this new birth given by the Spirit be understood as purely "spiritual" and in no way connected to physical childbirth? What is included in this second birth? Reading this passage in light of the experience of childbirth provides a way of considering this passage anew. In the Old Testament, the metaphor of childbirth is associated with universal and personal crisis and includes the possibility of pain and death. When dealing with John 3, this element of the metaphor is often overlooked; yet elsewhere in John's Gospel the same understanding of childbirth as a metaphor for crisis is present. For example, in John 16:21, Jesus describes the experience of his death and resurrection as being like a woman who when she is giving birth has pain because "her hour has come" (which echoes "his hour had come" in reference to Jesus' death), but when her child is born, she does not continue to recall her pain (even if she remembers it), because now she has the joy of the newborn child.

The language used in John 16:21 mirrors the language used in Isaiah 42:14 by the use of the same verb "to give birth." In the same way that Yahweh is pictured like "one giving birth" in Isaiah 42:14, the experience of Jesus' death will be for the disciples like a woman who "gives birth." John 16:21 also uses language that echoes John 3's discussion of "birth from the Spirit" with its use of the verb "born." The ability to enter the kingdom in John 3 through the "birth" of Spirit is also similar to John 16 which compares the experience of the joy following the resurrection to the joy of when a child is "born."

Reading with an awareness of the echoes between John 3 and John 16 helps correct the general conception of the birth metaphor in John 3. Many commentaries speak of the "birth" in John 3 as simple and painless because it is spiritual rather than physical, as though a spiritual stork dropped the child off in a nice neat package. Yet it is unlikely an ancient reader would have read the birth metaphor apart from its original implications of crisis, particularly if the reader were a mother or mother-to-be. Even Nicodemus' response suggests that ancient readers would think of physical childbirth when they read John 3. Jesus' clarification that this birth is spiritual and not physical does not necessarily remove the implications of possible pain and/or crisis. Metaphors often move from an original physical referent (like physical birth) to something more abstract (like spiritual birth), and to understand the metaphor, one must understand the physical referent first.

In fact, two other indicators in the passage suggest that pain and crisis may be a part of the metaphorical entailments of being "born again" of the Spirit. First, Jesus' description of the movement of the Holy Spirit as unexpected in terms of its comings and goings may reflect the unexpectedness of the birth process. There is a sense of expectancy in labor and a constant sense of unknowing. In ancient times, one did not know specifically when labor would occur. The same is true for mothers today. The baby comes when it wants and with it comes the pain of childbirth, but also (as Jesus points out in John 16:15) the expectation of great joy to follow.

Another indicator of the pain and crisis involved is how the metaphor of birth is joined to the metaphor of the Son of Man being "lifted up" for the purpose of "eternal life." Repeatedly in John, this concept of the Son of Man being lifted up refers to the hour of Jesus' death, that is, his "lifting up" upon the cross by crucifixion. The reader is told that this is the means by which "everyone who believes will have eternal life in him." Not surprisingly, birth and life are interweaving metaphors, but this second birth and this eternal life must be precipitated by Jesus' death and suffering on the cross. Similar to John 16, this picture of death and resurrection, suffering and exaltation of the Son of Man should be understood as part of the underlying imagery of the second birth pictured in John 3.

This has particular impact as one continues reading John 3 and sees the description of the Father giving his Son in John 3:16. When one thinks in terms of the potential loss of life inherent in childbirth and then combines this with the notion of inheritance, the idea of God the Great King giving his one and only Son highlights the dashed hopes that families felt frequently with the death of a newborn son. Such a hope was writ large in the situation of ruling families. For the Father to give up his only Son could potentially mean the loss of every hope, yet the second-half of John 3:16 immediately turns this possible loss into absolute hope. Because this Father has given *his only Son*, all other fathers and mothers have the hope of *their children* never perishing.

Beth M. Stovell is Assistant Professor in Biblical Studies in the School of Theology and Ministry at St. Thomas University, Miami Gardens, Florida, United States.

A READING OF JOHN 3:16

Shirley Phelps-Roper (United States)

God loves everyone is *the* single greatest lie that man or Satan has ever told and John 3:16 is always cited as support for it. It is the central theology of all phony Christians worldwide. Have you questioned how many times the actual words "God loves everyone" appear in the Bible? Or who said these words? Or how many times Jesus said, "God loves everyone"? As a matter of uncontroverted fact, the phrase "God loves everyone" never appears in the Bible. Period. In other words, the most famous Christian notion of God of our time—repeated without measure or limit in this sinful and adulterous generation—NEVER APPEARS IN THE BIBLE!

What about John 3:16? Does it say anything remotely close to "God loves everyone"? Of course it does not! It says, "For God so loved the world that he gave his only begotten Son..." The word translated "world" is the Greek word *kosmos*. It does not refer specifically to humans, certainly not to all humans, and certainly not you individually. In my experience most of the faux-Christians who cite John 3:16 stop halfway through the verse. This is where they would like the verse to stop. Here is the part they leave out: "*that whosoever* believeth in him should not perish, but have everlasting life."

It is clear, then, that if you do not believe, you do not obtain everlasting life and in fact Christ says just two verses later that you are "condemned already" (3:18). That's right; many of this world are walking dead men, condemned to eternal damnation and in the fullness of time will land in hell as condemned men! What does Christ say about the condemnation of man as John 3 continues? He states "that men love darkness rather than light because their deeds were evil," and "*everyone that* doeth evil hateth the light, neither cometh to the light, lest his deeds should be reproved" (vv. 19–20). The Holy Spirit closes John 3 in a dramatic and unambiguous fashion that blows straight to hell the notion that God loves everyone: "He that believeth on the Son hath everlasting life: *and he that believeth not the Son shall not see life; but the wrath of God abideth on him.*" God's hatred is his perfect determination to send the unrepentant to hell for eternity.

Satan concocted "God loves everyone" to ensnare the ungodly and the children of disobedience to believe there is no accountability in this life or the life to come for their filthy sins. The Prince of the Power put it in the hands of sinful men so they could multiply their stupid words to obfuscate the Consuming Fire's great Day of Judgment. But Satan, the great deceiver, says there is no wrath coming! This generation thinks the mere assertion of "God loves everyone" will wash away their adultery, fornication, sodomy, idol worship, abortion, murder, thefts, and drunken reveling. Here is what the servants of God say with all their hearts: "RUN! THIS DOOMED AMERICAN THEATER IS ON FIRE! RUN! FLEE THE WRATH TO COME!"

"God loves everyone," really? Here is how it all turns out according to Revelation 21:8: "But the fearful (cowardly Christians), and unbelieving (Jews, Muslims, Hindus, etc.), and the abominable (Sodomites), and murders (abortionists, the military, and criminals), and whoremongers (fornicators, adulterers, Sodomites), and sorcerers (drug addicts, alcoholics, witches), and idolaters (those that make and worship graven images and bow down to Santa Clause and the like), and all liars shall have their part in the lake which burns with fire and brimstone: which is the second death." God obviously does not love these people whom he daily torments in the fiery lake of hell.

So who is to blame for this bogus reading of John 3:16 and the proliferation of the "God loves everyone" lie? The pastors of this generation are to blame! They are paid fat salaries and fat pensions to lie and to gloss over the sins of fornication, homosexuality, remarriage after divorce, killing on the battlefield, and paying homage to all forms of godless consumerism. God condemns the preachers that scatter his flock, just as he condemned the false prophets in Old Testament times (e.g., Jeremiah 5 and 23).

It was not always so.

The famous American Puritan and Congregationalist pastor Jonathan Edwards (1703–1758) wrote about God's wrath as God's dominant characteristic in his sermon "Sinners in the Hands of an Angry God":

> The God that holds you over the pit of hell, much as one holds a spider, or some loathsome insect over the fire, abhors you, and is dreadfully provoked: his wrath towards you burns like fire... You are ten thousand times more abominable in his eyes, than the most hateful venomous serpent is in ours. O sinner! Consider the fearful danger you are in: it is a great furnace of wrath, a wide and bottomless pit, full of the fire of wrath, that you are held over in the hand of that God.

Edwards as representative for his generation took the Bible seriously and concluded that God hates people. You may have heard it said that "God hates sin, but loves the sinner." The Bible never says that anywhere. That is yet another lie propagated by wicked Christian leaders. Not only is God's hate of sinners implied in his wrath toward them, but God explicitly states that he hates workers of iniquity in texts such as Psalm 5:5. Furthermore, God simply appoints some humans for his hatred, having done neither good nor evil, before they were born, in order to fulfill God's purpose. God, for instance, declares his hatred for Esau in both Malachi 1 and Romans 9. The Bible not only does not say that "God loves everyone," but it includes assertions to the contrary: God hates some people (some before they were even born).

So, who does God love? From one end of the Bible to the other, including in the Gospel of John, we find one repeated answer: Those who obey God. Among the many passages we could cite are John 14:21, "He that hath my commandments, and keepeth them, he it is that loveth me" and 14:23, "If a man love me, he will keep my words: and my Father will love him."

God loves only those who believe in Him and obey His commandments. The rest will burn in eternal torment. Therefore, run from the "God loves everyone" farce, as your soul depends upon it!

Shirley Phelps-Roper is an attorney and servant of the God of all creation in the last minutes of the last days.

QUESTIONS

1. In light of Ansari's observations concerning Islamic texts and traditions, speculate as to why there is "a lack of religious ministry" for Muslim women in prison.

2. How does a group-oriented, honor–shame culture compare to your cultural context?

3. Reread the story of Nicodemus in light of Stovell's observations. What "spiritual pain" might be involved in being "born again"?

4. Assess Phelps-Roper's reading of the biblical text. How would the "wicked preachers" of this generation respond to her?

CHAPTER 9

GOSPEL OF JOHN (PART II)

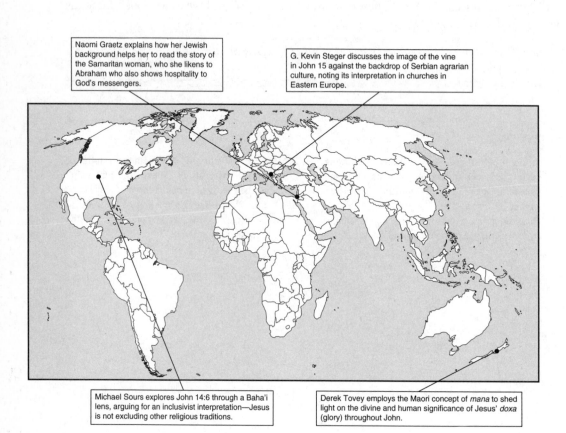

Naomi Graetz explains how her Jewish background helps her to read the story of the Samaritan woman, who she likens to Abraham who also shows hospitality to God's messengers.

G. Kevin Steger discusses the image of the vine in John 15 against the backdrop of Serbian agrarian culture, noting its interpretation in churches in Eastern Europe.

Michael Sours explores John 14:6 through a Baha'i lens, arguing for an inclusivist interpretation—Jesus is not excluding other religious traditions.

Derek Tovey employs the Maori concept of *mana* to shed light on the divine and human significance of Jesus' *doxa* (glory) throughout John.

READINGS

The Samaritan Woman from a Jewish Perspective
Naomi Graetz

The Image of the Vine in Serbian Agrarian Culture
G. Kevin Steger

An Inclusivist Interpretation of John 14:6 through a Baha'i Lens
Michael Sours

The Maori concept of *Mana* and *Doxa* in John
Derek Tovey

THE SAMARITAN WOMAN FROM A JEWISH PERSPECTIVE

Naomi Graetz (Israel)

At first glance, the Gospel of John creates a problem for me because it appears that Jesus reveals himself as a God. This is not always the case in the other gospels. So the first thing I have to do is suppress this thought—since obviously I, as a Jew, do not believe that Jesus is a God, son of God, or a Messiah figure. There also seems to be an anti-Jewish bias in John's Gospel. This also presents a problem for me, even though intellectually I know that when the Gospel of John speaks of Jews negatively, it is a reflection of the later dissension between the synagogue and the early Christians and not an accurate portrayal of Jesus himself. It appears that John uses the Jews as a symbol or metaphor for powers and authorities who oppose the belief in Jesus as the Messiah. But symbols and metaphors are not merely symbols and metaphors: They have intrinsic power. Indeed, we should not underestimate the power of John's language, and we should remember how his language was appropriated on occasion by Christian anti-Semites. Women especially should be aware of the dangers when one group speaks in judgment against another group.

When I read the story of the Woman at the Well in John 4, I find many familiar elements. First, there are a number of well scenes in the Torah—for example, with Jacob (Genesis 24, 29) and Moses (Exodus 2). Usually well scenes in the Bible are sites of matrimonial match-making, but clearly that is not Jesus' intention here in John, although he does manage to find out that the Samaritan woman has no husband. Perhaps to prevent her from trying to capture him as a possible mate for herself, he tells her she already has had or has five husbands. At any rate, it is clear from the well scenes in the Bible that the oriental laws of hospitality demand that we slake the thirst of those who ask for water—in fact we do not wait to be asked. We run and satisfy thirsty travelers immediately.

Second, the concept of "living water" is not new to me either. It is a frequent metaphor in the Bible. In Jeremiah 2:13, God is described as a "fountain of living waters" and of course the Torah is described as living water. I also can easily connect with the woman at the well, as I identify with the Samaritans, who are outside society—much as are the Conservative Jews, of whom I am a member. I too am not recognized by mainstream Judaism in Israel. Our rabbis are discriminated against.

Third, the issue of not eating food prepared by gentiles is also one that I can understand. In John 4:8; 31–33 there seems to be reference to this. Although the woman is shocked that Jesus is willing to drink water from her well, the text makes clear that "his disciples had gone into the town to buy food." And later when they come back and urge him to eat and Jesus says, "I have food to eat that you do not know about," the disciples are suspicious and ask each other "has someone been bringing him food?" The suspicion of eating food prepared by non-Jews has ancient origins. There are laws dating back to Mishnaic times and there is the famous saying of R. Eliezer b. Hyrcanus (early second century): "He that eats the bread of the Samaritans is like one that eats the flesh of swine" (M. Sheviith 8:10). The laws of Kashrut continue to be a cornerstone of

Judaism today. And the war over Kashrut observance and standards continues unabated; non-Jews and even Jews whose standards are less stringent than those on their right are excluded and discriminated against by those whose observance level is higher.

There are also other Jewish themes in this story which are relevant. First of all in Jewish tradition, there are many powerful women who talk back and hold their own in male society: Beruriah, a woman scholar who lived in Palestine in the second century and was the wife of Rabbi Meir, is one who comes to mind. There are many tales about her that show she had considerable rabbinic knowledge and understanding of sophisticated methodology. The tale clearly related to the Samaritan woman appears in the Babylonian Talmud when R. Yose the Galilean met Beruriah and asked her, "Which way to Lod?" and she famously answered, "Did not the sages say not to 'talk too much to women'?" The Samaritan woman echoes this when she says to Jesus, who is on his way back to Galilee: "What! You are a Jew, and you ask me [a woman], a Samaritan, for a drink?"

There are other tales that reveal Beruriah's awareness of rabbinic misogyny. Precisely because she is so knowledgeable and in command of her tradition, she is able to mock it. Because a learned woman was an anomaly, the rabbis told stories about Beruriah and projected their own mixed feelings about her. Her learnedness, a result of her father's teaching her Torah, which according to R. Eliezer's dictum results in licentiousness, made her a threat to male institutions. Eleventh-century scholar Rashi, as part of his commentary to the Talmud (B. *Avodah Zarah* 18b), has her getting comeuppance by being seduced into committing adultery, which led to her suicide.

If we compare Beruriah with the Samaritan woman, we find an attempt to lower her worth by implying that she too may be guilty of adultery (having five husbands). But unlike Beruriah, she continues to influence the people; for her testimony was well received by many (John 4:39) and she does not come to a sad end. The Samaritan woman is ordinary and possibly illiterate, unlike the highly educated Beruriah, but the Samaritan woman has life experience: witness her questions, her confidence, and her marital history. In the end, the Samaritan woman is almost on the same level as the apostles (her powerful testimony), whereas Beruriah dies a wanton. There seems to be an inverse connection between a simple woman's attaining spiritual power and the downfall of an educated woman's studying Torah. The legend of Beruriah is thus an ambivalent acknowledgment and denial of women's autonomy and intellectual achievement.

The position of women in the rabbinic system is that women are the intellectual and moral inferiors of men. In tractate Ketubot, it is said that women are flighty, easily seduced, and because of their looseness, inherently seductive. Women's hair, their movements, their voice, their clothing all entice. Women in short are viewed as aliens, as outsiders who unfortunately present a problem since they still inhabit the male culture. Even rescuing a man in captivity takes precedence over saving a woman (Mishnah Horayot). The less visible the woman, the more praiseworthy.

Thus this public conversation between Jesus and the Samaritan woman is scandalous, as the woman herself notes: "How is it that you, a Jew, ask a drink of me, a woman of Samaria?" (4:9). She knows that a Jewish man should not talk with a woman, or drink from her vessel. The scandal is noted also by the disciples when they arrive at the well (4:27). They are amazed that Jesus, a Jewish rabbi (4:31), speaks in public with a woman, and a Samaritan no less. Their protests reflect traditional cultural and social conventions and expectations, which Jesus appears to be challenging.

The Samaritan woman engages in a good deed when she brings water to Jesus. In that way she is like Abraham who runs to feed the angels when they come to visit him as seen in Genesis 18. Both she and Abraham do not recognize that Jesus and the angels come bearing God's message. Both of them offer drink/food to the god-like figures. In Abraham's case it is clear that the angels ate (Genesis 18:8). But did Jesus actually drink water from the Samaritan woman? For him to have asked for water and then not drink it would be a slap in the face to her oriental hospitality. It is clear to me that the author of the text has in mind Abraham's greeting the angels in the "heat of the day"—note the "high noon" setting in John 4: 6, which explains why water is offered and undoubtedly drunk. It is the drinking of water, not mentioned but assumed, that gave him the energy boost to deliver his sermon.

How can we apply this new interpretation to the Samaritan Woman? The writer of the text is aware of Abraham's hospitality and the whole tradition of oriental laws of hospitality. Those who perform the commandment of hospitality are blessed and godly and able to converse with the Gods, as Abraham did. Both Abraham and the woman are involved in creating new kinds of societies where acts of loving-kindness will be encouraged and where all will be welcome. Jesus' policy is of open doors, welcoming all—including women and other outsiders.

Naomi Graetz taught English for 35 years at Ben Gurion University of the Negev, Israel; she is the author of a number of books on women in the Bible and Midrash.

THE IMAGE OF THE VINE IN SERBIAN AGRARIAN CULTURE
G. Kevin Steger (Serbia)

My mother was raised on a farm in Northeast Texas. She had regular chores to do including stereotypical things like milking the cow and weeding the garden. She grew up with an understanding of the relationship man had with the land. My wife's parents were also raised on farms in East Bell County in central Texas. They grew up feeding the chickens and planting seeds in that seemingly miraculous black dirt that would grow anything. They developed calluses on their hands pruning cotton plants and picking that white gold, so they also understood the necessary connection man has with the land. Different from so many of my parents' generation, I grew up in town. I attended school, church, and cub scouts, all within a few blocks of our home in a nice neighborhood in the good part of town. The only connection I had to the land was that it tethered me to a lawnmower every Saturday whether I liked it or not. I remember asking my Sunday school teacher why Jesus taught so often with agricultural themes. The kind old Mr. Alex explained, "Well, it's because that's what the people knew." He continued, "Everyone in Jesus' day was dependent upon the produce of the land, so in one form or another, they were all connected to it."

I understood about as much as a 10-year-old could, but it would be many years later, as a young man stepping foot in Eastern Europe that I really began to understand the significance of passages like John 15:1–8. After visiting Serbia for the first time, I understood the significance of the image of the vine. The subsistence culture of so many in Serbia is directly tied to the land and its stewardship. Consequently, there is a deeper understanding of things like pruning and harvesting. On my way to Serbia, I passed through beautiful river valleys in Central Europe covered in vineyards that were initially planted by the Romans 2,000 years ago. Across Europe, wine and spirits are important parts of their culture, mainly because they are products of their ancient land. Each region has their own varietals of which they are very proud, having an understanding of the hard work involved in their production as well as the emotional investment in creating something uniquely their own. In Serbia, grapes are used certainly to make wine, but perhaps more importantly they are also used to make *Rakia. Rakia* is to the Serbian people what Vodka is to the Russians. Every family makes their own version and serves it in shots before every meal, including breakfast. They believe it promotes healthy digestion. The connection they feel to the fruit of the vine is an integral part of their identity as Serbs.

In John 15:1, Jesus explains to the disciples, after they have just shared the Last Supper, that He is the vine and His father is the gardener. He used this metaphor because the vineyard, the grapes, and the wines of the local area were an important part of the community's identity just like for the Serbs. They understood the sanctity of the growing process; therefore, Jesus chose the metaphor of the vineyard.

Jesus spent an incredible amount of time in his days on earth challenging the hypocrisy of the Pharisees. He was especially concerned that the Pharisees seemed more concerned about appearances than actual spirituality. Jesus' vine metaphor includes a sharp statement against hypocrisy stating that the gardener "cuts off any branch in me that does not bear fruit." According to Jesus, those who look as though they belong in the family of faith, those who seem to be attached to Him, if they bear no fruit, are cut off from the vine. Perhaps they were never actually part of the vine in the first place.

Eastern Europe's evangelical population is small. They are small because they must compete with the state-supported Orthodox Churches. Any religious group that does not fall into the very strict government definition of acceptable religious organizations is considered a cult. So, most of the evangelical groups in countries like Serbia and Bulgaria are considered a cult. They have no official classification or acceptance from the government.

Because the evangelical churches in Eastern Europe are often persecuted, their leadership places a high value on church identity. If a member of the church is bearing no fruit, they are confronted by the church leadership and encouraged to participate in the life of the church or be cut off. Church discipline is certainly encouraged in John 15, but few churches today genuinely practice it, except for these churches in Eastern Europe. While teaching a course at the Novi Sad Theological College in Novi Sad, Serbia, I became aware of a rather high-profile church disciplinary action in the area: One of the leaders in a prominent evangelical church was a wealthy businessman. In their annual review of contributions, the Board of Elders discovered that this man did not tithe. The elders confronted him and gave him an opportunity for repentance, which he disregarded. After some time passed, they made a further decision to excommunicate him. Across the larger evangelical community in the region there was general agreement that the action taken by the elders was not only appropriate but also necessary. Every member of the church—as a "branch" on the vine—has an important role to play, and if they are not participating, then they must not be a genuine Christ follower and are cast out from the fellowship. Those that remain "in the vine" are expected to bear fruit.

G. Kevin Steger (D.Ed.Min.) is the CEO/Founder of Light over Europe Ministries, Inc., an organization dedicated to the advancement of the Gospel of Jesus Christ all over the European Continent.

AN INCLUSIVIST INTERPRETATION OF JOHN 14:6 THROUGH A BAHA'I LENS

Michael Sours (United States)

I was baptized in the Church of England and spent my formative years growing up in the American "Bible Belt." In this Christian-dominated culture the Gospel was readily available and was ever present in daily conversations. However, by the time I was a teenager I began to learn about other faith communities, in particular Hinduism, Buddhism, and Islam. I became fascinated with Buddhist and Islamic art. I was impressed by the teachings of the Buddha and the anticlerical poetry of Muslim mystics like Hafez. But early in this journey of discovery, I learned that many of my Christian family and friends viewed my interests in other faiths as troubling. I was soon schooled in a conservative form of Christian exclusivism. Stated concisely, Jesus claimed that He was the only way to God, the only truth, the only life. Verses like John 14:6 were interpreted to mean that the followers of other faiths were lost, doomed to perish in Hell or in a lake of fire in the final days. Some of my Christian friends even believed this gruesome fate awaited other Christian denominations, such as Catholics and Mormons.

If it were possible to look beyond the confines of Christianity and find only God-haters perpetrating cruelty and injustice, reading John 14:6 in such an exclusive way might be easier. But this is not reality. There are people in other faraway places who are just as devoted to God, just as charitable and caring as Christians in Texas. In many parts of the world, deeply religious people pass their lives without ever hearing the message of the Gospel. In fact, this has been true for most of human history. Can it be that God is so uncharitable and His grace so limited that He cares so little for the souls He created? And would God judge harshly even those who have encountered Christianity and rejected it when it came to them alongside the barrel of a gun or with foreign diseases that decimated their populations and destroyed all that was dear to them? Why do some people get to learn about Christianity in the most favorable circumstances while others only encountered it in ways that would convey the opposite of Jesus' own example? I could not imagine that God would be less compassionate, less fair, and less understanding than mere human beings.

At an early age, the problem of religious pluralism became one of the central questions of my personal religious life. It was Bahá'u'lláh's answers to this problem that attracted me to the Baha'i Faith. At the core of Bahá'u'lláh's teachings is the belief in the oneness of religion. Bahá'u'lláh taught that all the religions have "proceeded from one Source, and are rays of one Light." But if they are one, why are they so different? He explained that each successive revelation unfolds in accordance with "the varying requirements of the ages in which they were promulgated." In effect, there is only one religion and Bahá'u'lláh's followers, the Bahá'ís—like Jews, Christians, Buddhists, Hindus, Zoroastrians, and Muslims—all belong to this same true religious heritage.

Buddha, Moses, Jesus, Muhammad, Bahá'u'lláh, and others were like the sun, shining light on all peoples each new day. We can give the sun a different name each day, but no matter how many days the sun sets and rises again, it is always the same sun. It is the same light that gives life wherever it shines. This more loving view of God explains both why religion is so universal and why some differences exist between them. And with these teachings in mind, I could understand why every Faith proclaimed itself as the "only way."

Many Christian friends were unsatisfied by such general explanations. They wanted me to reconcile my acceptance of other religions with the particular claims of Jesus Christ found in the Bible. Because Bahá'u'lláh presents a forceful defense of the Gospel in His writings, a Baha'i cannot brush aside Jesus' claim as unreliable. Bahá'u'lláh stresses that God's redemptive testimony is available to everyone. He ardently defends the Gospel against its critics who claim that the true record of Christ's teachings has been lost or corrupted. God protects and renews His redemptive message. It is a theological principle that can be applied to the scriptures of any Faith. And its truth is demonstrated in the spiritual efficacy of the message that still survives in the different holy books. All Faith communities have pious believers, remarkable leaders, inspired mystics, saints, and martyrs. And those personal transformations were inspired and informed by Scripture regarded as sacred and authoritative. If we argue that one community possesses the genuine Word of God and others do not, then where is the superiority of that sacred book over other books that have shown the same transformative powers?

Bahá'u'lláh provides the principles for reconciling the age-old claims that have divided the followers of other Faiths. And, for His followers, it becomes an act of faith to read the Scripture—all world Scriptures—through a lens that is free from cultural prejudices. Just as Christians have reconciled seemingly conflicting verses between different books because they regard them as holy and authoritative, a Baha'i can read the Scriptures of many faiths as the one Word of God. He writes, "Purge thy sight... from all earthly limitations, that thou mayest behold them all as the bearers of one Name, the exponents of one Cause, the manifestations of one Self, and the revealers of one Truth." If we can see past the outward names and cultural differences, we can come to know the Buddha in Christ and Christ in the Buddha. We can hear the same way, truth, and life—the same one voice of God speaking through them all.

When I read the Gospel of John, the book Christians cite most often to convey an exclusivist message, what stands out most is the Gospel's prologue that describes the Messiah, the "Christ," as a preexistent reality and light of the world. Jesus is both the historical Messiah, and also much more—the one divine Reality that transcends place and time. In His example, as recorded in the Gospel of John, Jesus lives a life of devotion to God, compassion, and self-sacrifice. He rejects materialism and violence, and urges social justice and virtuous living. In John's description of Jesus' significance and in the particulars of His teachings and example, Jesus provides a theological and ethical way for understanding His words, "I am the way, and the truth, and the life; no one comes to the Father but through Me." In context, Jesus is not making a distinction between Christianity and Judaism, or Christianity and Buddhism, or Christianity and any other religion, but a distinction between the Light he represents and the darkness of materialism, the ethical and virtuous way that leads to God and the ways that do not. It is a distinction between morality and immorality, between truth and falsehood, between love and hatred. It is about "the Way," "the Truth," "the Life," not about the different names used by Jews, Christians, Buddhists, or Muslims to designate the same reality. The context isn't other religions. Rather than rejecting Judaism, Jesus affirmed it. When he criticizes, it is the conduct of followers, not the Faith itself.

Understanding John 14:6 in this way liberates us from a view that inevitably reduces God to an image of our own prejudices. And, instead of feeling like the members of an exclusive and superior club, this interpretation calls us to live fuller and more meaningful lives as believers, whatever religious tradition we follow. Rather than a mere matter of ideological correctness or believing in a particular theology of Jesus or belonging to the right group with the right name, this interpretation means that the way of salvation requires that we follow Jesus' example. It is an interpretive approach that can be applied to similar "exclusivist" verses in the Scriptures of other Faith communities.

The oneness of God and the oneness of religions are central Baha'i teachings, and the promotion of fellowship between faith communities is important to the Baha'i mission of promoting world peace. This makes understanding these types of verses and being able to explain them important to Baha'is.

Michael Sours is a Baha'i and an award-winning author of a number of books on the relationship between Christianity and the Bahá'í Faith; he has been involved in many interfaith activities.

The Maori concept of *Mana* and *Doxa* in John

Derek Tovey (New Zealand)

Among the strategies and the rhetorical devices that the author of John uses to present his understanding of Jesus is his use of the concept and language of "glory" (*doxa*). This concept provides a way of establishing the status and honor of Jesus, both as a character in the story and as portrayed in the dynamics of the narrative, so that readers, by understanding Jesus' honor and status as both ascribed and achieved, may accept the Gospel's claim for Jesus as the Christ and as God's Son (20:30–31).

Here I examine the concept of *doxa* (glory) by drawing analogically upon the Maori concept of *mana*. Not only does this help to illuminate the Gospel's use of *doxa*, but it also provides a way of mediating the dichotomy between a "theological" understanding of Jesus' glory which emphasizes his divine status over against a "view from below," which sees that *doxa*, or "glory," as manifest in and through a human character. I must state at the outset that I write as a Pakeha (European) New Zealander, and I am very dependent upon secondary literature, by both Maori and non-Maori scholars, for my understanding of *mana*.

The noun, *doxa*, is used 18 times in John's Gospel (and the verbal form appears in a variety of cases and tenses 22 times). In ancient secular Greek, it had two basic meanings. One was "opinion" in the sense of the perspective or thoughts on a matter that one held and was prepared to defend. The other sense of *doxa* referred objectively to one's standing or repute in the eyes of others. This sense most likely contributed to its choice by the translators of the Greek Septuagint (LXX) to translate the Hebrew word *kabod*. This could refer to a person's status, importance, worth, dignity, rank, and position of power: It conveyed the sense of a person's *gravitas*, a person's inherent authority and prestige. In the Septuagint, *doxa* was also used of God's glory, and so represented God's radiance, and divine mode of being.

Mana, like *doxa*, is a big concept. It has a wide range of meanings that cannot quite be captured in English. To have *mana* is to be a person who has prestige, status, charisma, dignity, and influence. To have *mana* is to have authority and power of control (sovereignty) over people or something (like land), or to have authority and control in certain contexts. Furthermore, as a concept *mana* is closely associated with *tapu*, which itself has a range of meanings. It can refer to the fact that a person or thing is placed under a religious or spiritual restriction, so that the person or thing that is *tapu* is "holy," or even "consecrated" and "set apart," or that the person or thing is off-limits as "polluting," or "unclean," even "dangerous," depending on the context. The fundamental feature of *mana* is that it is ultimately something that is received from God (or "the gods" in ancient Maori understanding); the power from which *mana* is derived is spiritual and supernatural in nature.

It is important to understand that, though everyone is born with *mana* inherited from one's parents and inherent in being human, the degree of *mana* inherited depends upon one's parents' rank and social status. While individuals of high rank in ancient Maori society inherited an initial store of *mana* by birth, they could increase or decrease their *mana* by their own actions. Moreover, *mana* was also "given" to an individual by the community: It derived from the recognition and respect given to an individual by others. Hence, *mana* as a social value was both *ascribed* (by one's birth or primogeniture and by the recognition of others) and *achieved* by one's own actions and abilities.

The pertinence for our reading of John's Gospel in drawing an analogy between *mana* and the concept and language of *doxa* lies precisely in the way in which the concept of *mana* sees a link, or continuum, between the human and divine. In John, the *doxa*, or *mana*, of Jesus is seen "from below" through his works or "signs," for instance, as much as it is portrayed "from above" through the claims made by the narrator, or by Jesus himself. The narrative portrays honor as both ascribed to Jesus and as achieved by Jesus. As characters are challenged by Jesus to accept his status, or *mana*, as demonstrated by his works, so the reader is to understand and recognize Jesus' *mana* on the basis of the narrative.

The prologue in John 1:1–18 is, *par excellence*, an example of how the narrator outlines Jesus' ascribed honor, that is, his status as "the Word" who is the same as God, and who is, in fact, God's only begotten Son. Is it too much to say that this is the narrator's way of establishing Jesus' "primogeniture"? I would argue that the author of the Gospel begins precisely in this way in order to establish that Jesus' status as God's Son is ascribed. When the narrator says that the Word has "lived among us" and that "we have seen his glory, glory as of a father's only son" (1:14), he does not just mean that we have seen in him the divine splendor of God shining forth, but rather we have seen and come to understand his true status, we have recognized his *mana* as One who is one with the Father. This "oneness" with the Father is something that Jesus asserts again and again in the Gospel, in different ways and contexts. In John 17:5 we have an instance where Jesus directly claims this honor: "So now, Father, honor me in your own presence with that status/honor/*mana* that I had in your presence before the world existed."

It is the achieved, or acquired, status or honor of Jesus that the author is particularly concerned to convey to the reader. The signs, those miraculous deeds that Jesus does, are intended to make clear to all who have eyes to see (e.g., 10:31–39) what Jesus' status really is: the true *mana* that he has. This, I suggest, is made explicit in the very first sign Jesus performs (2:1–11). At the conclusion of this event, when Jesus has turned the water into wine, the narrator comments that in this first sign Jesus revealed his "glory" (his honor/status/*mana*) and his disciples believed in him. In 11:4, at the outset of what may be taken as the last miraculous sign, Jesus says that the raising of Lazarus will function to bring "glory"/honor both to God and "the Son of God" who will be "glorified"/honored through it. In this way the author has the "glory" (*mana*) of Jesus revealed in his actions as a human being: "Flesh" and "glory" combine, just as the two words appear "side-by-side," as it were, in 1:14.

The Gospel also shows Jesus engaging in verbal defense of his *mana* through challenge and riposte, claiming that those who are truly alive to the import of his actions would recognize the "honor" that he is due, and the honor that he shares with God (e.g., 5:39–47; 10:31–39; 14:11).

It is important to note that the rhetoric about Jesus' honor particularly coheres around his "hour," a theme that is developed in such a way in the narrative leading up to Jesus' crucifixion that the reader is led to see that Jesus achieves honor through the dishonor of what is done to him in his "hour of suffering" (cf. 12:20–28, esp. vv. 23, 28; 19:1–3, 5, 16–25). The author of John presents the human character Jesus who attains honor by his actions. But these actions bespeak a *mana* that is more than merely human: This true, divine status of Jesus is reinforced by the narrator, who refers to Jesus' ascribed honor in the Prologue, and by the discourse of Jesus in which Jesus also makes claims for this divine status, and challenges his interlocutors to accept this on the evidence of his works. But, above all, this is a *mana*, and a style of seeking honor, that subverts human conceptions of honor.

Derek Tovey is Lecturer in New Testament at the College of St. John the Evangelist, and the School of Theology at University of Auckland, New Zealand.

QUESTIONS

1. Articulate why it is important for Graetz to compare the Samaritan woman to Beruriah and to Abraham.

2. How would religious groups in your culture react to the excommunication of the wealthy businessman discussed by Steger? What is your response?

3. How might an exclusivist reading of John 14:6 attempt to refute Sours's interpretation?

4. Is there a concept analogous to *doxa* or *mana* in your cultural context that might be brought to bear on a reading of Jesus in John?

CHAPTER 10

CRUCIFIXION OF JESUS

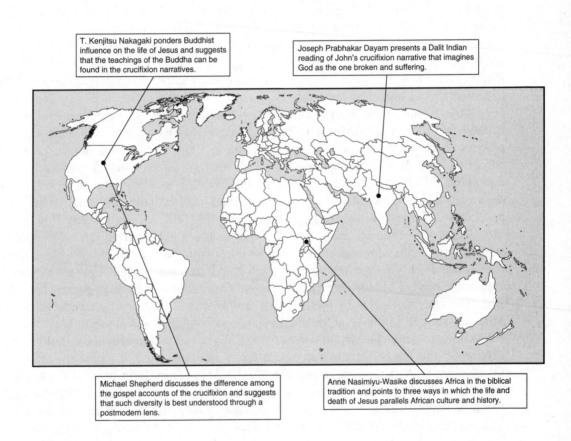

T. Kenjitsu Nakagaki ponders Buddhist influence on the life of Jesus and suggests that the teachings of the Buddha can be found in the crucifixion narratives.

Joseph Prabhakar Dayam presents a Dalit Indian reading of John's crucifixion narrative that imagines God as the one broken and suffering.

Michael Shepherd discusses the difference among the gospel accounts of the crucifixion and suggests that such diversity is best understood through a postmodern lens.

Anne Nasimiyu-Wasike discusses Africa in the biblical tradition and points to three ways in which the life and death of Jesus parallels African culture and history.

READINGS

The Crucifixion from a Buddhist Perspective
T. Kenjitsu Nakagaki

Dealing with Differences in the Crucifixion Narratives
Michael Shepherd

A Dalit Reading of the Cross
Joseph Prabhakar Dayam

The Suffering of Jesus and Suffering in Africa
Anne Nasimiyu-Wasike

THE CRUCIFIXION FROM A BUDDHIST PERSPECTIVE

T. Kenjitsu Nakagaki (United States)

When I first started to learn about Christianity as a college student, I was first introduced to the story of the crucifixion of Jesus Christ. Having grown up with Buddhist teachings, I could not help but compare the life of Shakyamuni Buddha to the life of Jesus Christ. One key difference stands out: Shakyamuni Buddha lived a long life of 80 years, and died naturally and peacefully surrounded by disciples, humans, various animals, gods, bodhisattvas, and various buddhas. Jesus Christ lived a short life of 33 years, and died violently by crucifixion, surrounded by Roman soldiers, local people, family, and a few disciples. The crucifixion of Jesus Christ, of course, is central to Christianity, so I wanted to learn more.

After I came to the United States, I realized that I had not studied much about Buddhism's journey from India to the West, though I had intensively learned the process of the spread of Buddhism from India to China and other Southeast Asian countries, and then later from China and Korea to Japan. Once I started reading about Buddhism's interactions with the West, I saw how much Buddhism seems to have influenced the teachings of Jesus and the story of Christ's life. It has been documented that King Ashoka (304–232 B.C.)of India sent Buddhist missionaries to Greece, Iran, Syria, Turkey, and Egypt during 262–258 B.C. Buddhist teachings were therefore available during this time in the regions surrounding Jerusalem. Jesus may have encountered Buddhist teachings during the so-called "missing years" of his life. We also know that Greeks were in India beginning in 323 B.C. The Gandhara style of Buddhist art was clearly influenced by Greek culture. This can be seen in the Gandhara-style statues of Buddhas and Bodhisattvas which have Greek features. The world where Jesus Christ lived was international, culturally diverse, and interactive. India was not so far away at that time. It has been said that St. Thomas the Apostle came to India in 52 A.D. Many stories of Christ's life parallel those of the Buddha's life such as virgin birth, bathing/baptism in a river, overcoming demonic temptations after 40 days (Jesus) or 49 days (Buddha), fasting, and more. The similarities also extend to Christ's teachings such as the Sermon on the Mount (Matthew 5–7), parts of which are nearly identical to the Buddha's teachings of practicing love and compassion even for one's enemies, controlling anger, and doing unto others as you would have them do unto you. The major difference is the crucifixion, the violence of which stands in contrast to the peacefulness of Christ's teachings and the peacefulness of Buddha's passing into *parinirvana*.

This poses the question, How many of the details of Jesus' crucifixion really happened or even did the crucifixion really happen at all? We know that the Gospels of Matthew (26, 27), Mark (14, 15), Luke (22, 23), and John (12–19) have detailed narratives of the crucifixion. Yet, each gospel is slightly different. Even Jesus' last words on the cross are different in the four gospels. We also know that gospels were written at least 40 years after the death of Jesus Christ. Paul said very little about the crucifixion; for him all that seems to matter is that Christ died for our sins in accordance with the scriptures.

The Q document and the Gospel of Thomas, which might be earlier documents than Paul's writings, have no narratives, and no story of crucifixion or resurrection.

Since the life of Jesus Christ is not taught as part of Buddhism and therefore has little meaning for Buddhists, there is no standard Buddhist interpretation of the crucifixion narratives. Yet it is still possible, I believe, to understand the crucifixion narratives from a Buddhist perspective. One way is that the crucifixion narratives can be seen as a story based upon historical facts that also mix in symbolic episodes as a means to reveal the fundamental teachings of Jesus. The other is to see it as a completely imagined story with the same purpose.

Buddhist texts explain that Buddha's mother, Queen Maya, became pregnant when she dreamed of a white elephant coming into her body. The baby Buddha was born from under Queen Maya's right arm, and the Buddha walked seven steps immediately after his birth. Is this story historical truth? There is historical evidence that the Buddha was born in Lumbini in present-day Nepal, but what about the rest of the story? Different Buddhist traditions have different views on how literal the story is to be taken. In mine, it is seen as a metaphorical tale. The white elephant in India represents a pure and sacred animal, the right arm a sign of a higher sacred birth, and the seven steps represent going beyond the six realms of deluded existence. It may not be historically true, but symbolically the story represents the "truth" of the teachings of the Buddha. Similarly, written details of the crucifixion narratives may not be historically accurate, or may or may not have even happened at all, yet even when taken as dramatic metaphor, they convey a universal truth through Christ's teachings that perhaps is more important.

In Buddhism, there are various Buddhas. One of those, "Amida" or "Amitabha" is a central Buddha in Pure Land Buddhism, the lineage from which my sect derives. In the sutras or Buddhist scriptures that describe Amida, the life story of this Buddha is similar to that of the historical Shakyamuni Buddha. Like Shakyamuni, Amida was born a royal. After becoming aware of suffering, he became a monk, took the name Dharmakara, and established and practiced a great vow to liberate all beings. Though Dharmakara is described as if he is an historical person, his existence is a symbolic one which is meant to guide us to the boundless wisdom and compassion of the Buddha.

Can the teachings of the Buddha be found in the crucifixion narratives? Can we see Jesus as a Bodhisattva, an enlightened being who comes to guide others to awaken to the dharma truth? For me as a Buddhist, the betrayals, unfair trial, and lies told about Jesus represent the illusive world, the delusion of human beings filled with self-centered evil passions; his suffering from the crucifixion represents the painful inner struggles that we all go through as we try to live our lives; and the earthshaking that was said to have occurred at his death represents the true transformation or true liberation to overcome outer and inner suffering. With compassion, the Bodhisattva Jesus will come back to guide all beings in a form of resurrection. His dramatic story awakens us to the true nature of ourselves, and that we all have potentiality to be enlightened through our own transformation. In Buddhism we say that we all have "Buddha nature" within us in spite of all our blind passions, just as Christians say we all have Christ within us in spite of all of our sins. Both emphasize transformation from evil into goodness. What is the essence of Bodhisattva Jesus? They are the teachings of wisdom, love, and compassion that Jesus shared in the Sermon on the Mount, and other occasions. This is the essence of both Buddhism and Christianity.

T. Kenjitsu Nakagaki is an ordained Jodoshinshu Buddhist priest and is Vice Chair of the Interfaith Center of New York; he formerly served as Head Resident Minister of the NY Buddhist Church for 16 years and president of the Buddhist Council of New York.

DEALING WITH DIFFERENCES IN THE CRUCIFIXION NARRATIVES
Michael Shepherd (United States)

As global migrations and telecommunications have created a more interconnected world, the dynamic of cultures interacting with each other has dramatically increased. Living within the convergence of cultures, different perspectives will exist along-side each other more frequently than they have in the past. Homogenous communities are rapidly declining and an emphasis upon unique cultural identity is growing due to postmodernity. This philosophical shift from the assumptions of the European Enlightenment era creates a new framework to understand and interpret reality. As Christianity has shifted to become majority within non-Western cultures, the Eurocentric assumptions of theology are no longer universally valid. There is a question of how different cultures, each with particular of rules for determining truth and meaning, can interact with biblical texts and self-determined theology.

The existence of four distinct gospel narratives and different perspectives of the crucifixion provide a template for appreciating this context of pluralism of cultures and the theological diversity of the world church. This multiformity is best appreciated through a lens of postmodern interpretation.

Each of the gospel narratives takes a different approach to communicating the significance of Jesus, his ministry and teaching, and ultimately the events of his crucifixion and resurrection. The differences in the narratives reflect the contextual location of the author and audience. Attention to these particularities will help us to appreciate each gospel writers' understanding of Jesus.

Reading with a postmodern perspective reiterates the importance of holding multiple views simultaneously rather than attempting to merge the distinctive narratives into a singular story. To create a fifth gospel, compiled from pieces of the received texts, attempts to engineer a unified view yet creates a document that is no longer faithful to any of the four canonical texts. Rather than pursuing an artificial unity, the postmodern perspective allows for a more faithful interpretation to the scripture.

This tension is especially poignant in the recounting of the death of Jesus and its spiritual significance. The authors selectively include details of this monumental event, such as the setting, day, progression of events, and the words of Jesus. The crucifixion is central to the Christian faith, yet the explanation of what happens and how atonement works is starkly absent from the gospel narratives. The brief summaries below represent only one possible interpretation of each narrative within a diversity of perspectives.

Matthew presents the ministry of Jesus as a new Moses. He presents him as giving a new law, leading a new Israel, and initiating a new covenant. The crucifixion is interpreted in light of the Passover, in which sacrificial lambs protected the Hebrews from the tenth plague and in light of the covenant sacrificial system, in which the blood of sacrificial animals covers the sins of the community.

Mark portrays Jesus as a divine figure, frequently including stories of healing and miracles to substantiate the claim that Jesus is the son of God. The events of the cross stand in juxtaposition to this divine power, as Jesus does not resist or overcome his oppressors. The crucifixion displays a suffering Jesus, not Jesus as a representative of the power of God.

Luke has the least developed atonement theory present in his narrative. Taken as a combination with the book of Acts, the death of Jesus is significant mainly as it helps to establish the identity of the early Christians. In the same way that Jewish leaders reject Jesus, they reject the community of Christians who are subject to persecution. The narrative points to God's status-reversal in establishing a universal kingdom of God and restoration of creation.

John presents an image of Jesus as one who brings life by giving up his own life. The Hebrew concept of *akedah*, or giving of your life for others, takes on added connotation in the identification of Jesus' role as a Passover lamb. Jesus' crucifixion adds significant details lacking in the other accounts, such as indicating that the time of the crucifixion coincides with the lamb sacrifices, the ceremonial hyssop and washbasin at the cross, and the soldiers who do not break Jesus' legs. As Jesus is sacrificed, he is "raised up" as a sign to the people that God's work has been accomplished, as Jesus announces with his final words, "It is finished."

Different theologians throughout the history of the church have posited atonement theories although the subject is noticeably absent from both the Apostles' and Nicene Creeds. The gospel authors each wrote autonomously, even though it is likely that they shared source material or incorporated elements from one another. By the second century, most of the church used the fourfold canon and numerous scholars have attempted to harmonize the four gospels into a single narrative, beginning with the *Diatesseron* by Tatian in the second century.

The breadth of theories attempting reconciliation of these differences reiterates the tension that exists within the received text. The author, occasion, and audience for each gospel were born and shaped in a particular cultural context. The differences that exist provide a template for how differences can exist within Christian theology without necessitating a singular, universal standard.

As divergent formulations of Christian theology develop, groups that emphasize the internal continuity of scripture often raise concerns that these differences may contradict each other and thereby nullify the validity of both expressions. The biblical precedent, however, demonstrates that the significance of textual interpretation is not contingent on accord but its ability to communicate the Christian message and affect the transformation of a community to respond in faith. Seeing the way that the gospel authors adapted their narrative in order to be effective storytellers provides the confidence to creatively adapt the gospel today for a particular faith community. Indeed, the four different gospel accounts of the crucifixion anticipate the different cultural expressions of theology and faith that can stand alongside one another today without the need to derive a singular perspective.

Michael Shepherd is a graduate of Hope International University and Fuller Theological Seminary; he is editor of GlobalTheology.org, a collaborative online journal for world expressions of Christian theology and biblical interpretation.

A Dalit Reading of the Cross

Joseph Prabhakar Dayam (India)

On the Christmas Eve of 2007 Dalit Christians in Khandamal in Orissa, India, were brutally attacked. While they were preparing to gather around the manger to celebrate life found in the baby Jesus, they were paraded to the outskirts of their vicinities. The persecution that began on that Christmas day continued and found greater expression in the year that followed. At least 50 people were brutally killed and several thousands displaced. It was told by the victims that some were butchered and at least one was buried alive. A nun was raped and several were forced to renounce their faith. Churches were set on fire and priests were beaten. Their houses were looted and fields were burnt. The symbol that strikingly conveys their context is the gruesome cross with the grotesque body of Christ on it. One may write off this incident as an isolated one. Mass murders like that in Khandamal may not occur every day. However, Dalit (those who were considered as untouchables and polluted in the caste structure that determines the identity and social location of an individual and communities) life in India is marked by suffering.

In a context of such despair and death, where do we, as Dalit Christians, locate hope? John 19:38–42 echoes the faith of the Church about Christ. Both the Apostle's creed and the Nicene Creed profess that Christ, the God incarnate, had suffered, died, was buried, and was raised to life. Such is the faith of the Dalit Christians as well.

In this text the writer brings together three Christian symbols which were central to the faith of the Church. He was crucified, buried, and raised to life again: Golgotha, grave, and the garden. These were the occasions for the Son's glorification.

It is intriguing that even though Christ as God incarnate is the central theme of John's Gospel, he does not mention any of the birth or the infancy narratives. Rather, his passion narrative is quite lengthy. He describes the way in which the powers of the day collided and unjustly put Jesus to death. He makes the slyness of the scribes, prejudice of the priests, and the cowardice and the cunningness of Pilate responsible for the death of Jesus. The place where he was crucified was a public place where everyone could see what would happen to a blasphemer and one who engages in treason. Sure it was a political murder of someone who was presented as a breaker of the law, as a rebel, a subversive usurper, and pretender. John painstakingly narrates the gruesomeness and paints the picture of the grotesque body hanging on the cross. The way of the cross in this Gospel is an excruciating journey. It was a painful political path for Jesus. For his disciples who left everything and followed this man, it was a betrayal of their hopes. The one whom they believed would institute God's reign is hanging there, being mocked, pleading for a drink, and finally giving up his spirit. The one in whom they supposedly experienced the presence of God hangs on the cross naked and God-forsaken.

While the cross of Christ depicts the grotesqueness of his death, the grave declares the irrevocability of it. It appears to be the end of any hope for the community of Jesus. It looks as though his movement was a failure, the hopes that he evoked were fake. He is like any other messianic pretender. The one who is supposedly the Word of God which creates all that is and on which all reality constantly depends has fallen silent. It is the absolute abandonment of God experienced by the One who claimed to be present with the Father in eternity.

Incongruously, it is in these sites of God's absence that the Gospel writer locates God's presence. It is through these shameful and ridiculous symbols that John unfurls the wisdom of God: a scandal to the worldly wise and the power of God to the one who is being saved. For the Gospel writer, Jesus unveiled God by living among humans, proclaiming and practicing the good news of God's presence among us, walking the way of the cross, and finally by being interred. He was God crucified and God buried.

The Gospel of John alone mentions that there was a garden in the place where Jesus was crucified. Accordingly, the place where Jesus was crucified was also the site of his resurrection. It is likely that by placing the grave in the garden the Gospel writer has his eye on the resurrection morning. While Golgotha and the grave obscure any view of the horizon of hope, the garden where the grave becomes empty opens up a new horizon of hope. By raising Jesus from the dead, God declares him to be the Son who was with him from eternity. By the raising of the Son from the dead, by turning the grave—the location of death, into a location of life, God gives meaning to the cross and the grave.

By placing Golgotha, the grave, and the garden together, the Gospel writer suggests that these three sites are revelatory symbols. If Christ is the God incarnate, he is God crucified, God interred, and God raised to life. It is in and through these sites that God manifested God's perfections.

How do they relate to the context of the Dalits?

1. It opens up a possibility to imagine God as the Dalit. In the event of the Father experiencing the death of the Son and the Son experiencing the abandonment by the Father, the human experience of pain, suffering, and death are taken into the very life of God (Jürgen Moltmann). God who is manifested in the incarnation of the Son is the God crucified and God interred: the one who is pierced, broken, torn asunder, killed, and buried. God is the broken one who took upon Godself the Dalitness (the word "Dalit" literally means, the broken, crushed, and torn asunder which is used by the "untouchables" in naming themselves). If in the cross of Christ God has identified and expressed God's solidarity with the extremities of human predicament and pain, I suppose it is theologically legitimate to engage in such imagination. In the incarnation of God in Christ, not only did God come to us, but humanity also is taken into the life of God. In this passage of human into the life of God, God takes into Godself the human brokenness, pain, and pathos. Therefore one could imagine God as the Dalit.

Both for a Jew and a Greek, and for an Indian alike, the grave is a polluting site. For a Jew, since contact with anything dead is a "polluting" act, the holy one of Israel could never enter into such a site. For the Greek, since the spirit is eternal and matter is evil, an interred God is unthinkable. Christian faith in the one who is crucified, buried, and raised brings pollution into the language of the perfections of God. If incarnation is a necessity in the life of God for God's self disclosure, then I suppose pollution is a necessity in the life of God. In the death, burial, and resurrection of Christ, God manifests Godself as the Pained and the Polluted One, the Dalit. Perhaps, one could imagine pathos and pollution as the divine perfections.

2. Dalit lives are characterized by pain and death. These are the lives, symbolically speaking, nailed to the cross and interred. Their lives seem to be Godforsaken and God seems to be an abandoning God. How do Golgotha, grave, and the garden speak to us in such a context? Could we suggest that in Dalit persecution Christ is persecuted, in their cry for liberation Christ is shouting aloud: "Why God, Why God, Why have you forsaken us?" In this cry, God experiences the death of God's children and turns their graves into a garden. Surely God would raise them to life. It is precisely in these grave-like situations God acts, bringing life to the dry bones, turning the grave into a garden. This habitat of the Dalits is the location of Christ's resisting and God's life-renewing activity.

Joseph Prabhakar Dayam, a theologian and an ordained minister of the Andhra Evangelical Lutheran Church, is an Associate Professor in Christian Theology at the United Theological College, Bangalore, India.

THE SUFFERING OF JESUS AND SUFFERING IN AFRICA

Anne Nasimiyu-Wasike (Uganda)

The Crucifixion narratives speak to the African experience in many ways, as the suffering of Jesus parallels the sufferings on this continent. The innocent majority of the African people are challenged by numerous situations which leave them helpless and with little hope. The state of Africa and the states in Africa confront the daunting challenges of extreme poverty, the devastating HIV and AIDS pandemic, cruel and dehumanizing dictatorship and failing leadership, ravaging civil wars, human trafficking, uncontrolled corruption, and unstrained economic exploitation of the masses. The explanations given for Africa's state range from the harm inflicted from the outside, that is by slavery, imperialism, colonialism, neo-colonialism (in the form of the so-called trade liberalization and globalization), to inherent reasons of cultural or, as some still argue, "genetic" origin (the latter being a modern form of perpetuated racism). Whatever the causes, it results in ever-worsening and painful life experiences for many in Africa, which can be compared to the crucifixion of Jesus Christ in the biblical narratives.

But first we should note the prominent biblical witness of Africa: Jacob and his family were economic refugees who out of hunger sought and were freely granted refuge in Egypt, Africa (Genesis 42–47). In two great times of trial, God looked for a continent to protect and help His son. Africa was that chosen continent: When Herod tried to kill the baby Jesus, God sent Jesus and his family to Africa (Matthew 2:13–14). When Jesus was struggling to get to the hill of Calvary, it was a man from Africa— Simon from Cyrene, that is, Libya—who assisted(Matthew 27:32). Indeed, a discussion of the state of Africa would be incomplete and misleading without a consideration of its ancient history, with the enormous blessings and hope represented in Africa. Africa, the cradle of humankind, has brought heroes and heroines in the fight against injustice and oppression in the world; she has produced world-class politicians, theologians, intellectuals, artists, musicians, and athletes influencing and shaping the rest of the world. Africa has some of the youngest democracies, and also some of the most vigilant and creative debates are going on throughout this continent. Some African states are regarded as having the best and most progressive gender-sensitive constitutions in the world. Although Africa is a place of wide cultural diversity, it is also place of *Ubuntu*, where a person becomes a person through the community with others.

But there is another lens through which to view the Bible and Africa today, namely the life and death of Christ as it parallels the African experience. There are at least three ways in which this is the case:

First, in the Holy Scriptures we meet Christ suffering as a refugee in Africa (Matthew 2:13–23). This scenario is evidenced in the refugee crisis in Africa. Africa has experienced uprootedness because of numerous wars, civil conflicts, and genocides like the one in Rwanda 18 years ago. In African cities, "informal settlements" are evidence of the uprootedness our people are experiencing. Many go to cities looking for greener pastures only to experience poverty, hunger, and homelessness. Lack of basic needs and education opportunities, unemployment, and the devastation caused by the HIV and AIDS pandemic has caused many people to be homeless. This has led to conditions of depression, mental problems, and drug and alcohol abuse. Indeed, the uprootedness of Christ is like the uprooted and the homeless in Africa.

Second, in the scriptures we see Christ betrayed by one of His trusted disciples—Judas (Mark 14:10–11). The same has been true for Africa. African leaders have betrayed the masses that elect them by benefiting themselves and their cronies while closing their eyes to the needs of the people. In most of the African countries, the contrast between luxurious wealth and extreme poverty is visible everywhere. This scenario needs to be challenged seriously so that the countries' distribution of resources is justly done.

Third, Isaiah 52:14 prophesies about Jesus when it says, "His appearance was so disfigured." In the New Testament, we learn that the body of Christ was damaged and broken on the cross. All His natural beauty was torn away (Luke 23:26–38). The same has been true for Africa. Again and again outsiders have divided up the land as suited their economic, political, or religious agendas. The natural resources have been taken to other lands, and the human resources decimated for trade. Even today, politics mars and disfigures the lands, destroying economies, roads, schools, and lives. Not all this disfigurement has been from outside. Africa herself has torn and broken herself, in endless tribal conflicts, which still persist today.

In many parts of Africa, Christianity is attempting to address people's needs in a holistic manner. Schools and hospitals have been built and peoples' needs are being met. During the struggle for independence and even after, the church has continually played a significant role in providing scholarships to the young people. As the church plays these roles, we believe that it is the redeeming wok of Christ.

In Africa people are burdened by conflicts, epidemics, and constant displacements that in many cases could be prevented by implementing appropriate strategies and programs based on the respect of human life and dignity. To resolve this distressing situation, what is required is the establishment of local and international orders inspired by justice and enlivened by a sense of brotherhood and sisterhood.

Anne Nasimiyu-Wasike is General Superior of Little Sisters of St. Francis, Kenyatta University, Uganda.

QUESTIONS

1. Nakagaki explains how his knowledge of Buddhist texts has shaped his reading of the stories about Jesus. Are there other narratives or texts that come to your mind which shape your reading of the crucifixion stories in the gospels?

2. Evaluate Shepherd's "one possible interpretation" of each gospel's crucifixion narrative. What specific elements in each Gospel lead to Shepherd's interpretations?

3. What texts from John does Dayam have in mind when he says that "John painstakingly narrates the gruesomeness of the cross and paints the picture of the grotesque body hanging on the cross"?

4. What other elements of the crucifixion narratives might Nasimiyu-Wasike bring to bear on life in Africa?

CHAPTER 11

RESURRECTION OF JESUS

Matthew 28, Mark 16, Luke 24, John 19–20

Robert E. Shore-Goss offers a queer reading of the Emmaus story in Luke 24, explaining how it serves to encourage and empower that community.

Øyvind Strømmen questions the historicity of the resurrection narratives, concluding that it simply comes down to belief.

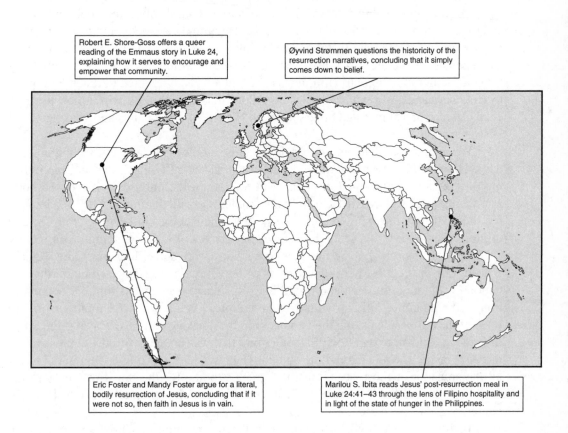

Eric Foster and Mandy Foster argue for a literal, bodily resurrection of Jesus, concluding that if it were not so, then faith in Jesus is in vain.

Marilou S. Ibita reads Jesus' post-resurrection meal in Luke 24:41–43 through the lens of Filipino hospitality and in light of the state of hunger in the Philippines.

READINGS

A Case for the Historicity of the Resurrection
Eric Foster and Mandy Foster

Questioning the Historicity of the Resurrection
Øyvind Strømmen

Jesus' Post-resurrection Meal and Filipino Hospitality
Marilou S. Ibita

A Queer Reading of the Emmaus Story in Luke 24
Robert E. Shore-Goss

A CASE FOR THE HISTORICITY OF THE RESURRECTION

Eric Foster and Mandy Foster (United States)

When examining the numerous accounts of Jesus' resurrection from the dead, the question of whether or not it was a literal, physical, bodily resurrection often arises. According to the Scriptures, it most certainly was. Even though Jesus was clearly able to materialize out of thin air, sending his disciples completely into shock and panic, he also offered proof that He was not a ghost. He bore the scars of His recent crucifixion. He ate bread and fish. In John, the disciple that Jesus loved describes for us Mary and Thomas' accounts. It is fair to assume that Jesus would not have had to tell Mary Magdalene not to hang onto Him unless she had at least attempted to touch Him prior to His command. And while there is no record that anyone took Him up on it, Jesus even offered for Thomas and others to touch His nail-scarred hands and place hands in His spear-pierced side.

When Jesus said He would tear down "this temple" and raise it up again in three days, His disciples eventually figured out that He meant Himself and not the building of worship standing in Jerusalem. But that is not the only reference to the body as a temple in Scripture. In 1 Corinthians, bodies are called temples when readers are reminded of how they should care for and treat their bodies in keeping from sin and in glorifying God. In his second epistle, Peter speaks of his impending death merely as putting off his earthly tabernacle, as if his body were something worn like a cloak. Indeed, one of the most pertinent aspects of the Gospels is Jesus' own claim that the temple would be torn down and raised back up. There was a very important connotation to the tangible, solid structure of the temple. Even when the temple was in the form of the tabernacle during the exodus or in the portable edifice of the ark, the Spirit of God was known to dwell within something that was created with the express intent of being indwelt. God charged the ancient Hebrews with crafting His temple, but for all the splendor of those structures, the greatest home for the Spirit of God was the Son of God. And the God-man's reference to the temple, when referring to Himself, could only have been the man aspect.

If, however, we hold to the idea that the resurrection of Christ was more than spiritual, but still find ourselves skeptical of a bodily resurrection, then we are left with the belief that Christ was as dead on Sunday morning as He was on Friday night. This would require that the skeptic discount a large number of personal accounts as either mass hysteria or, as is more commonly asserted, a complicated element of a large conspiracy that was concocted in order to validate Christ's prophesies about His own death. But the principle question remains: What happened to the body?

Some believed in the months following the crucifixion, as some do today, that the disciples moved the body. After all, the Jewish and Roman bureaucracies were both best served by a dead Jesus. The only contemporaries of Christ that would profit from His resurrection were the disciples, who had gained identity in Jesus and whose faith would be in vain if His claim as the Messiah was proven false after that third day.

These same disciples, in order to pull off the greatest hoax in history, would have had to coordinate corroborating stories in order to document Jesus' prophesies about Himself. They would then have had to do the same after his crucifixion, including the assembly of multiple crowds that would either agree to conspire or be able to be duped by a double that they would mistake for the Christ that they so diligently followed under threat of death as the fledgling church.

All of this would have been difficult enough, but there is still the problem of a corpse that needs to be removed from behind a massive boulder that is flanked by a trained Praetorian. And these disciples would have had to storm this tomb some four days following their own self-serving desertion and denial of allegiance. Referring back to John's account, the disciples would have then immediately lost this courage after assaulting the tomb, as they were gathered in a home, scared for their lives. Rather than appear to them in bodily form and speak, under our conspiracy hypothesis, Christ's corpse would have been stashed away in the hopes that the rumor of the resurrection would last longer than Rome's resolve to find it. (The Pharisees could not be involved in such a search, as Jesus' corpse would have been unclean, so their Roman occupiers would have been given the dirty work. The body had supposedly been taken under their watch, after all.)

Given the alternatives, the bodily resurrection of Christ starts to become the easiest-to-believe option. However, if eternal salvation and life-more-abundant are the stakes, the student probably should avoid pinning all his hopes on Ockham's razor. It would seem that it is a better pursuit to match up eyewitness accounts with millennia-old prophesies and determine whether Christ fits the bill of Messiah and whether a bodily resurrection is necessary for that description to hold. Isaiah discusses the prolonging of the Messiah's days after the offering up of His soul. While this is also indicative of a bodily resurrection, as the body has regard for days and the soul does not, it also speaks to the Messiah's mission. Christ could have risen and immediately ascended while still accomplishing all that was necessary to commence the new covenant, but He prolonged His ministry by days. And in those days, He showed multiple world-changing, indisputable proofs that He was alive. Those proofs were documented by the apostles, posited and elaborated on by Paul, and believed today by millions. To disbelieve in the resurrection of the body of Christ is to claim that the Bible is flawed. And if the Word of God is either the product of a flawed God or not His word at all, then hope in Christ is good for this life only, and, to quote Paul in his letter to Corinth, "we are more to be pitied than anyone in the world."

Now consider this: John describes in Revelation, Jesus, the Lamb of God, as having an appearance of a lamb that had been slain. Even in Heaven, arrayed in splendor with the Name "King of Kings and Lord of Lords" written on His thigh, Jesus still bears the scars of the price He paid for the sins of the world. Jesus Himself was pure and spotless, so His earthly tabernacle that died—yet, as prophesied by King David in Psalm 16, saw no decay—is the only one that will remain forever and ever. It will be the same body that died on the cross—the one that over five hundred eyewitnesses in the Bible saw walking around, speaking, eating, materializing, disappearing, and rising up into the clouds. And it will remind the Redeemed every time they look upon the only scars found in the new Heaven and new Earth of eternity that they owe their salvation to the Holy One who raised Himself from the dead, having paid the price they should have paid, but never could.

Eric Foster is a consultant in the group health and welfare field; Mandy Foster is a mother, private voice teacher, and author of books and dramas for faith-based organizations.

QUESTIONING THE HISTORICITY OF THE RESURRECTION

Øyvind Strømmen (Norway)

Norway is often seen as a bastion of secularism, and even of atheism. And it is true; to most Norwegians religion plays a very limited role in daily life. Only about 3 percent are regular churchgoers. In one poll, 44 percent said they believe in God, 29 percent said they are in doubt, and 27 percent said that they do not believe in God at all. The Norwegian Humanist Association is one of the largest such associations in the world, and it is by far the largest such association per capita.

And yet, this is only half the story. Eighty-five percent of Norwegians remain members of the Lutheran State Church. And what about myself? I did not grow up in a Christian family, but I did grow up in a community with many conservative Christians and Christianity was omnipresent in my school. Thus, a rebel was born, and as a youngster I was a hard-line atheist, doing my best to annoy the theologist we had as a teacher in religion in secondary school, secretly enjoying the fact that it was a subject I'd soon be able to avoid in its entirety. How naïve? Just a few years later, I became gradually more interested in religious studies. Why? As many scholars have pointed out, some of them with quite a bit of embarrassment, the secularization process which for some time was seen as inevitable turned out not to be inevitable after all. In 2013 religion still plays a major political and societal role. Without studying religion, how can one even hope to understand many current events?

For me, increasing respect came with my studies; and with respect, came doubt. I became an agnostic. Thus, it is as an agnostic that I approach the central story of Christianity, the resurrection narrative, an event placed sometime around 30 A.D. And it is as an agnostic I will have to conclude that it does not and *can* not come down to anything other than belief.

First, regardless of what certain Christian apologists may claim, we do not have strong historical sources regarding the event, or—for that matter—on Jesus as a historical character at all. Most of us might agree that he did in fact live, that he was regarded as a teacher and a healer, that he was a Jew, and that he was crucified on the charge of sedition; but otherwise, we do not really know much about the historical Jesus of Nazareth.

According to traditional Christian understanding, the Gospels of John and Matthew were written by eyewitnesses. Modern research, however, has shown that there are good reasons to doubt this claim. In any case, it does not seem likely that any of the Gospels were written before 70 A.D., 40 years after the reported events. There might have been earlier writings, such as the hypothetical Q source seemingly used by both Matthew and Luke, but if there were, they have been lost. This of course raises an interesting question: Would you today believe a story about a man rising from the dead in the 1970s, a story not written by an eyewitness, a story published 40 years later and peddled to you by a rather small—yet increasingly successful—new religious movement? Or would you consider it, perhaps, as a fanciful fable?

If you are a Christian, and this *does* provoke you (it should not, really), you might want to consider a very real parallel, namely the question of the historicity of the prophet Muhammad. Once again, we have few sources except distinctly Islamic ones, most of which are of a later date. There is a Greek anti-Jewish text called *Doctrina Iacobi* from around 640 A.D., which mentions "a false prophet amongst the Sarasenes." There is a Jewish apocalyptic text from the late eighth-century mentioning a prophet of the Ismaelites. And there is a mention of Muhammad by the Armenian bishop Sebeos, recorded around 660 A.D. While this certainly gives us reason to consider Muhammad as a real historical person rather than as an imagined hero, it does not tell us much about the historical Muhammad, and I have met quite a few Christians who regard his prophethood as nothing more than a fanciful fable.

As with Muhammad and the Muslims, it is possible to find some non-Christian sources mentioning or, at least, referring to Jesus or the Christians. The Jewish historian Flavius Josephus mentions him twice in his *Antiquities of the Jews* from 93 A.D. The Babylonian Talmud mentions "Yeshu" a few times. Pliny the Younger advises on how to deal with Christus-worshippers in a letter to Emperor Trajan from around 112 A.D. None of these sources mention the resurrection, though. The first non-Christian to even touch upon that topic was Lucian of Samotasa, a Greek satirist—think of him as a Jon Stewart of his age—writing in the second century. He ridiculed the Christians, portraying them as gullible fools. Then came Celsus, who wrote the first known comprehensive attack on Christianity—a work called *The True Word*—sometime around 170–180 A.D. The work itself has been lost, but fragments are known—thanks to a reply written by Origen, a later Christian scholar. Celsus disregards the resurrection as a story from "a half-frantic woman, as you state, and some other one, perhaps, of those who were engaged in the same system of delusion."

Of course, none of this disproves the resurrection narrative. It does show, however, that there is no such thing as historical *evidence* for the story, regardless of what the Gospels say, and regardless of numerous daring claims made by Christian apologists. It shows that the story itself was so fantastic, that it was met with disbelief even in a time when *magic* was considered as a very real phenomenon and where *Gods* were seen as active participants in the world of men.

It is worth noting that there are many early Christian texts which do not share the focus on resurrection. The Gospel of Mark, for example, by scholarly consensus originally ended at 16:8 (all the earliest manuscripts end there). Verses 9–20 appear to have been added later in an attempt to bring it in line with the other three Gospels. It is indeed striking that the earliest written biblical gospel does not (at least originally) contain a story of Jesus' resurrection. The aforementioned hypothetical Q source used by Matthew and Luke focuses almost exclusively on the teachings of Jesus and does not include a resurrection story. The noncanonical Gospel of Thomas—which has been dated as early as 60 A.D.—merely contains a number of sayings by Jesus, and mentions neither miracles nor the resurrection. Likewise, the Gospel of Mary seems to present Jesus' teachings as a way to inner spiritual knowledge and it rejects the idea that Jesus' suffering and death provided a path to eternal life. Indeed, one could argue that if it were not for Paul's focus on the significance of the death and resurrection of Jesus that those beliefs would not have become central to the faith. Even Paul's own understanding of the resurrection is not entirely clear. Some have reasoned that he believed only in a spiritual—not bodily, physical—resurrection based on passages such as Acts 9 and 1 Corinthians 15.

None of this tells us much more about the historical Jesus or about the historicity of the resurrection narrative, of course. It does, however, reveal that the story of early Christianity is a story of heterodoxy, rather than of orthodoxy, of conflicting ideas rather than of a shared faith, which leads to a final point: Even the four Gospels do not agree on what happened that first Easter morning. Four conflicting accounts do not make for good historical evidence. But one can still believe.

Øyvind Strømmen is a journalist and writer; he has studied religious history, and is currently particularly interested in the impact of religion on dietary habits.

Jesus' Post-resurrection Meal and Filipino Hospitality

Marilou S. Ibita (Philippines)

The post-resurrection meal in Jerusalem (Luke 24:41–43), often eclipsed by the meal at Emmaus (vv. 13–32), contains a very significant detail as the *last* of the 10 meal scenes of Jesus in Luke's Gospel. It affirms and sets the evangelist's seal to the theme of table-fellowship that evokes a specific picture of Jesus, sheds light on an aspect of his proclamation of the Kingdom of God, and presents a challenge to discipleship. Hence, reading the Lukan meal scenes, especially Luke 24:41–43, as a Filipina Christian with our meal-oriented culture vis-à-vis the problem of hunger in the Philippines is a challenging task.

One of the most important expressions of Filipino hospitality is table-fellowship with friends and family, expected and unexpected visitors, and even with strangers. *Kain tayo!* (Let's eat), *Salo tayo!* (Let us partake [of food and drink]) are variations of an invitation to table-fellowship. It could be an elaborate or everyday meal, a simple snack or a sharing of whatever meager food one has. The list of venues is endless: one's own home, a food chain outlet, a park, a beach, a bus, or a place under a mango/coconut tree. Differences in economic and social backgrounds influence the quantity and quality of what is offered. However, the driving force behind it remains the same: to share food and drink with others because one is a *kapwa* (the other is a person like one's self).

The level of *pakikipagkapwa* is detectable in Filipino table-fellowship through the kind of food and drink served, the type of tableware, and the way guests and hosts relate to one another. *Pakikipagkapwa* is humanness at its highest level where the *kapwa* (other) is *sarili na rin* (oneself). *Pakikipagkapwa* is rooted in the concept of shared inner self and recognition of shared identity, not just smooth interpersonal relationships. *Kapwa* embraces both the categories of *ibang tao* (outsiders) and *hindi ibang tao* (insiders). In table-fellowship, one can detect the level of relationship between partakers. The *ibang tao* (outsider) category moves from *pakikitungo* (level of amenities) to *pakikibagay* (level of conforming) and *pakikisama* (level of adjusting). The *hindi ibang tao* (insider) category consists of two levels: *pakikipagpalagayang-loob* (level of mutual trust) and *pakikiisa* (level of fusion, oneness and full of trust). The progression of relationships from being an outsider to an insider is evident in the quality of relationships expressed in the meals, with *pakikitungo* as the shallowest and *pakikiisa* as the deepest. The food and drink served varies from elaborate and expensive ones in the *ibang tao* (outsider) category when the parties involved try to gain each other's confidence to that of being able to serve daily fare in the *hindi ibang tao* (insiders) category. The tableware changes from those infrequently used to those that are utilized daily as partakers become more at home with each other. What I want to highlight here is how the visitor grows from being a guest toward becoming a cohost with the host and a coservant at table when the deepest level of relationship has been achieved, enabling the former guest to be one with the host and help serve the new guests.

Yet the richness of the meal-sharing culture questions and challenges the state of hunger in the Philippines. We have enough food but not everyone has the power to buy food. The November 2010 survey indicates that there are about 3.4 million Filipino families who suffer from hunger. This report shows that we lag behind the UN Millennium Development Goal (MDG) No. 1 of eradicating extreme poverty and hunger by halving the proportion of those who suffer hunger between 1990 and 2015. Our own context, nevertheless, is but a small reflection of the shocking news in 2009: mid-way through the UN MDG drive that began in 2002, we have reached the 1 billion mark of people suffering chronic hunger worldwide.

How does this contrasting background influence my reading of Luke's meal scenes? First, I want to focus on Jesus at table with different kinds of people and explore Luke's characterization of Jesus, of God's kingdom, and of discipleship in these texts, particularly in 24:41–43.

In dialoguing between the meal scenes where Jesus is the protagonist and my own context, I notice that the Lukan Jesus' role at table keeps on changing. In Galilee, Jesus is first the guest of Levi, a despised tax collector (5:29). Then he is a guest of Simon, a law-abiding Pharisee (7:37). Does Luke imply that just as Jesus can be the guest of these seemingly extreme examples, he can be a guest of those who fall in between? Nevertheless, at the close of his Galilean ministry, the Lukan Jesus changes his role to that of host and feeds a hungry multitude (9:15). In this part of the journey, Jesus is not confronted directly by those against his kind of table-fellowship.

In Jesus' ministry on the journey to Jerusalem, he is pictured as the guest of many people: of women (10:38–42), of another Pharisee (11:37–54), of a ruler who belonged to the Pharisees (14:1–24), and of a chief tax collector, Zacchaeus (19:1–10). It is notable that just before entering Jerusalem, the last two hosts of Jesus remind us of the first two hosts that he had. However, there is an intensification of the characters with whom Jesus shares table-fellowship since one is a *ruler* who belonged to the Pharisees and the other a *chief* tax collector. At this juncture and in contrast with his Galilean experience, Jesus addresses direct antagonism from people he dines with (11:53–54; 14:1) and from all others who disapprove of his brand of meal-sharing (15:2; 19:7).

Despite the disapproval of many, Jesus continues his inclusive table-fellowship. In Jerusalem, there is only one meal scene but it epitomizes an inclusive table-fellowship: his farewell meal or the Last Supper (22:14–38). Here Jesus is the host who gives himself to his disciples, even if one will betray him and another will disown him (vv. 14–23, 31–34) and the rest will abandon him. With his disciples' misunderstanding of roles at table, Jesus affirms that he is among them as one who serves (v. 27). In Luke, Jesus' table-fellowship contributes to his crucifixion.

Luke, however, continues to emphasize table-fellowship in the post-resurrection accounts showing that Jesus and his brand of table-fellowship overcome death. The disciples recognized the Risen Jesus at table as a guest who is also a host (24:13–35, especially 29–31). Then in the next scene in 24:41–43 Jesus is back to his initial role as a guest, indicating an invitation to follow him in the cyclical roles at table.

From the foregoing, I glean that the Lukan Jesus can be characterized as cyclically changing his roles at table. It reminds me of the changing roles at table in Filipino table-fellowship. Jesus as a guest shows that we are guests, recipients of God's providence just as Filipinos strive to serve the best for their guests. Yet, Jesus changing roles suggests that we cannot be guests forever. We are called to be hosts, too, like Jesus at the end of his Galilean ministry and at the Last Supper. Lest one become conceited for providing food and drink, Jesus shows that being a host is coupled with being a servant. Hence, Luke portrays his post-resurrection appearances by underscoring table-fellowship in Emmaus and ending with the one in Jerusalem. Jesus' cyclically changing role as guest–host–servant at table consequently challenges his disciples to follow what I call Jesus' meal-ministry that proclaims a facet of God's kingdom as a banquet for all.

How do these insights relate to hunger? They ask Christians to be cognizant of their own table-fellowship and the changing roles of Jesus at table. The dialogue creatively challenges them to embody his example in the different contexts in which they find themselves whether as a guest or a host or servant at table. To do so, Christians and Christian communities need to be informed and active participants in the demanding, complex issue of hunger by contributing in ways that uphold economic, political, and sociocultural rights that affect the food security, food self-sufficiency, and food sovereignty of peoples. In this way, everyone, not just a few, can have enough nutritious food at table every day. The UN MDG goal of reducing the number of hungry people in the world and eventually eradicating hunger can be achieved. This would indeed be an expression of God's dream of a banquet for all.

Marilou S. Ibita is a Filipina, Roman Catholic Christian, and a doctoral researcher at the Katholieke Universiteit Leuven, Belgium; she has served at the Institute of Formation and Religious Studies at Maryhill School of Theology and St. Vincent School of Theology, Quezon City, Philippines.

A QUEER READING OF THE EMMAUS STORY IN LUKE 24

Robert E. Shore-Goss (United States)

Concerning the Emmaus story in Luke 24:13–35, John Dominic Crossan writes, "Emmaus never happened, Emmaus always happens." (*Jesus: A Revolutionary Biography* [Harper: San Francisco, 1994], 197). Crossan considers the Lukan narrative unit a metaphoric condensation of early followers of Jesus who continued to experience his resurrection appearances over a period of time and associated his presence with his actions of interpreting the scriptures and the continued practice of commensality.

The story of Cleopas and the unnamed disciple walking toward Emmaus has long been recognized in queer faith communities. For queer Christians, the two disciples are separated from the main body of Jesus' male disciples, huddled in Jerusalem. They are physically outside the inner circle, and they may have left in sadness and disgust over the failure of the body of disciples to be present to Jesus at his crucifixion. The death of Jesus has become a crisis, generating emotions of fear and anxiety mixed with feelings of loss and grief. Clearly, the text is a story of grief over the loss and death of Jesus.

The two disciples are grieving at the loss of Jesus, but they are joined by a stranger who walks with them, and the disciples speak to the stranger about their hopes, dreams, betrayals, and deadly loss. They express to him how they have given their hearts to Jesus, his message and practices, and how they had hoped that Jesus would set them free. The two are astounded by the reports of the women who went to the tomb. They are separate from the mainstream male leadership in Jerusalem; they are queer outsiders, perhaps even two lovers. They raise the women's story with the stranger because they are processing the death of Jesus with the proclamation of the empty tomb. They tell their story to the stranger on the road. It takes a stranger to hear the story of two outsiders.

The stranger explains from the scriptures how Jesus had been charged with perverting the nation and queered all religious expectations and that through his ministry, suffering, and death, the Christ entered into glory. God has not disappointed them, for God raised the queer Christ. The stranger speaks to their estrangement and alienation, but they are also emotionally open to speak about the pain of their lives. Many translesbigay folks feel out of place within many churches since those churches have taken Jesus away from them with their exclusionary practices. Churches have absented Jesus from their lives by directly excluding them from community or making it impossible to love and remain within the community.

Stopping at Emmaus, the two queer disciples invite the stranger to stay with them for the night and share a meal with them (queer folks love meals as a time to deepen their communal bonds of friendship). They extend the stranger hospitality at their table. Their hearts yearned for Jesus' presence, and as outsiders they intuitively recognized and felt an embodied connection to their own experience. They included him in their meal with openness and a warm welcome—remembering that open table hospitality was a significant feature of Jesus' ministry. Jesus practiced an egalitarian commensality, an inclusive lived practice of the parable of the Great Supper (Luke 14:15–24). During the meal, he "takes, blesses, breaks, and gives" them the bread. These gestures are mimetic rituals that Jesus set up during his ministry of open commensality and during his last meal. Jesus took and blessed, but they clearly recognize him in the distinctive last gestures—breaking and giving. These were the functions of women and slaves. The risen Jesus takes the role of a woman or slave in breaking and distributing the bread. The eyes of the disciples are opened, and they recognize Jesus in the transgression of social roles.

Their eyes were opened with the mimetic rituals. They function as a memorial linking object that evokes a memory of Jesus that actualizes a sense of presence. Their lives changed, for they complete the ritual of the bread, recognizing Jesus in the midst and in their own life experiences. The disciples recognize their lives in the bread. Jesus takes bread; blesses their experiences of brokenness, pain, exile, and alienation; and transforms the bread of their lives into himself. The breaking of the bread creates hope, actualizes the presence of the risen Christ, and forms them into church. The risen Jesus is not the possession of the community back in Jerusalem alone but also abides in the word of scripture, in the bread broken, and queer embodied lives in community. Though physically absent, Jesus is present through scripture, the breaking of the bread, and the community fostered by a memorial practice linked to Jesus' original practice of open commensality. The moral of the narrative is "Do not neglect to show hospitality to the stranger, for the stranger can be the risen Christ." It is also a warrant that exclusion is not a practice of open commensality.

Their queer experience finds hope in God's vindication of Jesus' queer ministry and death, for Jesus was charged by the high priests with "perverting the nation" (Luke 23:2). Their hearts were once again set on fire as they once heard Jesus' proclamation of the good news in his ministry. The despondent community of the male apostles did not enkindle the fire of hope but the simple repetition of the hospitality and kindness reconnected them to God and the risen Christ. The story of Emmaus highlights that the risen Christ walks with us in our human pain, grief, and confusion.

The story of Jesus is not finished as the opening quote from John Dominic Crossan: "Emmaus always happens." Crossan's insight is correct that the followers of Jesus then and even now encounter the risen Christ in the ways Luke describes. The narrative is repeated in queer Christian lives. One such story is that of the founder of MCC (Metropolitan Community Church), the Rev. Troy Perry.

Perry took an ad out in a gay Los Angeles magazine, *The Advocate*, announcing a worship service for gays and lesbians. At that first service on October 6, 1968, 12 people responded to the ad and came to the service. Toward the end of the worship, Perry offered a prayer over the bread and grape juice and invited those who had been excluded to come and receive communion. He dramatically and spiritually ritualized the inclusion of those queers excluded from their churches' politics of the table. They had been denied access to the ritual Christian meal because of their sexual orientation. Rev. Perry opened a sacramental gateway for not only gays and lesbians but also for bisexuals, transgendered folks, and alienated heterosexuals.

This ritual is now repeated in all MCC Sunday worships at the end of the communion table prayer with the invitation: "You neither need to be a member of MCC, nor any church nor even be a Christian. All are welcome to God's table." In that simple ritual proclamation, there is embodied a mimetic invitation of open inclusion and egalitarian commensality—that the unconditional grace of God is available to all people and equally available to them. God surrounds all human beings from birth to death with unconditional love and compassionate care. This gift of love is nothing other than God's self-communication of divine love and forgiveness. There are three notions embodied in MCC's ritual to the open commensality. First, God's grace is radically inclusive and without conditions. Second, no one is turned away. Finally, every person is loved equally by God. This ritual invitation has become the core mission of MCC: radical inclusive love.

Queer folks look for the risen Christ outside many denominational Christian churches. They have discovered the absence of the risen Christ in the lack of welcome and hospitality in hostile and exclusive churches. As they discover Christ outside the traditional faith communities in open commensality, they realize their responsibility to journey back to the community. Their healing, openness, and reflection lead them to follow the trajectory of Cleopas and the unknown disciple. With courage and renewed lives, they leave their exile to tell the story how Jesus was found in their queer lives and stories and how the breaking of the bread made them into a community, empowered by the risen Christ. The risen Christ's breaking of the bread transforms the two queer disciples into church. Each time queer followers gather together in faith and remember the meal that Jesus celebrated, they create a queer Church.

Just as Cleopas and the unknown disciple, the queer church travels back to the mainstream churches, bringing the message of the power of Christ's resurrection discovered in their embodied, erotic experiences. They embody the risen Christ in radical inclusive churches, and the recognition of their embodiment of the queer Christ motivates them to return to the larger community to bear witness to the queer Christ in their own lives and inclusive practices of table hospitality and love. They now have the power to transform the despondent and disembodied community, to change the hearts of its members so that they can recognize the presence of the risen Christ embodied in queer disciples. It is only their embodied return that prepares the community to welcome and hear the risen and embodied Christ in their midst.

Robert E. Shore-Goss (Ph.D., Comparative Religion and Theology, Harvard University) is the gay Pastor of the MCC Church in the Valley; he is author of Jesus ACTED UP: A Gay and Lesbian Manifesto *and* Queering Christ: Beyond Jesus ACTED UP.

QUESTIONS

1. What are Foster and Foster's best arguments for a bodily resurrection? Which of their arguments are weak?
2. What might constitute evidence for the historicity of Jesus and his resurrection? Why does Strømmen say that his observations should not provoke Christians?

3. Examine carefully each of the biblical texts discussed by Ibita and assign each character or group to one of the categories from Filipino table-fellowship.
4. Assess carefully Goss's handling of the biblical text, not his ideological orientation..

CHAPTER 12

ACTS (PART I)

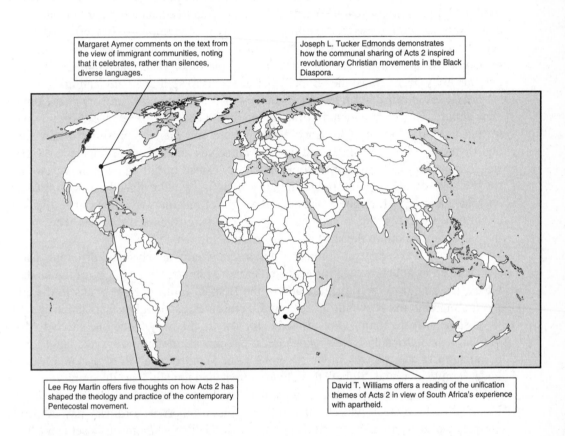

Margaret Aymer comments on the text from the view of immigrant communities, noting that it celebrates, rather than silences, diverse languages.

Joseph L. Tucker Edmonds demonstrates how the communal sharing of Acts 2 inspired revolutionary Christian movements in the Black Diaspora.

Lee Roy Martin offers five thoughts on how Acts 2 has shaped the theology and practice of the contemporary Pentecostal movement.

David T. Williams offers a reading of the unification themes of Acts 2 in view of South Africa's experience with apartheid.

READINGS

Pentecost from the View of Immigrant Communities
Margaret Aymer

Acts 2 and Revolutionary Christian Movements in the Black Diaspora
Joseph L. Tucker Edmonds

The Unification Themes of Acts 2 and South African Apartheid
David T. Williams

Five Thoughts on Theology and Practice in the Pentecostal Movement
Lee Roy Martin

PENTECOST FROM THE VIEW OF IMMIGRANT COMMUNITIES

Margaret Aymer (United States)

When one is an immigrant, voluntarily or involuntarily, any trace of home can draw your attention, distracting you from whatever it was you were doing. This is particularly true for the sounds of home, words of a language or a dialect you may have not heard used publicly for many years. We immigrants are used to exchanging our languages for that of our host country, either learning an entirely new grammar or having our dialects "corrected" to match the dialect of the majority culture. All nations do this in one way or another. It is a way of gaining control over "the other" and maintaining a sense of national unity over against the "Babel" that threatens to split apart any nation.

And so, in our daily lives, we speak and act as though we are part of the dominant culture. However, when we immigrants come together, when we drop the need to translate ourselves into someone else's culture and their accents and music, food and rhythms of home emerge, and we find ourselves suddenly emancipated. We find freedom in being able to affirm all of ourselves, instead of hiding parts of who we are for the sake of the uncomfortable majority. It is no wonder that those who fear the encroachment of us foreigners blanch at the sight of our flags flying at our festivals or cringe when we sing "their" national songs in our languages and rhythms. They sense the palpable freedom in the air that comes from being whole.

In many ways, Roman-dominated Jerusalem would have been no different. Those who walked its streets would have spoken either Aramaic, the language of the land, or Greek, the language of commerce and of the Roman military. Immigrants to the city, like immigrants today, would have found themselves exchanging their languages for those spoken by the majority of residents, for only in this way could one survive. Most of them would probably have spoken Greek. Greek was, in many ways, the language of domination. It was the way in which Rome gained control over all of disparate groups under its rule, over the "Babel" that always threatened to split apart the empire.

Against this context, the Pentecost narrative stands in stark relief, like the bursting of a Mediterranean-wide "ethnic festival" on an otherwise ordinary day. As Luke narrates the story, after the Spirit descends on the Galileans, themselves set apart from Judeans by their accents (Luke 22:59), they begin to speak in other, or as we might say today "foreign," languages. The languages are quite distinct and represent a roll call of the nations from around the Mediterranean basin (Acts 2: 9–11).

The sound of languages other than Aramaic or Greek would have been a curious enough sign of something different and potentially holy afoot. But a more poignant moment happens when the languages are heard. For, at the sound of their languages being spoken, immigrants to Jerusalem do what immigrants always do when they hear the sounds of home. They turn toward the languages to hear more. The coming of the languages is not simply a sign of the power of God. It is, as many immigrants can attest, a signifier that this "new thing" is a place of emancipation, of self-expression, of home.

To be sure, these are immigrants (2:5), and not pilgrims in town for the Pentecost feast, as is often proclaimed. It is these immigrants, outsiders and foreigners with "strange" maternal languages and flags and accents, that make up the congregation for Peter's famed sermon and that constitute the first members of the early church in Acts 2. They come together not because they feel the need to translate themselves in order to survive, but rather because the Spirit of God has chosen to translate the good news and the church to them, to signify that the sounds of the church are sounds of home.

Of course, the gathering drew mockers. Gatherings of "others" always do. The charge of drunkenness, of being somehow less than upstanding aimed both at the Galileans and tangentially at the accents and languages so strange to majority ears, is a polemic intended to reset the dominant order. Not unlike the unkind mocking of accents that so many of us know, the charge is that something in these different sounds and words is not quite right.

In response to this charge that somehow the sounds of difference are harmfully transgressive, Peter declares, in the words of the prophet Joel, the kinship of all of the languages present: the majority and minority ones, the silenced and the spoken. For, in Peter's proclamation that God will pour out God's Spirit on all flesh, sons and daughters, old and young, Peter is also declaring that all present, yes even the immigrants, are witnesses to that greatness in their maternal tongues and dialects, accents, and rhythms.

In Acts, the promise for salvation changes the rules about immigrants; for Acts does not require of us self-translation and it does not need, as empires do, to silence Babel for the sake of control. Indeed, Acts celebrates Babel in all of our rich linguistic diversity. And into the polyphony, God translates God's own self through the Spirit for the sake of the people. And all over Jerusalem, heads turn and people gather. For they hear the sounds of home.

Margaret Aymer is Associate Professor of New Testament at the Interdenominational Theological Center, Atlanta, Georgia, United States.

ACTS 2 AND REVOLUTIONARY CHRISTIAN MOVEMENTS IN THE BLACK DIASPORA

Joseph L. Tucker Edmonds (United States)

While capitalism is dominant in the contemporary global village and is often conflated with freedom in its Western formulation, capitalism is not without its detractors and critics. For a number of groups the narrative of capitalism has not only included the trade of goods and items that enrich their lives, but for many in our global neighborhood, capitalism has been rooted in the trade of certain people and insensitivity to the needs of many. Capitalism for certain communities has been a narrative of horror, disenfranchisement, and violence. As a result, many of these communities have looked to the Bible for resources to challenge and reshape capitalism. The book of Acts, and especially the second chapter of Acts, continues the countercultural narrative of the gospel that challenges the exclusivist (especially among religious elite), imperial, and masculinist biases of the first century and beyond. Acts pushes the boundaries of the biblical narrative (especially the Gospels) where the individualized acts of the miracle-working Messiah and his small group of disciples is extended from the inner circle to a larger group of men and women who are charged to speak prophetically and transform creatively the very contours of local and global communities. It is in the Acts narrative that power and control are effectively loosed and shared. Moreover, the loosing of the tongues (glossolalia) on the Day of Pentecost functions as a metaphor for the decentralization of power and the locus of control from the elite to the entire community. It is a radical re-visioning of autocratic and dictatorial forms of control, and it signals a shift to democratic and power-sharing modalities. Here I will address the ways in which democratic participation and communal modes of power and profit sharing in the first-century community were as countercultural then as they are now. I will also suggest that the *post-glossolalia* moment led to a reorganizing of the early church community and provided compelling options for revolutionary Christian movements in the Black Diaspora in the twentieth century.

The "glossolalia event" or the speaking in tongues moment (Acts 2:4) is critical in the biblical narrative, for it represents an important shift in who has access to divine revelation and what happens when divine revelation rests in the hand of the many rather than the few. This moment reflects a radical reordering as it not only signals a critique of the elite-dominated Jewish community but is also an expansion and fulfillment of the biblical and gospel narrative. The quoting of Joel 2:29 by the leader of the nascent Christian community highlights the unique and auspicious nature of this moment. God is pouring out God's self not only on the elite or well connected but also on the Galileans who could be understood as the weak, marginalized, and oft-forgotten group of Israel. More importantly, in this moment not only is it poured out on the weak and marginalized men, but also this revelation from God is given to both male and female Galileans in the presence of those who might otherwise degrade or ignore them. The revelation that is given to the "servant" or the weak in Acts 2 is one that is not only heard by the elite and the Jewish community that is meeting in Jerusalem for a high holiday, but also it is understood by them and signals a shift in their orientation. Moreover, the shifted orientation of the early Jewish/Christian community from elite-led and indifferent to suffering to communally focused has relevance for Black Christian movements and their quest for freedom in the modern era.

The particular shift that is highlighted in this passage is a reconception of power and participation that challenges the foundations of what would in the first century be understood as imperial or elite rule and in the modern era is conceived as the foundation of capitalism. While we tend to focus on the glossolalia event, the important part of the Acts narrative for many Christian movements in the twentieth century is the reshaping of their freedom projects in light of the voices (the Galileans, the servants, the women) that are now audible in the postglossolalia moment. Black freedom as described by Christian or Christian-derived projects like Rastafarianism and the Nation of Islam in the beginning of the twentieth centuries, Martin Luther King and the civil rights movement in the middle of the twentieth century, and the anti-apartheid Christian movements in South Africa in the latter half of the century was a critique of elite-dominated, profit-oriented structures and practices. Freedom was not a continuation of the modern project and the way that it had previously unfolded, as that project was one that denied and degraded Black and Africana subjects and was predicated upon individual ownership and profit maximization at all costs. The postglossolalia moment in the Africa Diaspora re-visions the very parameters of freedom and participation by listening to those people that had either been commodified, destroyed, or ignored by the elite or those committed to profit maximization. The communal ethos of Rastafarianism and their commitment to local and communal self-sufficiency, the mass boycotts during the Civil Rights and apartheid eras, and even the emergence of small tight-knit communities based on shared economic empowerment like the Nation of Islam and the early Black Pentecostal communities argued for a rejection of profit and self-interest in favor of holding many things in "common" and working together to "give to anyone in need" (Acts 2:45). The Acts narrative in these communities became a space for disenfranchised and often disempowered people to lay claim to God's voice and to use it radically to resist the forms of modernity and capitalism that desired to destroy them and people like them. In this regard, the Acts narrative or Pentecost is not simply about the spiritual act of speaking in tongues, but it is the ways in which God's revelation to God's people can be connected to acts of liberation and freedom for everyone, even, or especially, the weak and disenfranchised among us.

Joseph L. Tucker Edmonds is Assistant Professor of Africana Studies and Religious Studies at Indiana University-Purdue University, Indianapolis, United States.

THE UNIFICATION THEMES OF ACTS 2 AND SOUTH AFRICAN APARTHEID

David T. Williams (South Africa)

The essence of the political problem is how to get people who are different in so many ways to live together. How can they be persuaded to treat each other in a humane way without injustice and oppression?

The last half of the twentieth century witnessed a solution to the problem in South Africa that was to become notorious, and to add a word to the global vocabulary, "apartheid." It was the expression of a belief that peaceful coexistence was not really possible, so the best solution was to keep peoples apart. Although obviously inspired by political and social ideology, the sadness was that attempts were made to justify it biblically. At the same time, although it could have been established in justice, it was not, and the blatant inequality and oppression outraged many in South Africa and the world.

The experiment ended, after a long struggle, with elections in 1994, and the emergence of what Nelson Mandela and Desmond Tutu envisioned as a "rainbow nation" with the welding of disparate elements into one nation. Will the South African attempt succeed when so many other nations have continued to experience tremendous internal friction, and when the splitting of countries has been a not infrequent event? Welding different groups together is by no means a simple endeavor.

The second chapter of the book of Acts starts with the recognition of the existence of several distinct groups, which had come to Jerusalem with one purpose, but which were decidedly different. Yet by the end of the chapter there had been the emergence of a group which was characterized not by the word "separation," but by its opposite, "together" (2:44, 46).

In itself what was recorded in Acts 2 was dramatic enough, but the rest of the book relates something even more striking, for the world of the day witnessed the practice of an apartheid beside which the South African version fades into insignificance. Jews maintained a rigid separation from Gentiles, especially from their neighbors in Samaria. Perhaps there was a similarity of cause in that the Jews saw their distinctiveness in a belief that God had chosen them (Deuteronomy 7:7). Likewise, even if it may be argued that the British must be reckoned culpable in their attitudes to the nonwhite population of South Africa, the belief of the Afrikaners that they were the chosen people of God reinforced and motivated an ethos of separation.

What emerged from the events recorded in Acts 2 was not a dull uniformity. The early Church was not a manifestation of communism. Even if there was an amazing practice of sharing, it was not equality, but an expression of love, the fruit of the Spirit, so that nobody was any longer in need. It was not very long before the original enthusiasm of sharing came under pressure in the story of Ananias and Sapphira (Acts 5), but the very existence of the story witnesses to the continued existence of private property. The story highlights that at the same time there was an openness, both in the sense of willingness to share material possessions, but also of not hiding personal secrets from each other. What had been produced was called *koinōnia*, active sharing (2:42), through which differences between people were not just removed, but that the needs of all would be met. Paul would later describe the interaction of people in the Church in terms of the members of one body (1 Corinthians 12:4f), where each is distinct, but where there is a process of mutual interaction and support.

This vision prefigures the dream that Nelson Mandela and Desmond Tutu have of a South Africa renewed after the horror of apartheid. The picture that is often used is of a rainbow nation, where color is obviously prominent in a way in which it was not in the early Church, but where the key idea is of diversity in unity.

But there may be an unfolding tragedy in South Africa. The dramatic events of Acts 2 can only be explained by the coming of the Holy Spirit. He has been described as *vinculum amoris*, "bond of love," where his action in the world is an expression of his role in relating the Persons of the Trinity. Later theology spoke of *perichōresis*, the interpenetration of the Persons so that they are absolutely equal while preserving distinction. It is this that he produced in the early Church.

Churches were very active in the transition from apartheid. The process of struggle was undergirded by an enormous amount of prayer both within and outside South Africa. The transition was held up as morally correct and in accordance with biblical norms. Then after the transfer to democracy, there was a process of "Truth and Reconciliation," inspired and chaired by Desmond Tutu, again an acknowledgment of God's hand in the whole process. This was only to be expected in a country where the majority of the country claimed to be Christian.

But South Africa has declared itself a secular state, and the accepted policy is pluralistic, no doubt acknowledging the existence of significant minorities from other faiths. The modern ideal of tolerance is upheld, and there is no longer a belief in the correctness of Christianity; it is one belief among others, as is common in the Western world. A not insignificant factor is the belief that Christianity was used to justify apartheid. Religious education is no longer a school subject; theology in universities is diminishing and under pressure. The contrast with the attitudes of the apostles is striking.

The society that is emerging is one of disparity. Far from the sharing of the early Church, South Africa is one of the most unequal societies in the modern world, with all the associated danger of unrest and conflict. The divisions are no longer rigidly along racial lines, although race is far from insignificant, but the economic divide is just as painful, even if it is seen not in skin color but in expensive clothes and cars.

While Peter, in his initial sermons, could trumpet the resurrection of Christ as evidence for the reality of the gospel, and while the "resurrection" of South Africa can likewise be seen as evidence for the reality of the action of God in the world, the appeal that Peter made to accept and to change, to "save yourselves from this crooked generation" (2:40), is increasingly falling on deaf ears.

Nonetheless, the miracle of Acts 2, and the subsequent miracle of 1994, provides hope, even confidence, that God would act again. While praying for, and expecting this, as they were at the start of Acts 2, Christians should emulate the disciples, who, although they could not really anticipate the coming events, were nevertheless acting in a way consistent with them, anticipating them as they were "together in one place" (2:1).

David T. Williams, originally from the United Kingdom, has served as a missionary in Southern Africa since 1971; he is currently professor of systematic theology at the University of Fort Hare, South Africa.

FIVE THOUGHTS ON THEOLOGY AND PRACTICE IN THE PENTECOSTAL MOVEMENT

Lee Roy Martin (United States)

"PENTECOST HAS COME TO LOS ANGELES" was the front-page headline for the inaugural issue of *The Apostolic Faith*, the newspaper published at the Azusa Street Mission by African American pastor William J. Seymour. The Azusa Street revival included extraordinary expressions of worship and witness, such as glossolalia, miracles, dreams, visions, healings, and prophecies. Many people questioned the validity of these experiences—opponents labeled the revival as fanatical at best and demonic at worst. Sympathizers were curious, but they were also puzzled about the meaning and significance of the manifestations. Seymour's paper was an attempt to defend the revival against its critics, to encourage the faithful, and to articulate for the inquisitive the meaning of the miraculous events. Seymour concluded on the basis of Acts 2 that Los Angeles was experiencing a last days' outpouring of the Holy Spirit that was meant to restore Apostolic Christianity to the world.

Seymour and other Pentecostals observed in Acts 2 a parallel to their own experience. The disciples of Jesus were filled with the Holy Spirit and began to speak in all kinds of tongues. The Jewish pilgrims who were in Jerusalem for the annual feast of Pentecost were astonished at this unexpected behavior. It was not a part of the usual Pentecost ritual; rather, it was something new and different. Many in the crowd, made uncomfortable by the disciples' vigorous praise of God, scoffed at them and accused them of debauchery. They said condemningly, "These people are drunk." Others were curious and asked, "What does this mean?" Peter stood forth and offered an answer to the question. Citing the prophet Joel, he declared that the unusual events signaled God's intent to pour out his Spirit upon all people. Furthermore, this Holy Spirit was flowing from Jesus Christ, whose crucifixion and resurrection ushered in the day of salvation.

Following the lead of Peter and of early Pentecostals, I would offer at least five answers to the question, "What does this mean?" First, the events of Pentecost mean that God is faithfully fulfilling his promises. Through Prophet Joel, God had promised that in the last days he would pour out his Spirit "upon all people" bringing charismatic gifts and activities such as prophecy, dreams, and visions to "sons and daughters," to young and old, and even to the poor and marginalized. The promises of Joel are echoed by John the Baptist who, in reference to Jesus, declares, "He shall baptize you with the Holy Spirit" (Matthew 3:11). Jesus himself assures his disciples saying, "I will pray to the Father, and he shall send you" the Holy Spirit (John 14:15). Then, just before his ascension into heaven, Jesus instructed them, "wait in the city of Jerusalem until you are clothed with power from heaven" (Luke 24:49). Therefore, in answer to the question, "What does this mean?" Peter responds, "This is that which Joel predicted and which Jesus promised." Peter insists further, "This promise is for all of you, for your children, and even to everyone who is far away" (Acts 2:39). Consequently,

Pentecostals understand that we are living in the last days, that God is now faithfully fulfilling his purposes, and that Jesus Christ continues to pour out his Spirit upon believers everywhere.

Second, the events of Pentecost signify that Jesus Christ is alive, that he is active in the world, and that he has been exalted as Lord over all. Everyone in Jerusalem knew that Jesus had been crucified and buried, but only a few had knowledge of the resurrection. On the basis of the Spirit's outpouring, Peter argues that Jesus is alive (2:32–33). According to Peter, the Holy Spirit has come on behalf of the Lord Jesus to empower and guide the Church's witness to the world. The ministry of Jesus and the Kingdom of God would not cease, but it would continue through the Spirit-empowered ministry of the Church.

Third, God's outpouring of his Spirit means that he is offering his love and grace to the entire world. Another section of Joel's prophecy that Peter cited promises, "And it shall come to pass that whosoever shall call upon the name of the Lord shall be saved" (2:21). Peter extended the offer of salvation to his listeners saying, "Repent and be baptized… and you shall receive the gift of the Holy Spirit" (2:38). This Pentecostal version of salvation declares that God's power is available and sufficient to deliver from any power that binds or oppresses. In most cases, salvation is a spiritual work, and those who repent will be delivered from the power and corruption of sin. Salvation can also mean deliverance from the power of drugs, alcohol, and other life-controlling substances and addictions. In still other contexts salvation might mean liberation from political and social oppression.

Fourth, the events of Pentecost mean that God continues to work in new, exciting, and surprising ways. The Church can at times appear to be fossilized, predictable, and powerless. In such times we may attempt to produce vitality and spectacle through our own ingenuity and creativity, but in Acts 2, the spectacle was of divine origin—"there came a noise from heaven like a rushing mighty wind" and "there appeared tongues like fire." These heavenly signs were demonstrations of God's visitation with inbreaking, transforming power. On the Day of Pentecost the onlookers were "amazed and perplexed" (2:12). Like those spectators, we do not enjoy uncertainty and ambiguity. It seems that the Church has now excluded any manifestations of God's presence that might result in amazement and perplexity. We are unsure how we should evaluate and respond to the signs that accompany God's visitation. God, however, desires to visit us in surprising ways; we must not attempt to confine him in our theological box. Only when we entertain him in new ways will we be able to recognize his contemporary presence and relevance. We must overcome any overreliance upon the familiar, the traditional, the certain, the ritualistic, and the predictable. We must invite and welcome divine interventions, prophecies, healings, miracles, and other manifestations of God's presence. For Pentecostals, this means that we should expect to be filled with the Holy Spirit just as the apostles were filled on the Day of Pentecost, and we should expect the same kinds of miraculous manifestations that occurred in the book of Acts. We pray for the sick with the expectation that God will heal them. We anticipate that our worship services will include utterances of tongues and prophecies from clergy and laity alike.

We assume that, at any time, God may speak directly to us through a dream or a vision. As God pours out his Spirit, he continues to show himself to be the God of the present.

Fifth and finally, the outpouring of the Holy Spirit transforms Jesus' followers into a community of prophets that bears witness to the gospel. On the Day of Pentecost, the Spirit-filled believers "spoke in other tongues" (2:4) and proclaimed "the wonderful works of God" (2:11). The prophetic gift is not confined to select individuals; it is for "all people." It is not limited to certain categories of leaders or to particular classes of people. Joel foresaw the day when men and women of all ages and all social groups would prophesy (2:17–18). It is Jesus' own prophetic ministry of "miracles, wonders, and signs" (2:22) that serves as the paradigm for his Spirit-filled Church.

In sum, when Joel speaks of new voices and new visions, he anticipates neither the perpetual rote repetition of the old voices nor the nostalgic recitation of old visions; instead, he announces the eruption of new voices and new visions—sons and daughters will prophesy; new dreams and visions will break the old wineskins; and those on the margins will find themselves at the center of God's exploits, as he again brings salvation. The new voices and new visions seek to refresh and reshape the ancient theologies and usher them into new contexts. The universal and indispensable Pentecostal testimony is that God never ceases to be intensely active; that is, he continues to speak and work through and among his people for the sake of his Kingdom in the world. From Azusa Street until now, Pentecostals everywhere have insisted upon the present reality of God's presence to save, sanctify, fill with the Holy Spirit, heal, and reign as coming king.

Lee Roy Martin (D.Th., University of South Africa) is Professor of Old Testament and Biblical Languages at Pentecostal Theological Seminary, Cleveland, Tennessee, United States.

QUESTIONS

1. Is there an imposed dominant language in your cultural context? How might Aymer's comments on language be brought to bear on the place in which you live?

2. Explain what Edmonds means by the "post-glossolalia moment." How does his reading integrate both a political-economic and spiritual dimension?

3. What parts of Acts 2 support Williams's statement that the Christian community was not "a manifestation of communism"?

4. Evaluate Martin's application of Acts 2 to spiritual and religious life today. What insights does such a connection bring? Are there possible problems in making such a link?

CHAPTER 13

ACTS (PART II)

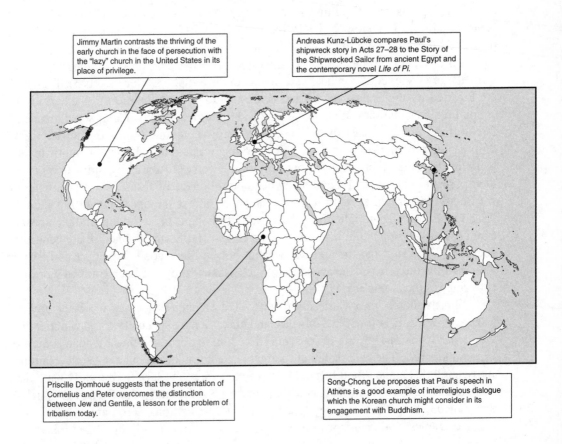

Jimmy Martin contrasts the thriving of the early church in the face of persecution with the "lazy" church in the United States in its place of privilege.

Andreas Kunz-Lübcke compares Paul's shipwreck story in Acts 27–28 to the Story of the Shipwrecked Sailor from ancient Egypt and the contemporary novel *Life of Pi*.

Priscille Djomhoué suggests that the presentation of Cornelius and Peter overcomes the distinction between Jew and Gentile, a lesson for the problem of tribalism today.

Song-Chong Lee proposes that Paul's speech in Athens is a good example of interreligious dialogue which the Korean church might consider in its engagement with Buddhism.

READINGS

The Church in Acts and the United States
Jimmy Martin

Paul's Shipwreck in the Context of World Literature
Andreas Kunz-Lübcke

Cornelius and Peter as Models for Overcoming Tribalism
Priscille Djomhoué

A Lesson from Paul on Interreligious Dialogue
Song-Chong Lee

THE CHURCH IN ACTS AND THE UNITED STATES

Jimmy Martin (United States)

Ever watched a movie or read a story that just abruptly ends? Then you wait and wait for a sequel. Well that is what we have with Luke and Acts. Luke ends rather abruptly and Acts picks up the storyline from there. What better sequel could there be? Acts begins with Jesus bestowing the Holy Spirit upon the apostles and then ascending into Heaven; a biblical version of "I'll be back," if you will. From there the apostles fill the hole in their ranks by voting in Matthias, and then they get to work.

Unfortunately things don't go smoothly. The persecution of the church begins immediately. Peter and John heal a lame man in the temple complex (Acts 3). Then they are arrested by the Sadducees. When Peter and John come before the Sanhedrin, the council realizes that they are "uneducated and untrained" men, so after some menacing threats, they simply release them (Acts 4). What did Peter and John do? They kept right on preaching the name of Jesus, which of course was a real risk to their safety since it had already gotten them arrested once. With the power of the Holy Spirit upon them, their preaching is successful and many become followers of Jesus. It is not long before the Sadducees are filled with jealousy, and they arrest the apostles and put them in prison (5:17–18). That night, the angel of the Lord opens the jail doors and the apostles simply walk out and begin preaching again (5:19–21)! So the Sanhedrin convenes and decides to let Peter and the apostles go, but not before a good flogging (5:40). Upon their beating and release, the apostles "rejoice because they had been counted worthy of suffering for the Name" (5:41).

Shortly thereafter, a Christ-follower named Stephen is accused of blasphemy and seized. He appears before the Sanhedrin and makes a long speech (Acts 7) which indicts the Jewish leaders. They are furious and stone him to death and thus Stephen is the first Christian martyr. Then we read that "a great persecution broke out against the church in Jerusalem" (8:1), and "Saul began to destroy the church" (8:3). So the early Christians scattered from Jerusalem and took their message throughout the Roman Empire. At every place along the way, they faced trials and opposition. Herod arrests Christians, executes James, and imprisons Peter (Acts 12). Acts recounts Paul's three missionary journeys, which are filled with false accusations, incarceration, physical suffering, ship-wreck, and trials. But still, Paul, Silas, Barnabas, and others soldier on. Indeed, it can be said that one of the main themes of Acts is to show the triumph of Christianity in the face of bitter persecution. What a triumph it was; a few hundred years later the Roman emperor Constantine made Christianity the official religion of the empire.

While Christianity is obviously not the official religion of the United States, we as Christians in this country enjoy tremendous privilege and opportunity. That is not necessarily a good thing. If Christianity thrives under persecution, as in Acts, then it tends to flounder and wilt under freedoms, as in America. Christianity has been so embedded in American culture and history that it appears as though the church has gotten lazy. Who shot at you today? Did you have a high-speed chase to get to where you are sitting now? Did masked marauders attempt to kidnap you, cause you harm, or kill you? The simple truth is none of this has happened because we have it good. Yet the reality is that many Christians around the world live with those possibilities; sometimes *probabilities*. In many parts of the world, people take their safety, their family's safety, and even their lives into their own hands for simply uttering the name of Jesus. They risk severe punishment should they be found with a Bible, or simply a portion thereof. Despite all of these obstacles and threats to their safety, people *choose* to follow Christ.

Here in the United States, we get up on Sunday morning and happily drive to the local church. You can't do that in other parts of the world, where to do so is an act against the government that could cost your life. Yet people in those places continue to make this choice because they know what most Americans have managed to forget: The only path to salvation is complete and total obedience to Christ. Jesus commanded: "Give up everything you have and follow me." That is a choice and it is one many people take seriously—to the point of death.

For Christians all over the world the persecutions seen in Acts are a daily reality. Americans have freedom of religion, the freedom to worship, and the freedom *not* to worship—at least in theory and at least for now. Which hard choices have you made lately? So, while you sip your latte from Starbucks playing on your tablet of choice in your warm comfy place of residence trying to decide if you will or will not go to church next Sunday, someone on the other side of the world sits in a prison because they chose to believe and follow Christ. What have you given up to follow Him? What are you willing to give up if it comes to that?

Jimmy Martin is a Christian husband and father of three; he works with any and all Microsoft technologies and loves guns almost as much as his Bible.

PAUL'S SHIPWRECK IN THE CONTEXT OF WORLD LITERATURE

Andreas Kunz-Lübcke (Germany)

The Mediterranean Sea connects and divides Europe and Africa simultaneously; likewise, it permits travel between Asia and Southern Europe. Paul, the missionary of Asia Minor and southern Greece, traveled a great part of his journeys on land. His last journey to Rome, as a prisoner of the Romans, takes place by sea.

A number of commentators have argued that Paul's shipwreck and the snakebite incident should be separated into two independent stories. They use arguments such as it is unlikely that 276 passengers (Acts 27:37) were present at the campfire scene (28:3), rain and cold weather (28:2) are not indicative of Maltese climate, and the description of the island's inhabitants as "barbarous people" (28:2) would be implausible due to the close proximity of the Italian mainland. In this view, one must overlook the fact that the sequence of events constitutes a progression commonly seen in shipwreck narratives, namely the outbreak of a tempest; nautical maneuvers and initiatives; sinking or destruction of a ship; rescue and subsequent jeopardizing of the rescued person by dangerous persons, animals, or beasts; and the final rescue of the hero(s).

One of the oldest shipwreck narratives in world literature is the Story of the Shipwrecked Sailor from the Egyptian Middle Kingdom (twelfth Dynasty). In an autobiographical narrative, the hero records his adventures of a sea voyage where his ship comes into distress. The (excellent) crew tries everything to save the vessel; however, despite all attempts, the ship sinks and the hero lands on an island as the only remaining survivor. The island itself proves to be an ambiguous place. On one hand, it appears as an ambrosial paradise that guarantees nutrition and consequently survival. On the other hand, it is the residence of a hazardous creature:"Then I heard thunder, I thought it was a wave of the sea, trees were breaking, and the earth was trembling. When I uncovered my face, I found it was a serpent coming, his beard was bigger than two cubits, his skin was gilded, and his eyebrows were of real lapis lazuli" (Shipwrecked Sailor, 56—66).

The snake represents a deadly threat. Angry, he snaps at the hero:"Who brought you, who brought you, little one? Who brought you? If you hesitate to tell me who brought you to this island, I will make you that you will find yourself as ashes" (Shipwrecked, 70—72).

The hero shakes off his fear and explains how he came across the island. His speech transforms the angry animal into a friendly and sympathetic being. The snake explains his own story on the island and describes the loneliness he felt after a star had destroyed his 75 snake companions, including his little daughter, whom he obtained by prayer (Shipwrecked, 129). The shipwrecked sailor learns from the snake that "a (or the) God saved his life" (Shipwrecked, 113f.). The snake predicts that the hero will return to Egypt and that prediction shortly comes to pass.

The metamorphosis of the snake from a dangerous beast into a friendly helper and of the island from a place of loneliness and death into a place of survival and rescue appears in almost every shipwreck story. In Yann Martel's recent version of the shipwreck story *Life of Pi* (2001), the protagonist Pi is the single survivor of a shipwreck and a religiously ambitious adolescent who drifts several months over the ocean in a small lifeboat. His only companion is a Bengal tiger named Richard Parker. Similarly, the animal is a deadly threat as well as a rescue to the hero. Constantly threatened to be eaten by the hungry tiger, the hero must feed him with fish. Later, a second shipwrecked person enters the boat and tries to eat Pi; but Richard Parker saves Pi's life by eating the cannibalistic person. The ambivalent nature of the relationship between the shipwrecked and the animal, after the rescue in the end, turns into a glorified view of the former beast, "Richard Parker, thank you. Thank you for saving my life" (384).

Paul is also confronted with the phenomenon of foreigners during his adventure on the island of Malta. His survival of the snakebite and his encounter with the foreigners, the barbarous people (28:2), demonstrate two things:

1. Paul's journey to Rome is portrayed by Luke as a sea journey that ends in shipwreck with all the necessary components including an encounter with a dangerous beast. In other words, the shipwreck, the dangerous animal, and the encounter with the foreigners belong to the same story.

2. In this story a metamorphosis does not happen. The bite of the venomous snake does not affect him and this miracle proves that God is the helmsman of this journey.

In any given year it is estimated that 1,000 people drown in the Mediterranean Sea. In the last year, the riots in North Africa and the overthrow of the regimes in Tunisia, Libya, and Egypt have led to an increase of around 2,000 causalities. The open political future of North African countries, the hopeless economic situation, and the lack of rights granted to refugees from other African countries will force a great number of people into boats after the severity of winter storms decrease in the spring.

In 2004, the European Communion founded the European Agency for the Management of Operational Cooperation at the External Borders of the Member States of the European Union (Frontex). One of the goals of the organization is the coordination of measures to prevent illegal migrations into the European Union. One of the aims of this organization is to increase control of the Mediterranean Sea and thus avoid the arrival of immigrants onto European land.

According the international Maritime law, every person is obligated to help persons and ships in distress. Reports made by human rights organizations have documented cases of ignored SOS signals and calls for help. The nameless Egyptian Sailor, Paul, and Pi were all shipwrecked sailors who demonstrate an intensive faith, including the certainty that God himself would rescue them from death and loneliness (cf. Psalm 107:26–28). All the shipwreck stories, ancient and recent, are concerned with the same problem, namely, loneliness and perceived distance from God. The main point of the stories is that no shipwreck is outside the reach of God's help. Therefore, the hope remains today that God will be with the stranded sailors of our times on the seas of inhumanity.

Andreas Kunz-Lübcke teaches at University of Applied Sciences for Intercultural Theology, Hermannsburg, Germany.

CORNELIUS AND PETER AS MODELS FOR OVERCOMING TRIBALISM

Priscille Djomhoué (Cameroon)

Acts tell how, at instigation of the Holy Spirit, the Gospel spreads throughout the Roman Empire. This Gospel must exceed the Jewish world to reach the Gentile one, though Jews received it first. But how can that spread be possible if we consider the Jewish law which forbids any communion with the foreigners? "You yourselves know that it is unlawful for a Jew to associate with or to visit a Gentile"(Acts 10:28a). Acts 10:1–11:18 functions as a narrative of the reception of the Gospel by the Gentiles and works to break the dividing wall that existed between Jew and Gentile. This narrative is helpful because it can help solve the problem of tribalism.

This text, written by Luke, establishes a link and cordial relations between people from different origins: Jews and Gentiles. This is illustrated through characters, especially the characters of Cornelius and Peter. Acts 10:1–11:18 is particularly important in Cameroonian and African contexts, for it offers a way to reflect on the problem of tribalism, which has caused many divisions and civil wars. This passage stresses two different and separated worlds: the world of Jews and that of the Gentiles. Luke operates the rapprochement by building his characters as belonging to two worlds, and by putting them in dialogue.

Many details are presented concerning Cornelius: his name, job, religion, and situation. He is a centurion in the Italian Regiment, and yet he is also a pious God-fearer who gave alms to many people in need and prayed to God constantly. So, on the one hand, he belongs to the Roman world. The use of his Roman name places him in a cultural and religious sphere: the Gentile world. As a centurion, he is an officer in the Roman army who is not authorized to practice the Jewish religion, since working in the army was incompatible with the Jewish law. This portrait makes Cornelius a person who should not be approached by a Jew. But, on the other hand, he is described as a pious God-fearer. The adjective "pious" emphasizes his virtuous conduct which stems from his commitment to God. These two terms—"pious" and "God-fearer"—form a technical expression for Luke. They indicate the Gentiles who became attached to the Jewish religion. Thus, "God-fearers" function as a bridge between Judaism and Christianity. They belong to two worlds.

Furthermore, Cornelius is "just." This word means that he is not only faithful to the divine prescriptions but also a man of faith. The word "just" is often used in the New Testament to mean a Jew of good reputation, and Luke here applies it to Cornelius. His sympathies to the Jewish religion are manifest by his deeds: his charities and his prayers to God (10:2–4).

When the angel declares that the prayers and the charities of Cornelius rose in memorial in front of God, he emphasizes the fact that his worship to God is accepted in the same way as that of the pious Jew. This statement of the angel means that God has already broken the barriers that existed between Jews and Gentiles. By accepting the prayer of Cornelius, God establishes equality between the prayer and the charities of the Gentile and the sacrifice of the Jew.

In the narrative, the name Peter is used 13 times and Peter is called Simon four times. Luke uses the two names to note the distinction between Greek and Hebrew. Peter is a Greek name, while Simon is Hebrew. By emphasizing both names, the author highlights the ambivalence of the Jew–Greek distinction. Peter the Jew lives with the impurity. The angel sent to look for him goes to the tanner. Tannery is a job that involves contact with the dead animals, and thus is impure. How can we explain that Peter, observer of the laws of purity, was able to live in such an environment? Luke mentions the tanner as an initiatory moment during which Peter had to live with the impurity. Through the construction of his character, Luke has a single objective: to show that Peter belongs to two worlds, the world of purity and that of impurity—just like Cornelius. Luke's aim, again, is to put opposites together. Luke prepares the reader to gradually accept this reality (or reversal) by showing that the characters, in spite of their differences, have in themselves seeds of a rapprochement.

If there is a question to settle, it is "What is the real problem to be resolved in Acts 10:1–11: 18?" The answer, in my opinion, is found in the comment of Peter: "You yourselves know that it is unlawful for a Jew to associate with or to visit a Gentile"(10:28a), the brothers of Jerusalem ask Peter,"Why did you go to uncircumcised men and eat with them?"(11:3). The problem is the Jewish custom which forbids connections with the Gentiles. Luke illustrates the malpractice of this custom by putting together the characters of Cornelius and Peter, who embody each. By sending his messengers into the house of a Jew, Cornelius broke the law of separation. Cornelius goes toward Peter (10:25), then Peter toward Cornelius (10:27). It is the meeting of one uncircumcised with one circumcised, between the Gentile world and the Jewish world, between prohibition and licence.

We can say, then, that Luke uses this narrative to emphasize the building of a harmonious world without divisions. The descriptions and actions of Cornelius and Peter reflect the situation of the current world. Globalization inevitably creates contact between peoples, which leads to all sorts of exchanges. In Africa, specifically my country of Cameroon, one of those exchanges is in the form of intermarriages between people from different tribes. Can we really speak about "foreigners" in today's world? How can we transcend our differences and accept everyone mutually in our tribes and in this "big village"? Luke invites us to build relationships by making use of the experiences of Peter and Cornelius.

Priscille Djomhoué is Professor of Greek and New Testament Studies at the Protestant University of Central Africa in Yaoundé-Cameroon.

A LESSON FROM PAUL ON INTERRELIGIOUS DIALOGUE

Song-Chong Lee (South Korea)

In Acts 17, the apostle Paul provides an interesting showcase for interreligious dialogue. He practiced discourse with people of different religions and philosophies in a civil manner through engaging in rational conversations. This passage presents a powerful message particularly to the Korean evangelical church, whose relationship with Buddhism has recently soured to its lowest point.

Paul was in Athens, which was still the intellectual and cultural center of the world and full of great minds. Although a staunch believer in the messiahship of Jesus, Paul was not averse to engaging in dialogue with non- and anti-Christians. Nor was he reluctant in initiating his dialogue to utilize their religious and philosophical beliefs and claims. He believed that the truth could and should be communicated in everyday conversation using faith and reason. This belief naturally led him to a civil dialogue in which the speaker and the listener articulate their positions in a respectful and thoughtful manner and through which conversion happens in an environment of mutual respect and understanding.

In prompting dialogue, Paul did not have spatial limits. Nor did he focus only on religious people. He was willing to talk with anybody in any place about the truth. Paul reasoned with god-fearers in the synagogue and others such as businessmen, politicians, and philosophers in the *agora* and the *Areopagus*. He did not deliver formal uninterrupted speech as did ancient rhetoricians in Athens. He practiced a conversational *midrash* with Jews in the synagogues of Thessalonica and Berea, examining and explaining his Christian claims, and tried Socratic dialogues with Athenians. Paul did not mind the hostile environment or being called an "idle babbler." He started his dialogue with respect, calling his interlocutors "highly religious." In particular, he expounded Jesus and his resurrection on their ground. Paul handled the Epicureans' fear of inexorable fate with identifying their unknown god with the Christian God and the Stoics' ambiguous pantheism of logos or Zeus with presenting his God as the ultimate principle, source, and reason. When Paul said, "In him we live and move and exist" and "For we also are His children," he was quoting the Cretan philosopher Epimenides and the Cilician Stoic philosopher Aratus. Although spreading the gospel was the primary goal of his journey, Paul never lost his civil virtue in interacting with people of different cultures and religions. He carefully observed their place, studied and thought about their claims, and utilized dialogue for engagement rather than preaching. Paul's civil dialogue stimulated the Athenians' intellectual and spiritual curiosity (17:32) and ultimately made some of them his followers (17:34).

This story sends an urgent message to the Korean church, whose relationship with Buddhism was derailed by a series of defamations and acts of vandalism against Buddhist temples. Over the last few decades, Buddhism has been the prime target of the hatred of the fanatically devout Christians. Verbal assaults against Buddhism have frequently and systematically happened in their revival meetings and *nobangjeondo* (outreach events). The worship leader in *Again 1907*, a revival conference held in Pusan in 2007, to which President Lee, also a devout Christian, sent a supporting video message, said a belligerent prayer: "Lord, let the Buddhist temples in this country crumble down!" Assaults on Buddhist temples and facilities are far worse than the verbal. For example, in 1984, someone painted red crucifixes and smeared dirt on the murals of *Muryang* Temple and *Ilson* Temple in Mt. Samgak. The *Taejôkkwangjôn*, the main Dharma Hall at *Kûmsansa* Temple, which was the National Treasure 476, was completely burned to the ground allegedly by a Christian. Pyo Cha-jong, member of Busan Bethel Church, attempted to destroy *Seokgeulam* classified as *National Treasure No. 24*. In 1995, a Protestant pastor was arrested for painting a cross on the *hubultaenghwa* of the *Muwi* Temple in Gangjin. One of the Buddha statues in *Jeonggakwon* was severely damaged by a sharp object and painted with a red cross in 2000. The list goes on and on.

Although it is not easy to identify the root cause of the Korean Christians' incivility and inability to build amicable relations with Buddhism and other religions, a cultural-historical explanation is plausible. Since the North American missionaries started their full-fledged missionary work in Korea in the early nineteenth century, exclusivism has been the dominant attitude of the Korean Christians toward other traditional religions. For Korean people, who have long been enculturated by the Confucian ethos, which prefers unity to diversity, it is never easy to recognize the coexistence of two sets of truth claims. In particular, the Calvinistic theology that the majority of the early Korean Christians accepted as genuine and pure has made this ethos permanent. Its exclusive soteriology has made Korean evangelical Christians perceive the world as a spiritual battlefield where they continue to fight to keep their faith pure and believe that other religious people, called "the unreached," are simply the subject of their proselytization.

Therefore, interreligious dialogue has never been viewed as necessary and legitimate in the Korean church. It is always understood as a fancy way of putting pluralism and syncretism in the faith by liberal Christians. For example, the Association of Korean Presbyterian Church (*Goryeo Yejang Chonghi*) released a public statement in 2009 on the upcoming WCC tenth anniversary conference in Busan. The statement points out that the WCC's projects emphasizing interfaith dialogue are anti-Bible, anti-Christianity, and anti-church, disguised in the mottos of peace, environment, human rights, and unity. Professor Kim Young-han also warned in a forum held by the Korea Reformed Theological Society in 2011 that the interreligious dialogue of the WCC is seriously threatening the absolute claims of Christianity. Korean Christians' excessive loyalty to their truth claims has kept them from nourishing the intelligence and virtue required to build a healthy relationship with people of other religions.

Now is time for the Korean Christians to reflect on how their spiritual paragon, Paul, dealt with people of other religions. Korea is becoming like Athens due to her cultural power called *the Korean Wave*. More people are visiting and migrating to Korea and enjoying her pop culture than ever before. The above-mentioned distorted Confucian and Calvinistic ethos emphasizing homogeneity yet despising open dialogue could not deal with the country's multicultural future. While Dr. Chan Su, Lee, professor at Kangnam University, a private Christian university, was fired in 2006 for his bowing to a Buddha statue (a moderate expression of respect), Paul boldly went up to the *Areopagos* and engaged in dialogue with pagans and atheists, actively adopting and adapting to their logic and beliefs. Jesus himself set the tone for interreligious and intercultural dialogue. Just as Jesus took off his Jewishness to expand saving grace, Korean Christians should be able to consider transcending their doctrinal identity to reach people on the different paths. Just as Jesus engaged without hesitation in dialogue with a spiritually and morally despised Samaritan woman and tax collectors to show his love, Korean Christians should be ready to talk with anybody in any circumstance without calculating their missionary gains. Just as Paul and Jesus went deep into the life of the Gentiles, Korean Christians should not be afraid of leaving their comfort zone and engaging in dialogue with people who have conflicting faiths. The power of interreligious dialogue is not the exchange of dead letters but the encounter between *inseong-deul* (characters/personalities). Paul strongly believed that the true Christian message could be delivered not by the doctrines but by the whole person. Interreligious dialogue will help Korean Christians reach people of other religions through person-to-person contact rather than the missionary-to-potential convert. It will naturally reveal the message of Jesus and make the genuine exchange of knowledge and mutual understanding possible.

Song-Chong Lee is Assistant Professor of Religious Studies and Philosophy at University of Findlay, United States.

QUESTIONS

1. Are there religious traditions that face persecution—or prejudice—in your cultural context? If so, how does it compare to that faced by the early church, as described by Martin?

2. What are the implications of Kunz-Lübcke's assertion that Paul's story fits the pattern of shipwreck narratives?

3. Who are the people in your context who are analogous to Cornelius and Peter as presented by Djomhoué?

4. Reread Paul's speech in Athens in Acts 17 in light of Lee's perspective. Can you make counterpoints to Lee's observations? What might Paul himself say to Lee?

CHAPTER 14

ROMANS

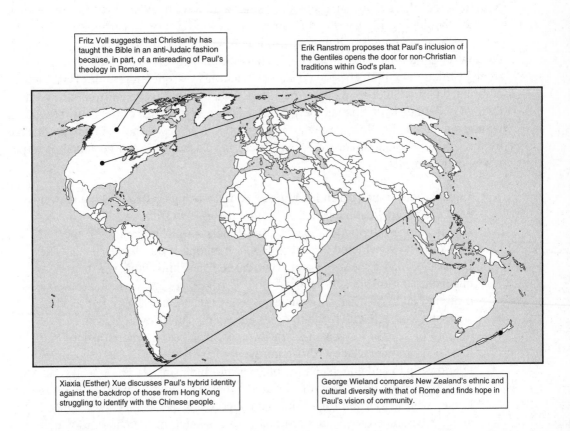

Fritz Voll suggests that Christianity has taught the Bible in an anti-Judaic fashion because, in part, of a misreading of Paul's theology in Romans.

Erik Ranstrom proposes that Paul's inclusion of the Gentiles opens the door for non-Christian traditions within God's plan.

Xiaxia (Esther) Xue discusses Paul's hybrid identity against the backdrop of those from Hong Kong struggling to identify with the Chinese people.

George Wieland compares New Zealand's ethnic and cultural diversity with that of Rome and finds hope in Paul's vision of community.

READINGS

Anti-Judaism and Paul's Theology in Romans
Fritz Voll

Paul's Inclusion of the Gentiles and Non-Christian Traditions
Erik Ranstrom

Paul's Identity and the People of Hong Kong
Xiaxia (Esther) Xue

New Zealand's Diversity and Paul's Vision of Community
George Wieland

ANTI-JUDAISM AND PAUL'S THEOLOGY IN ROMANS

Fritz Voll (Canada)

On the whole, Christianity has taught the Bible in an anti-Judaic fashion for 2,000 years, and it is still going on as if neither the Holocaust nor the foundation of the state of Israel ever happened. There is hardly a book on Christian biblical theology written before the 1950s and 1960s that is not anti-Jewish. When I discovered this in my own theological library, I had to throw out all books printed before this time. The New Testament cannot stand on its own; it is based on Judaism, its history, that is, on the Jewish Bible, the Church's "Old Testament." However, instead of admitting this freely, Christianity did its best to develop a "theology of contempt" (Jules Isaac) which dominated Christian thinking until the 1960s. What follows is taken from "Re-reading Paul—Guidelines for Christian clergy and teachers in their use of the New Testament with reference to the New Testament's presentation of Jews and Judaism" published by the Council of Christians and Jews, Victoria, Australia. It can be found at http://www.jcrelations.net.

What is clear from a careful reading of Paul's writings is that he would never have described what happened to him on the road to Damascus as a conversion from one religion to another, from Judaism to Christianity. To the end of his life he considered himself a Jew, a member of the People Israel. The Damascus road experience and what ensued, led him, however, to a new understanding of himself as a Jew and of Israel as God's people. It was a profound and enduring religious experience but it cannot be interpreted as signaling a breach with the faith of his ancestors. This is evident from a close reading of several key passages in Romans. It is also a crucial insight that must be acknowledged by Christians everywhere if they are to have a proper relationship to and understanding of Jews and Judaism.

To accept that Jesus of Nazareth, the man crucified under Pontius Pilate, whose followers he, Paul, had vigorously persecuted, was indeed alive, necessitated for Paul a profound reassessment of the nation to which he belonged. Just as, in the context of God's grace, it led to discovery in his own life of a hitherto unsuspected subtle sinfulness and resistance to God, it led also to a similar judgment on the nation as a whole, one that collapsed the vision of a holy nation separate from the surrounding nations of the world.

Let us be quite clear: This pessimistic view of Israel in moral terms was a judgment made by a Jew within Israel. It was a judgment made in earlier times by many of the prophets of Israel. It was one being made in Paul's time by other Jews who shared his apocalyptic worldview, such as the members of the community who wrote the Dead Sea Scrolls, the author of the Fourth Book of Ezra, and evidently by John the Baptist. It was a prophetic view that in no sense implied a rejection of the Jewish nation but rather a summons to conversion in view of the coming judgment of God.

Central to his personal experience of call was the conviction on Paul's part that it was his distinctive God-given task to summon the nations of the world to share in this movement of repentance centered upon but not confined to Jews. Israel had always acknowledged righteous Gentiles and, at the time of Paul, many people from the nations were attracted to the monotheism and ethical uprightness of Judaism. Paul, however, fought for and served a more radical vision, one that by no means all his fellow members in the messianic Jesus movement shared. In Paul's view, the nations of the world would come to the God of Israel, not as converts to Judaism but precisely as Gentiles. They were not to take on circumcision and the ritual obligations of the Torah. Nor, through a rigorous imposition of the purity laws, were they to be made to feel second-class citizens when the community gathered to celebrate, worship and eat (Galatians 2:10–21).

Paul found scriptural validation in his reading of God's dealings with Abraham. Jewish writers before Paul had pictured Abraham as the first proselyte. Paul took this notion much farther. In Abraham's simple faith in God's promise that he would have a son and heir contrary to all the evidence, a faith that put him right with God ("justified" him), Paul saw prefigured a pattern whereby the nations of the world could find acceptance and salvation. In God's promise to Abraham that all peoples would be blessed in his descendents (Genesis 22:18; 26:4) he found scripture's indication that the final people of God would be made up of Israel and a vast constituency of believers from all the nations. Paul's view of salvation history gives priority to the covenant God made with Abraham over that made with Israel at Mt Sinai through Moses. After all, Abraham was justified before, not after, he was circumcised—thus circumcision was not a requirement for justification (Rom. 4:9–11).

This new understanding did not diminish for Paul his self-understanding as a Jew; nor did it depreciate the role of the Jewish people. Rather, it emphasized the place of each in the conversion of the nations to faith in the God of Israel.

Paul rejects the imposition of Torah upon Gentiles for two basic reasons. In the first place, as already mentioned, that imposition destroyed Gentile identity in a way contrary to God's will as explained to Abraham. Secondly, and this is a more contentious point, he believed that as an instrument of moral regulation it could not stand up to the ingrained power of sin in human beings. Paul's analysis in Romans 5–7 (5:20; 6:14–15; 7:5, 7–25; also 3:20; 4:15) of the nexus between law and sin is where he gives greatest offense, seemingly intolerable offense, to Jews and Judaism. What he is trying to do, however, is to dissuade Gentile converts from looking to Torah as a sure means of restraining the impulses and temptations to return to their old pagan pattern of life. Against this, Paul believed that the law would for them be useless, indeed, counterproductive. It would actually provoke rebellion and make matters worse (Rom. 7:5, 7–13, 14–25).

Paul makes it abundantly clear that the problem lay not in the law itself, which he insists remains "holy and righteous and good" (Rom. 7:12), but in the indwelling power of sinfulness in unredeemed human nature. So, for instance, when Paul speaks in Rom 8:2 of "the law of sin and death" from which "the law of the Spirit of life has set me free," he is in no way identifying the Law of Moses with sin and death. The "law" of sin and death is the regime of sin in human life, which the Torah, in his view, is powerless to remedy. That judgment about the Law's impotence is made, as noted already, primarily with Gentiles in view.

When Christians read Paul's remarks about the Law (Torah) as God's general abrogation of the Law and apply these remarks to Jews and insist that Jews have to become Christians, they in fact deny God's covenantal faithfulness to the Jewish people (Rom. 11:29). For almost 2,000 years, since its separation from Judaism and beginning with the Church Fathers, Christianity has taught an anti-Judaism that contributed to anti-Semitism and the Holocaust.

Deeply shocked by the murder of 6 million Jews perpetrated by mostly baptized German Protestants and Catholics, the Catholic Church and most mainline Protestant churches the world over have since the late 1960s repented and reconsidered their theology of Judaism, among them Anglicans/ Episcopalians, Lutherans, and Reformed churches. They now recognize the lasting validity of God's covenant with God's people Israel and have begun to reread the New Testament in light of this recognition. Some evangelical churches, however, continue their anti-Judaic teaching and try to convert Jews to Christianity.

It takes time for the countless official statements of the churches to filter down to people in the pews. Many people baptized and confirmed as Christians will continue to know the Bible only in an anti-Jewish interpretation, as they were taught as children in Sunday schools and confirmation classes, especially if they don't continue to attend church services any longer.

Fritz Voll established the website Jewish–Christian Relations (www.jcrelations.net), to which he contributes as translator.

PAUL'S INCLUSION OF THE GENTILES
AND NON-CHRISTIAN TRADITIONS

Erik Ranstrom (United States)

It is certainly worthwhile, even necessary, to consider whether the Bible itself has a global perspective. In our own time, the rise in popularity and increased legitimacy given to interreligious dialogue is pressuring Christians to relax and even eliminate claims of revealed truth. After all, as some have argued, hasn't the "pretension to be a 'chosen people, a royal priesthood, a people set apart' led to exclusivism, chauvinism, and expansionism"? The moral force of the question sometimes results in evacuating the meaning of the Bible altogether in favor of a shapeless, formless, least common denominator universal "religion" of morality and spirituality. Christians, however, should not renounce their faith or their belief in the truth of the biblical tradition in light of this challenge. The New Testament is not alien to such questions. The New Testament was written in pressure situations where "insider" and "outsider" debates generated interethnic and intrareligious conflict and debate. Much of this was caused by the New Testament God who worked in surprising and often unpredictable ways among those who were not thought to have anything to do with God (Gentiles). I believe that Paul's letter to the Romans has something to say to this contemporary, global sensitivity.

Unlike other correspondences that he had with churches throughout Asia Minor and Greece, Paul had never been to Rome and had no relationship with the Roman Christians. Paul was reaching out to them primarily because he needed to rally support for his missionary expedition to Spain. Establishing relations with the Roman Christians was going to be complex for Paul since it was his writings that in part had led to inflammatory relations between Gentile Christians and Jewish Christians there. The Gentile Christian community was most likely disparaging the venerable Jewish tradition, perhaps following an interpretation of Paul's legitimation of the Gentile mission and Gentile Christian identity in Galatians. The Jewish Christian community, indignant at being dishonored by the traditionally dishonorable Gentiles, responded with condescension by relying on stereotypes of the "nations" and their immorality. We can imagine Paul's situation very much like our own, interrelated, interreligious world, where our words and actions are never allowed the "privacy" of their limited audiences but get caught up in different, more strained contexts. Paul is very much like the "crisis" interreligious theologian today, having to do theology and address issues in a setting where much is at stake.

Paul begins Romans with a "plight" narrative in 1:18–32 that describes the Gentiles and their situation before God. God's grace and truth was indeed given to the Gentiles but was rejected. The Gentiles relied on their "lower nature" rather than on God's truth, and Paul introduces a laundry list of vices that ensued: wickedness, envy, evil, greed, malice, disorder. Now a first-century Jewish-Christian audience reading this opening to Romans would have nodded their heads in approval. What Paul narrates in 1:18–32 would have been a very familiar Jewish invective against the Gentiles and would have been viewed as an unequivocal victory for their claims to superiority. Finally, Paul had taken their side, and the Gentile Christians are put in their place. Yet, this is where Paul surprises them, for in the very next chapter, Paul accuses the Jews of failing to uphold the Law and deluding themselves that they would "escape God's judgment" (2:3). As Paul says, "For there is no distinction; all have sinned and are deprived of the glory of God" (3:23).

We can learn from this too, for often Christians compare religious traditions unfavorably; the Sermon on the Mount is compared to violence in other religious traditions, the "preferential option for the poor" is compared with the historical abuses of the caste system. When we maintain such lopsided comparisons and contrasts, we are making the same error as the Roman Jewish Christians, and need Paul to remind us of our sin, of our own lack of righteousness.

It is crucial to note that Paul in Romans doesn't stop with a universal condemnation. Condemnation in Romans serves only to undercut claims of superiority that were causing conflict and division within the community. It also sets the stage for the insight in the very next line (3:24) that Jewish and Gentile Christians both "are justified freely by his grace through the redemption in Christ Jesus." Just as Gentile Christians and Jewish Christians are impartially judged, they are also impartially redeemed in Christ. There are no exceptions in either judgment or salvation; all have fallen, all have been redeemed, and all are assured of divine forgiveness and divine presence. Now some will be quick to counter that this impartial redemption for Paul applies only to Christians, those who have through baptism entered into this universal community of salvation won by Christ. It can be argued by these well-intentioned contemporaries that in the ancient, Jewish-Christian world Gentiles may have been representative of inclusion, but more is required today.

But, I would argue, there needs to be a place for members of non-Christian religious traditions within God's plan. Anything less is too parochial. Now, Paul didn't have this question in mind in the first century, but today, we can bring the revelatory text of Romans into conversation with contemporary questions. To address this concern, let us discuss Paul's treatment of Abraham in Romans 4 and its contemporary, global, interreligious implications.

Paul had to answer the question, who is in the community of salvation? Only the Jewish Christians? Only the Gentile Christians? Paul mediates this conflict by hearkening back to the prototypical figure of Abraham. Abraham is the ancestor of God's community of salvation; everyone in this community is somehow related to Abraham. What aspect of Abraham's existence was deemed by God to be constitutive of the community of salvation? Is it available to all, or only to some? Paul maintained that what made Abraham righteous in the sight of God was Abraham's faith, so that whoever has faith shares in that same righteousness, now consummated in Christ. Paul's theology here was liberating for the Christian community at Rome because faith is not something exclusively tied into a particular ethnic identity; rather it is a human invariant. Therefore, Jew and Gentile are both kin in this community of faith.

Abraham is often referred to today as the "father" of Jews, Christians, and Muslims; this is in many ways quintessentially Pauline: Through Abraham all three of these faith traditions are united. But this can be extended beyond even the three "Abrahamic faiths" into other faith traditions and people of goodwill, keeping in mind the twentieth-century Catholic Christian German theologian Karl Rahner who spoke of the presence of the theological virtue of faith among non-Christian religious traditions and all people of goodwill. This faith is a mysterious reality, perhaps known fully only to God alone, but like Paul, Christians place their trust in the impartiality of God's favor and salvation, and bring healing and communion to a world torn by interreligious indifference, suspicion, and hostility.

Erik Ranstrom is a Teaching Fellow in the Department of Theology at Boston College, United States.

PAUL'S IDENTITY AND THE PEOPLE OF HONG KONG

Xiaxia (Esther) Xue (Hong Kong)

Some postcolonial scholars argue that an identity is not grounded in geography (where you are from), but rather in the retelling of the past. Hong Kong was under British (colonial) power for a century and a half before it was returned to Mainland China in 1997. For those of us from Hong Kong, it is difficult to identify with those Chinese people who haven't been under the British power because we have been highly influenced and even transformed by the British culture. One example is that we do not know how to speak the official Chinese language (Mandarin). For most of us, it is much easier to speak English than Mandarin. We somehow are stuck in between two cultural identities. On the one hand, we desire to be identified with our traditional Chinese cultural heritage, so we begin to learn Mandarin and build up relationships with people in Mainland China. On the other hand, Hong Kong culture has been Westernized. Thus, in some sense, we struggle between two cultural systems. Gradually we have come to realize our new hybrid identity by integrating our colonized cultural system into our current Chinese context.

It is in this context that I read the oft-discussed passage in Romans 7:14–25 where Paul, I propose, is also struggling with reconciling various religious and cultural identities. The members of the church in Rome to which Paul was writing contained both Jews and Gentiles who believed in Jesus as the Christ. Like those of us in Hong Kong, the Jewish people were subjected to foreign forces for centuries prior to Jesus. They experienced the various dominations of Assyrian, Babylonian, Persian, and Roman empires. During those periods, the Jewish people and their culture were transformed. One of the most notable influences is that the Seleucid king Antiochus IV (175–64 B.C.) attempted to abolish the sacral constitution of Jerusalem and Judaea and tried to assimilate his Jewish subjects culturally and religiously to the Hellenistic way of life. In 6 A.D. Judaea was made a Roman province, and it was given two-tier administration (an appointed Roman provincial governor and a Jewish high priest). Some of the provinces of the Roman Empire assimilated Roman civilization so that their inhabitants came to think of themselves as Romans. By some estimates, there were between 40,000 and 60,000 Jews in Rome by the beginning of the first century A.D., as many as in Jerusalem itself.

In the book of Romans, Paul, as a representative Jew who was torn between two cultures, is speaking to other Jews describing his struggle with his past cultural identity. As a Hebrew born of Hebrews, he was a zealot, a persecutor of the church (Philippians 3:5–6). Ruled by a pagan polytheistic Roman Empire, Paul's concern for the national and religious life of the Jewish people impelled him to seek the independence of the nation and the restoration of the glory of the temple by the Messiah. Paul was driven to purify the nation by totally observing the law and persecuting people who spoke against the law (Stephen). Also, it was important for an honorable Jew to maintain inherited status in the "limited-good" culture of the first century. So, Paul's insistence on adherence to the laws of his tradition shows his desire to seek his identity in the historical past.

However, Paul's encounter on the way to Damascus had a series of transforming consequences, namely the realization that his zeal for the traditional Jewish culture and law had been misguided. Thus, when Paul talks about "wishing to do good, but doing evil instead," he does not mean that he does not have the ability to perform good. What he is referring to is that he sought to follow the will of God by persecuting Christians and confirming his identity in the root of the Jewish tradition, but what he had done in reality was to oppose the true Messiah by persecuting the Church. Similarly, when in Romans 7:17–18, 20 Paul reiterates "sin dwells within me" and "nothing good dwells within me," he is not referring to his inner evil self, or the evil impulse inside human beings. Rather, according to Romans 1, the sin of human beings is the ignorance of God, and seeking one's identity within themselves. Thus, "they became futile in their thinking" (1:20). Paul's zealous behavior demonstrates his seeking to establish his own righteousness in the Jewish laws. This demonstrates the power of sin "dwelling within me," which can refer to a certain force driving from a culturally twisted social system to push people to achieve certain religious or political goals. This zeal for their original identity led Jewish people into conflict with the very God they wanted to serve.

In 7:14–25, then, Paul is retelling his past story from his Christian perspective. It is a description of the struggle for a new self-understanding and way of being peculiar to the Jewish believer in Jesus. It is crucial to note that Paul does not simply reject the system of his Jewish tradition (e.g., the law) when he retold his story. He admits the good of the law (7:12). Moreover, the law is spiritual (v. 14), and could do many things for those who embrace it. Paul delights in his innermost with the law of God (v. 22). Now, however, Paul has arrived at a new stage of his understanding of the law, namely that faith in Christ establishes the law. Therefore, the new identity that Paul wishes his Jewish people to understand is a hybrid identity. Paul challenges his hearers in the Roman church to define their past in light of the new story of being in Jesus Christ.

In sum, Paul and the first Jewish followers of Jesus experienced a crisis of their cultural identity reminiscent of that experienced by those in postcolonial Hong Kong. In Romans 7:14–25 Paul looks back on his preconversion identity as a zealot for the Torah. He explains how the very heart of his religious devotion led him away from the will of God. Paul's new identity in Jesus Christ made him realize that this conflict lies not only within Paul himself but also among his pious Jewish people. Akin to our post-colonial cultural identity, Paul views his new hybrid identity as not totally ruptured with his past, but rather continuous with it. Paul, after all, does not become a Gentile after his conversion.

Xiaxia (Esther) Xue was born in FuJian, China, and studied in Hong Kong for many years; she is now a New Testament Ph.D. student at McMaster Divinity College, Canada.

New Zealand's Diversity and Paul's Vision of Community

George Wieland (New Zealand)

Auckland is New Zealand's largest city, with a population of 1.3 million. With almost 40 percent of its population comprising people born outside New Zealand it is increasingly diverse. Currently around 11 percent of the city's population is of Maori descent (indigenous people of New Zealand), 56 percent is European (descendants of nineteenth-century settlers or more recent arrivals), 15 percent have Pacific Island heritage, and the most dramatic increase over the last two decades has been in Auckland's Asian population (from Taiwan, Hong Kong, South Korea, India, the People's Republic of China, etc.), which now stands at around 19 percent of the total.

Many of those who have migrated to New Zealand have brought with them strong traditions of Christian faith, and others have found faith here. Pacific Island churches are prominent in some parts of Auckland and more than a hundred Chinese and a similar number of Korean congregations meet, some in their own church buildings but most in local schools or in premises belonging to other churches. To those may be added Russian, Iranian, Vietnamese, Ethiopian, Brazilian, Japanese, Afrikaans, and many other groups. As in many cities around the world, however, immigration and increasing evidence of diversity has been challenging for some who regard themselves as "traditional New Zealanders" and fear a dilution of what they regard as their cultural identity. Such responses are also found in many churches, even toward immigrants who share their Christian faith.

Reading Romans in this context (I myself moved to Auckland from Scotland 11 years ago) has thrown into sharp relief aspects of Paul's message in this letter that I had paid little attention to before. Rome, like contemporary Auckland, was a large multicultural city. It was ethnically and culturally diverse, with the addition of multiple gradations of social status, political influence, and wealth. Christian faith had first been brought to Rome by Diaspora Jews, residents of Rome's large Jewish quarter who had made the journey to Jerusalem for the festivals and had experienced the astonishing events of Pentecost and the subsequent proclamation of Messiah Jesus. By the time Paul wrote his letter, the church had evidently spread beyond the Jewish community and there were several groups of believers meeting in various homes, probably ranging from crowded tenements to the villas of the better-off. It's quite probable that these home-based groups would have comprised clusters of similar people, with particular attitudes and ways of behaving, and that there might have been some reluctance to have much to do with other groups who were different.

That wasn't good enough for Paul! He pleads with them, "Welcome one another, therefore, just as Christ has welcomed you, for the glory of God" (15:7). The "one another" who come into view in Romans 14–15 are believers who have different opinions and practices concerning food and drink and the observance or otherwise of particular days. Reading in ethnically diverse Auckland, these sound very much like cultural distinctives, and specifically the different norms that would have shaped the attitudes and behavior of people brought up in various Jewish and Gentile environments in the Roman world.

Rather than being an argument purely about ethical choices among Christians who varied principally in their stages of spiritual maturity, the issue that Paul was addressing seems to have had a lot to do with the challenge of cultivating authentic community across barriers of social, ethnic, and cultural difference.

But why does this matter? If churches are growing, worshiping, and witnessing within their own ethnic groups, is intercultural fellowship really a gospel priority? Rereading the familiar text of Romans with such questions in mind brings to the fore a dimension of the gospel that a more individualistic focus obscures, namely, that in it God brings together into one people those who had been ethnically and culturally separate. The gospel is the startling message that through God's Son, the Davidic Messiah, the Gentiles—the *ethnē*, the nations of the world—are called to belong to the one people of God, receiving together the gift of salvation (1:1–6). Paul is not ashamed to take this gospel to the heart of the empire, the multicultural city of Rome, because it is the power of God for salvation to everyone who has faith, to the Jew first and also to the Greek (1:16).

This theme runs through the letter's magnificent sustained exposition of the gospel. Romans 1–3 argue that all, of whatever ethnic identity, are under the power of sin, and that God deals with all on the same basis, that of faith in Jesus Christ. Romans 4 demonstrates that Abraham is the ancestor not only of those who could claim biological descent from him but of all who share his faith in a God who gives life to the dead. Romans 5 traces the problem of sin back beyond the Law that was given through Moses to the first human ancestor, Adam, and declares that God's gracious answer to that problem in Jesus Christ meets the need not only of Moses' disciples but of Adam's whole family. Romans 6–8 expound the new identity and the new life of those who become children of God through union with Christ rather than through any particular ethnic affiliation. Romans 9–11 wrestle with what this new vision of a family of God means for the more exclusive understanding of Israel as God's family, and offers the illustration of Israel as the olive tree that God had planted and cultivated, from which unfruitful branches had been pruned, but into which wild, uncultivated branches from among the nations were now being grafted.

When Paul turns in Romans 12–15 to spell out what all this means for the Christian community in multicultural Rome, his appeal has to be heard as not directed primarily to individual believers and their ethical choices, nor even to house churches regarding their internal relationships, but to the whole diverse people of God in Christ in that city. They are to be a family living for the glory of God as they break free from the ungodly assumptions, attitudes, and ambitions prevalent in their environment and radically reshape their thinking according to what God intends for his world (12:1–2). So in place of pride and competitiveness there is humility and mutuality; in place of indifference or a desire to retaliate there is love and generosity; in place of self-protective withdrawal from wider society there is respectful participation and love in action (Romans 12–13).

This includes how the believers are to relate to one another. Romans 14–15 turn out to be not an afterthought, but a major goal to which the argument of the letter has been leading! If the gospel really is the power of salvation for all, then that astonishing scope has to be seen and experienced in the community of those who are being saved. This, says Paul, is how God is glorified: "May the God of steadfastness and encouragement grant you to live in harmony with one another, in accordance with Christ Jesus, so that you may together with one voice glorify the God and Father of our Lord Jesus Christ. Welcome one another, therefore, just as Christ has welcomed you, for the glory of God" (15:5–7).

A string of Old Testament quotations (15:9–12) reinforces Paul's point that it is God's intention to gather the nations together with Israel to receive his mercy, to praise him joyfully, to live as one people under the rule of his Messiah.

Looking across my city, I hear in Romans 14–15 a series of rebukes to the kind of attitudes that obstruct relating in Christ across barriers of difference. There are the judgmental attitudes toward Christians whose practices and opinions are different from mine (14:1–13), the woefully inadequate vision of the kingdom of God that focuses on those differences rather than what really matters (14:17), the failure to look for and do what builds up the community and particular people within it (14:19; 15:2). I glimpse in these chapters the exhilarating prospect of people of all cultures and languages praising God joyfully as one (14:11; 15:5–12). I recognize more fully than before that this diverse but united worshiping and mutually accepting community is what God intends and is the goal for which Christ gave himself (15:8–9). It is what Paul longed to see, and it must also be what I hope for and strive toward among the still too fragmented Christian community in Auckland.

George Wieland is Lecturer in New Testament and Director of Mission Research and Training at Carey Baptist College, Auckland, New Zealand.

QUESTIONS

1. Read carefully the relevant passages from Romans and assess Voll's argument concerning Paul and the Law. What, if any, counterpoints could be made?

2. In what ways are the writings/views of both Paul and Ranstrom a reflection of their particular historical and cultural location?

3. What are the strengths and weaknesses of Xue's reading of Romans 7:17–18, 20?

4. What are some of the specific challenges of "cultivating authentic community"? How and why might those in Rome and Auckland resist Paul's and Wieland's call for a "united worshiping and mutually accepting community"?

CHAPTER 15

1 CORINTHIANS

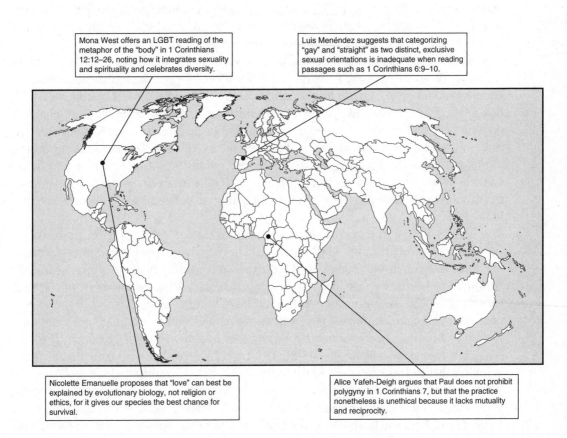

Mona West offers an LGBT reading of the metaphor of the "body" in 1 Corinthians 12:12–26, noting how it integrates sexuality and spirituality and celebrates diversity.

Luis Menéndez suggests that categorizing "gay" and "straight" as two distinct, exclusive sexual orientations is inadequate when reading passages such as 1 Corinthians 6:9–10.

Nicolette Emanuelle proposes that "love" can best be explained by evolutionary biology, not religion or ethics, for it gives our species the best chance for survival.

Alice Yafeh-Deigh argues that Paul does not prohibit polygyny in 1 Corinthians 7, but that the practice nonetheless is unethical because it lacks mutuality and reciprocity.

READINGS

The "Body of Christ" and the LGBT Community
Mona West

Challenging the "Straight/Gay" Divide
Luis Menéndez

Sexual and Marital Ethics in 1 Corinthians 7
Alice Yafeh-Deigh

Love and Evolutionary Biology in 1 Corinthians 13
Nicolette Emanuelle

The "Body of Christ" and the LGBT Community

Mona West (United States)

Lesbian, gay, bisexual, transgender (LGBT) people have a varied reading history with the Bible. We read it in order to protect ourselves from those who use the Bible to justify violence and hatred against us. We read it to find ourselves in the stories of Ruth and Naomi, Jonathan and David, and the Ethiopian Eunuch. We also approach scripture as resistant readers challenging the assumptions of gender, heteronormativity, and sexuality that we find either in the text itself or interpretations of it.

Paul's use of the metaphor of the human body in 1 Corinthians 12:12–26 to explain "varieties of gifts that come from the same Spirit" (12:4) and to emphasize diversity in Christian community is particularly rich for an LGBT reading. LGBT people are often marginalized in society and excluded from Christian communities because of what they do with their bodies: loving someone of the same sex, expressing one's gender identity in a way that does not conform to the strict binary of male/female, seeking ordination as a "practicing homosexual," wanting our unions blessed and sanctioned by the Church. What is hopeful to LGBT people about Paul's metaphor is the holy integration of sexuality and spirituality as well as the invitation to celebrate and welcome diversity in the body.

Paul's use of the body metaphor to speak about spiritual gifts points to an "embodied spirituality" for LGBT people. The way we express the Spirit's work in our lives is through our bodies or lived experience. Too often the word "sexuality" is limited to genital expression, but theologian James Nelson reminds us that sexuality refers to who we are in the world (and the Church) "as body-selves who experience the emotional, cognitive, physical, and spiritual need for intimate communion—human and divine" (*Embodiment: An Approach to Sexuality and Christian Theology* [Augsburg Press: Minneapolis, 1978], 18). LGBT people know in their bodies that it is impossible to separate one's spirituality from one's sexuality and we resonate with Paul's use of the human body as a metaphor to speak about how the gifts of the Spirit/spirituality manifest in the Church and the world for the work of the common good. In fact, LGBT people have a long history of sharing their spiritual gifts. In tribal communities throughout the world, LGBT people have functioned as healers and holy people. Their communities saw them as mediators between the worlds of spirit and flesh.

LGBT readers of this passage also embrace Paul's teaching on the importance of welcoming and celebrating diversity in the body. While the use of this metaphor in Paul's day would have been to convince people of different classes to stay in their place, Paul uses it in reference to the Church to talk about the need for diversity and the importance of interdependence among its members. This is good news for LGBT people who struggle not only to be accepted in the Church, but who want to make a difference in the life of the community by sharing their gifts.

Paul's baptismal formula in 12:12–13 (which is very similar to the one he quotes in Galatians 3:28) is an occasion for LGBT people of faith to remember their baptism and claim their place in this one body. We might even go so far as to offer an amendment to the formula: "For in the one Spirit we were all baptized into one body—Jews or Greeks, slaves or free, gay or straight—and we were all made to drink of one Spirit."

As resistant readers, LGBT people would question the assumptions Paul and interpreters of this text might make about the type of body used in the metaphor. Is it a heterosexual body? A male body? An "able" body? How would people who are deaf or blind find themselves included or excluded from Paul's metaphor when he asks in verse 17, "If the whole body were an eye, where would the hearing be?" When Paul speaks of the "less honorable" and "less respectable" members of the body in verses 23–24, he is alluding to genitalia. Where would eunuchs, castrated males in Paul's society, find themselves in this metaphor—especially when Paul's own Jewish tradition (Deuteronomy 23:1) excluded eunuchs from worshipping in the temple?

How would transgender people of today relate to this passage from Paul? The term "transgender" refers to someone who feels that their "gender identity" is different from the one assigned to them at birth based on their genitalia. Because transgender people may experience their genitalia as foreign to their body based on the way they understand their gender identity, it is possible that they might resist Paul's admonition that each body part belongs ("If the foot would say, 'Because I am not a hand, I do not belong to the body' that would not make it any less a part of the body"). Many transgender people undergo gender reassignment surgery by having breasts or genitalia removed or refashioned in order for their physical body to correspond to their gender identity. And there have certainly been those transgender people who have "clothed" (v.23) the "less honorable" parts of their body in ways that provide greater honor by cross-dressing or wearing clothes that match the gender they feel themselves to be rather than conforming to how they are expected to dress based on the gender they were assigned at birth.

An LGBT reading of 1 Corinthians 12:12–26 invites us to think about the many different kinds of bodies that are included in the body of Christ. There are healthy bodies, diseased bodies, gay bodies, straight bodies, male bodies, female bodies, able bodies, and disabled bodies. Paul claims in verse 26 that members of the body of Christ bear each other's pain and joy. To live into the diversity that Paul imagines means that we recognize the body of Christ as a transgender body or a body with AIDS just as much as it is a healthy body or a body with cancer, and all bodies share the same Spirit of God.

Mona West (Ph.D.) is a lesbian, formerly ordained as a Southern Baptist minister. She now serves as Director of Formation and Leadership Development for Metropolitan Community Churches; she is coeditor of Take Back the Word: A Queer Reading of the Bible *and* The Queer Bible Commentary.

CHALLENGING THE "STRAIGHT/GAY" DIVIDE

Luis Menéndez (Spain)

First Corinthians 6:9–10 has become one of the most interpreted, influential New Testament texts in biblical studies, theology, ethics, and politics. To talk about Christian sexual ethics today inevitably means quoting 1 Corinthians 6 together with Romans 1:26 and 1 Timothy 1:9–10. If the Hebrew Scriptures are included, Leviticus 18 and 20 and the Sodom and Gomorrah episode (Genesis 19) complete the anthology. First Corinthians 6 is also a paradigmatic example of how much interpretation matters in the real world, for as long as this text is taken into consideration churches will continue splitting, political debates will be polarized, and gays and lesbian will suffer marginalization.

The overwhelming majority of Western Christianity considers the issue to be quite simple: Paul condemned homosexuality, so shall we. Thus, arguments against legalizing gay marriage, which rest mostly on religious grounds, find support in biblical passages like this one. On the other hand, many progressive-liberal Christians, abetted by the finest scholarly arguments, argue that Paul is not referring to "homosexuality as we understand it" or that we should pay no more attention to Paul's reputed indictment of homosexuality than we pay to other issues that we do not read literally (e.g., women's roles in the assembly or view of slavery). Others, including nonreligious readers, conclude that a 2,000-year-old document, whatever its meaning, should not set the moral standards of a society struggling to cut its bonds from the religious grip.

In academia, positions differ little from the above-mentioned state of affairs: Many interpreters continue to hold a pervasive and inescapable indictment on homosexuality, while others have argued—successfully I think—that Paul's views on sexuality should not determine the present debate because they are informed by cultural assumptions that are no longer tenable. For instance, women are naturally inferior to men (7:4; 14:34), slaves are inferior to owners (7:21), and sexual pleasure is systematically dismissed (7:1). Importing wholesale Paul's views on sexuality would, as the argument goes, results in misogyny and racism.

As a self-identifying gay man who pursues academic work in Religion, I find fascinating the reactions that the biblical texts continue to trigger. I come from Spain where "same-sex marriage" became fully legal in 2005 and I am currently living in the USA, where similar disputes are taking place supported by almost identical arguments. Despite the radically different role that Christianity plays in both countries, one could say that Christian rhetoric, as far as sexuality is concerned, remains global. Gay and lesbian Christians continue to be hurt by such rhetoric whose outcome is in many cases fatal. On the other side of the spectrum, many Christians honestly feel that giving up their position on this issue results in a betrayal of their most cherished beliefs.

I think that, although religion is no private matter and it should not be, theological arguments should not determine which policies succeed politically. It is important that the debates go on, every side putting forward their position; but I have the impression that as these debates are carried out in the global context, two important features are not being sufficiently stressed. First, arguments about "homophobia" or "gay tolerance" are not solved exclusively according to reason; instead, "divine revelation" (the Bible) is taken into account. If reason were the means by which the issue is solved, the case would be closed very quickly, for homophobic claims—just as with racist arguments—are very easy to deconstruct one by one.

Second, theological reflection and church politics are missing one important issue when they reflect on the "gay question."We are accustomed to think of "gay" and "straight" as two distinctive categories of persons, two differing exclusive identity categories. As the argument goes, some people are straight, some are gay (and a few are bisexual). Although there are good reasons to think that most people would identify as such, there is much evidence that shows how fluid human desire is. "Gay" and "straight" are terms that classify people according to the gender of the person they are attracted to. Many people find this labeling useful for personal and political reasons. But the fact is that many persons do not follow such categorization and organize their desire following entirely different protocols. For some, gender plays no role whatsoever in the sexual realm: Certain body types, races, status, body parts, situations, settings, or bodily performances are the defining factors. To say it differently, while mainstream discourse would have us believe that everyone has a sexual orientation based on the gender he or she is attracted to, the reality is that many individuals skip such classification by way of organizing desires across multiple and differing axes. Craigslist's personal ads provide a vivid example. In the "homo/hetero/bisexual" model, how does one make sense of a "wmm" (white married male) who self-identifies as "straight," but yet seeks to have sex with certain ethnic types regardless of gender? Here, "bisexual" fails to capture the openness of desire because it continues to conceptualize desire in terms of gender. A bisexual, by definition, is someone who feels attracted to both males and females (gender axis), while here gender identity plays no role in the configuration of desire.

By focusing exclusively on the "straight/gay" divide we might be missing, in the end, a good opportunity to talk about desire in more comprehensive, real, honest, and inclusive ways. Because, in my view, desire skips such clear-cut identities, we need to expand Christian vocabulary to talk about sexuality in general. When all that churches have to say about sexual orientation revolves around the issue of "accepting gays," a wide range of practices, desires, and pleasures remains underscrutinized and, thus, under the privilege of invisibility.

Accustomed as we are to thinking exclusively of sexuality only in gender binomials, 1 Corinthians 6 is a perfect example of how our assumptions shape the text's meaning and not the other way around. After all, those who view Christianity as exclusively heterosexual need to come to terms with Paul's lukewarm, to say the least, recommendations on marriage (7:8–9) or his total lack of interest in procreation. Instead of resorting to specific Pauline passages to support our often judgmental reflections on sexuality, we might interpret Paul as providing instances of a variety of arrangements and, thus, of the virtually infinite ways in which desire can be configured.

Luis Menéndez is a Ph.D. candidate in New Testament and Early Christianity at Vanderbilt University; he taught Theology at Loyola College in Maryland in Alcalá de Henares (Madrid) and Hebrew Bible at Saint Louis University in Madrid.

SEXUAL AND MARITAL ETHICS IN 1 CORINTHIANS 7

Alice Yafeh-Deigh (Cameroon)

I am writing from my social location as a Cameroonian, middle-class, educated, and liberated black Christian woman living in the United States. My consciousness is equally shaped by my unique life experience as one who was a celibate nun for 15 years but who has now become a married mother. When I speak of my identity as a Cameroonian woman, I am referring to my cultural heritage as someone born and raised in Cameroon. Even more specifically, I am a member of the Bamessing ethnic group. The Bamessing tribe is a very small, relatively obscure tribe located in the North West province in Cameroon. In a hierarchically organized society such as that in Cameroon, the Bamessing tribe holds a disadvantaged position with virtually no political or economic power. In fact, I am among the very few who have been privileged to receive a higher education.

My claim to my Cameroonian identity and cultural heritage largely conditions my particular reading and appropriation of Paul's discourse on marriage and sexual ethics in 1 Corinthians 7. This claim acknowledges that my understanding and interpretation of Paul's sexual ethics is grounded in and mediated through my African cultural experiences, which are framed within a larger vision of Afro-womanist-feminist liberation hermeneutics. Furthermore, having lived on three different continents (Africa, Europe, and North America), my personal identity is intercultural and multidimensional with many variables intersecting and interacting in complex ways. Thus, I ground my reading and interpretation in my specific cultural experiences as a Diasporic woman.

As a child from a Christian polygamous relationship, a former celibate nun, and now a married mother, my reading of 1 Corinthians 7 problematizes what many easily derive as *the meaning* of the text. My tripartite experience not only recognizes the nuances and insights of what Paul is saying, but it also perceives the shortcomings of Paul's sexual ethics, particularly when read through the lens of a polygamous marriage in Cameroon. The central task of this essay is to reassess the problem of polygyny in ecclesial communities within the framework of Paul's theology of marriage and sexuality in 1 Corinthians 7.

It has long been recognized that Paul's discourse on the ethics of sex and marriage in this text exhibits a striking mutuality of conjugal rights between spouses. The distributive pronouns *hékastos* and *hékasté* ("each one") have been construed as having specific theological implications for the subject of polygyny. In addition to the *distributive* expression, the possessive reflexive pronoun *heautou* ("her own") and the strong adjective *idion* ("his own")in the context of his specific address to married spouses in 7:1–5 have equally been taken as a ban against polygyny. So, generally, 1 Corinthians 7:2 is seen by many as a bulwark against polygyny; it has often been adduced as fundamental for understanding the New Testament perspective on plural marriages. It is commonplace for interpreters to affirm that the verse condemns polygyny in favor of heterosexual monogyny.

Euro-American moral reasoning about Paul's sexual and marital ethics is inevitably grounded in a culture where monogyny is the normative framework within which sexual and marital ethics are analyzed and construed. They argue that the structure of Paul's arguments in 1 Corinthians 7:2–5 stresses the exclusivity of the individual relationship; hence Paul explicitly prohibits polygyny. Thus, Western exegetes traditionally assume that polygyny is tantamount to adultery. I argue, however, that the text itself does not directly address the issue of polygyny. In 1 Corinthians 7:2, the immediate context shows that the point of the phrase "his *own* wife," "her *own* husband," is to underscore the fact that the proper place of sex is within marriage. The emphasis is on the exclusivity of sex within marriage over against *porneia* (sexual activity outside of marriage). Thus, what Paul considers sexual immorality or fornication is sexual activity outside of marriage. Naturally, Cameroonian society does not regard polygyny as constituting fornication or sexual immorality, since it constitutes a recognized marital state. By necessity, a definition of what constitutes sexual immorality depends on readers' accepted cultural norms—even though cultural acceptance cannot be the exclusive norm for ethical correctness since history has shown that cultures are often willing to accept culturally egregious practices. Regardless, readers in a Cameroon-church tradition would hardly associate polygyny with sexual immorality. This does not, however, mean that because the practice is recognized, legal, and expedient, it is "ethical."

The only way to move beyond the stale debate between proponents and opponents of polygyny is to recognize that polygyny is by no means the focus or topic of Paul's discourse in 1 Corinthians 7, so neither side of the debate can stake legitimacy claims based upon explicit evidence from this passage. As context dictates the particular meaning of a word, the context of 1 Corinthians 7 emphasizes that Paul is confronting the problem of *porneia,* not polygyny. Therefore, in the specific context of this passage, the possessive pronoun should be construed in relation to the explicit problem of *porneia* and not as direct statements against polygyny. In my view, what the possessive pronouns undeniably prove is that Paul imposes reciprocal obligations and mutual consent between spouses in a marital relationship. To prevent *porneia,* Paul urges spouses to maintain sexual relations by mutual consent grounded in reciprocal authority. If Paul's vision of marriage is the moral principle of Christian communities, then any relationship that does not enhance mutuality and reciprocity is to be reproved, be it monogynous or polygynous.

Now, having said that, my contention is that when one situates the discussion of polygyny in the context of Paul's definition of marital love in 1 Corinthians 7, it is difficult, if not impossible, for polygynous relationships in general to fully embody mutual and reciprocal self-giving because the relationships operate within an oppressive, asymmetrical power system of patriarchy. Thus, basedon Paul's directives, the practice of polygyny is ethically inappropriate as an ideal Christian form of marriage principally because it is a structurally imbalanced practice that lacks mutuality and reciprocity. It is not because Paul is directly speaking to the specific situation of polygyny in the passage or that polygyny is tantamount to *porneia* (sexual immorality).

Ultimately, the moral norm of mutuality and reciprocity should serve as an overarching criterion for acceptable moral behavior among spouses in the Christian community. In approaching the problem from this angle, policy-makers will ensure that all marital relationships, not only plural marriages, should embody the ideal of Christian love.

Alice Yafeh-Deigh is Assistant Professor at Azusa Pacific University in California, United States.

Love and Evolutionary Biology in 1 Corinthians 13

Nicolette Emanuelle (United States)

First Corinthians 13 is a beautiful, inspiring, and well-known passage on love. It provides a wonderful guideline on how to love, but it does not reflect philosophically on the nature of love itself, which is what I aim to do here. As a nonreligious reader, I do not see any need to link the idea of love to religion in general, and certainly not to Christianity specifically. Rather love can be defined and conceived of primarily as a series of chemical reactions in our brain which have played a crucial and indispensable role in the perpetuation of our species. That is, love can be defined and understood in terms of evolutionary biology.

Love, indeed, is very complicated and has many different levels. We might say that we love our work, a favorite food, or sports team, our pet, our partner, our family, and ourselves. Surely, the word "love" has different meanings in each of these contexts. But when it comes right down to it, the amazing and exhilarating feeling of love—each and every kind of love—is the result of adrenaline, dopamine, serotonin, oxytocin, and other tangible, measurable chemicals in the brain and body. Numerous scientific studies have shown this. We are all familiar with this idea to some extent. For instance, it is well known that an increase in testosterone in men increases their desire for sex. We can also study the brain of people who are "in love" and find increased amounts of dopamine, which triggers an intense rush of pleasure. It actually has a similar effect on the brain as cocaine.

During childbirth, the female body releases oxytocin, which is crucial in breast milk production and also seems to create feelings of intimacy and connection. When scientists, for instance, block the natural release of oxytocin in sheep and rats, the animals will fail to take care of their own offspring. By contrast, if one injects oxytocin into female rats that have not had sex, they will be drawn to another female's babies and begin treating them as their own. Thus, oxytocin controls how much they "love" their young. Indeed, numerous scientific experiments have shown that we can influence an animal's behavior by injecting or withholding certain chemicals. The same is true of humans; the actions of love are the result of the presence or absence of chemicals in our body.

Evolution, then, has hardwired us to love. Feelings of love lead to mating, and mating leads to the perpetuation of one's genes; more feelings of love—triggered by more reactions in the brain—lead us to take care of our children so the next generation can survive. If you don't love, you don't survive. This is true on the macro-level of the evolution of species, and, more importantly, for our purposes in terms of 1 Corinthians 13, it is true on the micro-level of our human lives.

Paul is absolutely correct when he writes that love is patient, kind, giving, not self-seeking, not easily angered, and so forth. We teach each other to act this way not because of some divine revelation from God, not because some religious book or teacher tells us to do so. Instead, we act this way because, ultimately, our species has learned, it is what's best for us individually and collectively. We love because it gives us the best chance for a happy, meaningful life in community and harmony with others. We want what is best for ourselves and we know deep in our brains that we cannot ultimately get what is best for us by always seeking our own selfish desires. We must love self-sacrificially precisely as Paul outlines in this chapter. When we do, life in the long run is better for all of us.

For instance, we love our children—making numerous physical, emotional, and financial sacrifices for their well-being—because we know that it is advantageous for us personally and society as a whole to do so. Of course, we might not think of it in this detached way, but that is the best explanation. Child rearing is hard! And it takes a long time. Scientists, incidentally, have suggested that the concept of "love" developed among Homo sapiens because of the abnormally long time it takes human young to become self-sufficient. The offspring of most mammals can survive on their own in a few months or maybe a few years. Humans, by contrast, must spend a decade or more raising their young. That requires a lot of "love." Furthermore, think about how much better it is to have a partner in the child-rearing process, which, no doubt, accounts, at least in part, for the development of the idea of marriage among early humans. At any rate, the point is that we don't need a religious book to tell us to love our children; it's already programmed deep into our genes.

Beyond child rearing, all of our human relations require some degree of what Paul describes as love. As the saying goes, "I scratch your back. You scratch my back." When we scratch someone else's back, we are living out Paul's call to love. Again, we might not think of it that way. "I give without expecting anything in return," you might think.

And maybe in religious terms that is "true love." But at some fundamental level, all of your "loving" actions accrue some benefit to you—even if it is just making you feel good. If we put aside our own desires, we will find more peace within ourselves, which is advantageous to us. Moreover, feelings of "love" cause us to persevere in the face of indifference, fear, and heartache. "Love" gives purpose to our everyday lives and without it we may feel hopeless and without hope we may become depraved and destroy each other. Humans thrive when they see meaning and purpose in their lives. Love is purpose.

When we act on feelings of jealousy and anger—also the result of similar chemical processes in the brain—we not only hurt the person it is targeted toward, but we also injury ourselves. Look at how unhealthy our own lives and the world around us becomes when we fail to love. By contrast, if we follow Paul's advice and let love be something that always protects, always trusts, always hopes, and always perseveres, then we as individuals and as a society can reach our full potential.

In sum, 1 Corinthians 13 is a wonderful reflection on the importance of love. But we don't need the Bible or God to love; we only need each other.

Nicolette Emanuelle is a musician, producer, and performance artist who is native to the Southwest United States.

QUESTIONS

1. How does your own context and culture relate to West's notions of heteronormativity in the church?
2. Assess Menéndez's suggestion that Paul's views are based on cultural ideas that are outdated. What are the implications of such an argument?
3. Based on Yafeh-Deigh's observations, what do you think Paul would say about polygyny in Cameroon (and elsewhere) today?
4. How would Emanuelle comment on the statement, "God is love"? How do you view her claim that God is not necessary for love?

CHAPTER 16

GALATIANS

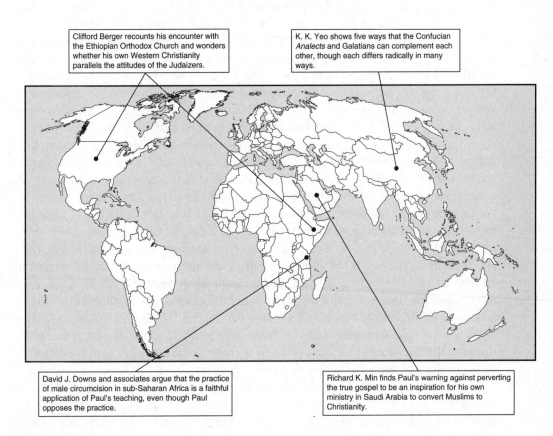

Clifford Berger recounts his encounter with the Ethiopian Orthodox Church and wonders whether his own Western Christianity parallels the attitudes of the Judaizers.

K. K. Yeo shows five ways that the Confucian *Analects* and Galatians can complement each other, though each differs radically in many ways.

David J. Downs and associates argue that the practice of male circumcision in sub-Saharan Africa is a faithful application of Paul's teaching, even though Paul opposes the practice.

Richard K. Min finds Paul's warning against perverting the true gospel to be an inspiration for his own ministry in Saudi Arabia to convert Muslims to Christianity.

READINGS

The Confucian *Analects* and Galatians
K. K. Yeo

The Judaizers and Western Christianity
Clifford Berger

Mohammed and the False Gospel
Richard K. Min

Male Circumcision and HIV/AIDS in Sub-Saharan Africa
David J. Downs, Lucas D. Fuunay, Mary L. Fuunay, Mary Mbago, Agrey Mwakisole, and Jennifer A. Downs

THE CONFUCIAN *ANALECTS* AND GALATIANS

K. K. Yeo (China)

Both Christians and Chinese treasure scriptures as authoritative rules of life, be they that of the Bible or the Confucian classics (such as the *Analects*). Although historical differences in linguistics, thought-pattern, and content exist between the Confucian classics and the Bible, the two scriptures share common ground in the areas of genre study, moral and spiritual teachings, redaction criticism, and commentary history. The varied contents of the texts allow for multiple points of dialogue and resonance. For Christian Chinese familiar with both texts, Chinese biblical interpretation will seek to fulfill Chinese texts with the Bible, just as Chinese scriptures will amplify the Bible. In reading the Epistle to the Galatians, we will here ground our interpretation scripturally, because the canonical texts will provide a more stable hermeneutical tool to construct a Chinese biblical interpretation that is helpful not only to itself but also to *global* biblical interpretation.

The *Analects* and Galatians can complement each other, though each differs radically. The argument between Paul's gospel of faith and his opponent's gospel of works, in Galatians, revolves around whether Christ or the law—or the rituals of Zhou dynasty for Confucius in the *Analects*—grants a life freed from evil and bondage. After Paul describes the temporary function of the law in salvation history—as well as the sufficiency of Christ in granting a life of righteousness and freedom (Gal. 2–4)—he still must prove how life in Christ can guide the *ethical life* of Jewish and Gentile believers. Moreover, after Paul has shown that the Gentiles are included in the covenant of Abraham and have become heirs of God through the endowment of the Spirit, he still must prove that the Spirit guides the communal life of God's people in an ethically vital way without the help of the law. Thus in Galatians 5:13–6:10, he explains how God's Spirit guides God's people to live *in unity and in freedom.* In other words, whether Christ or the law should best symbolize the identity of the people of God is ultimately to be determined by the virtuous life of the community.

A Chinese Christian intertextual interpretation of the *Analects* and Galatians concludes that God's Spirit is the initiator of virtue (*de* in the *Analects*), and that Christ's work shows human beings the divine paradigm for being a community. Christ's community lives out the virtuous life by imitating Christ and yielding to the Spirit. The Spirit grants freedom and out of that freedom comes the fruit of the Spirit. This is a Chinese Christian reading of the *theological ethics* of Confucius and Paul. This *theological ethics* of the *Analects* and Galatians has the following features:

1. It holds to the cosmogonic belief that the universe is theocentric; that is, the cosmos is initially created and sustained by a divine power of goodness. Though Confucian "heaven" (*tian*) as a naturalistic cosmos lacks personal narrative, the transcendent nature of heaven is thought to be *ren* (benevolence) of the moral order; the immanent nature of heaven is expressed in human nature as virtues. A balanced worldview that is theocentric *and* anthropo-cosmic is necessary; otherwise, religion becomes divorced from ethics, alienating divine grace from human endeavor.

2. It works toward an obedience of faith. Though the *Analects* assume neither Adam's fall (sin) nor one's existential estrangement with *tian* (heaven), both Galatians and the *Analects* seek to overcome social conflicts, moral collapse, and spiritual chaos. The difference between the two texts lies in Confucian virtue in self-cultivation and biblical faith in God's grace. However, the Confucian self-cultivation ethic grounded on *ren* (benevolence) and *li* (ritual propriety) can be subsumed under a biblical ethic that is based on the Spirit; together, these two traditions encourage a complete obedience of faith.

3. It transforms each other's worldview. The cyclical history of the *Analects* and the eschatological view of Galatians can mutually critique each other's "either space or time" interpretive assumption. Such mutual critique can move toward a more holistic and dynamic understanding of a multidimensional, spiral-movement universe.

4. It interacts and blesses one another's core being. Galatians' understanding of cruciform love fulfills the Confucian ideal of *ren* (benevolence); additionally, Confucian ethics on propriety (*li*) and music (*yue*) supplements Paul's theology that lacks detailed ethical explication.

5. It motivates all to be authentically human. The relationship between human nature/goodness and divine grace in the Bible and Confucian classics are antithetical; yet, both scriptures agree that only the love of neighbors expresses concretely how to be fully human (*Analects* 15:9) or to be holy (Leviticus 11:44; Matthew 5:48; 1 Peter 1:16).

As we have seen, the *Analects* and Galatians are fairly close at certain points while differing radically from each other. Holding their incommensurability in tension is a challengingly interpretive move of biblical Chinese interpretation that will fulfill each other's blind spots. Christ will complete or extend what is merely implicit in Chinese culture (theology, transcendence, spirit); without Christ, the Chinese ethic, for example, too quickly (even in early Chinese history) degenerates into a system of ritualistic behavior. But the Chinese ethic amplifies various elements of Christian theologies (e.g., community, virtues) underplayed in Western Christianity. The Christ of God (in the Bible) brings Chinese classics and cultures to their fulfillment while protecting the universal church from aberrations of Chinese history, and while protecting China against aberrations of Christian history and interpretation in the West. Chinese biblical interpretation has something to say to the universal church that needs to be heard by all. Chinese biblical interpretation will discover its *global* significance if it can be allowed to find its own biblical interpretation while listening to other contextual biblical interpretations.

K. K. Yeo is Harry R. Kendall Professor of New Testament at Garrett-Evangelical Theology Seminary in Evanston, Illinois, United States; and Academic Director of International Leadership Group, Christian Studies at Peking University in Beijing, China.

THE JUDAIZERS AND WESTERN CHRISTIANITY

Clifford Berger (United States, Ethiopia)

The Apostle Paul's letter to the churches in Galatia is an ancient writing, rooted in the culture and issues of its day, and yet it bears a contemporary message that speaks profoundly to the church in an interconnected world. Galatians can provide something of a template for considering questions such as: How do Christians regard and interact with those who come from different traditions and cultures? What are the essential elements of our faith that bind us together? What kind of influence does a dominant Christian culture try to exert on others? How do we decide what really matters?

I'm on a learning journey myself with regard to these questions. My own heritage and the starting point for my perspective is Western and American. I grew up in a Christian home, and have spent my life in evangelically rooted churches and ministry. This has shaped my understanding of what it means to be a Christian, what constitutes the church, and what is essential to the faith. My background, in fact, is in the churches of the American "Restoration Movement," among whom circulates the traditional axiom: "In essentials, unity; in non-essentials, liberty; in all things, love" (and yet how divided the church has been over what are "essentials"!). The chance to travel and experience some different cultures has, over the years, helped me realize the kind of "bubble" this background has created for me, and has made room for a larger view of the diversity within God's church.

To understand the message of Galatians, one must keep in mind that in the earliest era of the church nearly all Christians were Jewish. Not until Peter proclaimed the gospel to Cornelius and his household (Acts 10) was there a major precedent for Gentiles to embrace the Way (Christianity). Authorship of the Galatian letter is generally dated anywhere from 50–56 C.E.—roughly 20 years after the Christ-movement was launched at Pentecost (Acts 2). At this point the Jewish element in the Christian community would still have been an influential, if not a dominant force.

The Jewish/Christian influence was powerful enough that some of its teachers led a faction often labeled "Judaizers." These teachers proclaimed a rival version of Paul's gospel, in particular in the area of Asia Minor, where the Galatian churches were likely located. This teaching rested on the assumption that in order to become a follower of Jesus Christ, one first had to embrace the basic elements of the Jewish religion. This included, at the very least, submitting to circumcision as a sign of being a child of the covenant. Paul countered this teaching by stressing that disciples of Jesus are not bound to the law—not to any part of it. Rather, they are called to faith/belief in the life-transforming message of God's grace in Christ.

Considering that the original issues of circumcision and the Jewish law are no longer pressing issues for most Christians, Paul's basic theme of grace versus law in Galatians requires ongoing contextualization and application. So what are we to make of it? What are some "take-aways" from the ancient letter that can inform today's church, a church that is far more ethnically diverse and globally connected than ever before?

A fresh angle for getting at these questions may be to look at things from the standpoint of the Judaizers themselves. They are generally seen as the "bad guys" in the narrative (much the same as the Pharisees in the Gospels). While in no way excusing their false teaching which Paul so strongly opposed, it may be that they were simply doing what they thought was right—making sure that their "gospel" represented what was (to them) the dominant narrative of the Jewish roots of the Christian movement.

Believing that one is right, and that others need what you have, is a characteristic of those from a dominant culture. It is one of the things that has caused ethnic and cultural conflict even among Christians. It is what has caused Western missionaries at times to deal insensitively with indigenous practices or customs. For example, on a recent trip to Ethiopia with a cohort of doctoral students from the seminary where I work, we were guests for presentations by priests and faculty of theological colleges of the Ethiopian Orthodox Church, one of the world's oldest continuous forms of the Christian faith. Realizing that the Orthodox/evangelical conflict is likely complex and with multiple aspects to it, what was described to us was that when Western evangelical missionaries originally came to Ethiopia, rather than see the Orthodox Church as allies, they tended to treat them as prospects for evangelism. At least, that is how it was perceived and received, whether intended that way or not. In spite of their Trinitarian and generally biblicallybased doctrine, this was likely because of Orthodox beliefs and practices such as the veneration of Mary and of icons, the adherence to the Apocrypha as scripture, and the use of prayer shawls and unfamiliar liturgies. The missionaries may have been boxed in by their own ethnocentric point of view, imposing their priorities on others without listening, discernment, and weighing "essentials" against "nonessentials."

During that same trip to Ethiopia, our group visited a large Ethiopian Orthodox Church in Mek'ele during Sunday worship. We never actually made it inside, as much of the worship was taking place on the large outdoor portico. Men and women were on different sides, wrapped in white prayer shawls, reading from prayer books, some going up to kiss the wall of the huge stone building. The priest came out during the service and read scripture and preached to the people on the steps. These things, combined with the beggars at the gate and the donkeys wandering around, made me feel that the whole scene was something more like the Jerusalem temple in the time of Jesus than a church in the twenty-first century. It made me realize how very "North American" is our version of Christianity. How presumptuous it would be—even if we mean well—to impose our traditions, practices, and priorities on this ancient Christian culture where the love of Jesus also is evident.

I'm reminded of this when reading Galatians—that the problem Paul was addressing arose because a dominant group (the Judaizers) felt it necessary to impose their practices on others. Perhaps they meant well—but they failed to discern the essentials from the nonessentials. Likewise, as a Westerner, I must come to terms with my own beliefs, traditions, and practices, sorting them according to what is essential and what is not, and avoiding the temptation to impose my preferences on others. How tragic would it be if North American/Western Christianity, with its historic dominant influence, allowed the assumptions that can come with dominance to put us in the position—like the Judaizers—of being the bearers of false teaching.

The letter to the Galatians can help us with this sorting process, and fortunately, the list of "essentials" turns out to be rather short. Lumping all of the Jewish traditions together, Paul declares, "Neither circumcision nor uncircumcision means anything;

what counts is a new creation" (6:15). Furthermore, "You are all sons of God through faith in Christ Jesus, for all of you who were baptized into Christ have clothed your-selves with Christ; for you are all one in Christ Jesus" (3:26–28). By reminding us of the centrality of Jesus, and of the freedom found in grace and faith, Paul equips us with a polar star for discerning what "matters" and what does not.

Clifford Berger is Associate Director of the Doctor of Ministry Program at George Fox Evangelical Seminary, Portland, Oregon, United States.

MOHAMMED AND THE FALSE GOSPEL

Richard K. Min (Saudi Arabia)

In Galatians 1:6–9, Paul speaks his utmost and solemn warnings against any distortion or perversion of the gospel of Jesus Christ that he received and preached. Here Paul twice curses those preaching a different gospel. This passage has truly made a deep impression on me since the early days of my Christian faith and study. Many years ago, I would go out and share the good news of Jesus Christ in the streets of the Bronx, in New York City, and Georgetown, in Washington D.C. At that time I was a young professional at IBM Research Center, working on cutting-edge project in Artificial Intelligence. Little did I know that God was preparing me for ministry in Saudi Arabia years later.

My journey formally began when my senior pastor, upon hearing my Christian con-viction and passion, called me to teach a youth class. I took the call very seriously. It was the beginning of my Bible teaching and serious Bible study. Around that time, I also started to experience something very unusual. Whenever I heard someone preaching or whenever I thought of saying something about the Bible, I felt a tiny strange chill (as if there were a built-in alarm inside of me) warning me not to believe or say anything that might be con-trary to the scripture. I certainly did not want to be like the false preachers condemned by Paul in Galatians 1. This made me cautious and I prayed carefully about my formal Bible study and preparation as a pastor and teacher. In time, the Lord was gracious to me, and I received excellent biblical training and have now been in the ministry for the last 25 years.

In early August 2009, my wife and I were praying and waiting for the call of the Lord for our next ministry. We soon received an unexpected call from a small college in Saudi Arabia inviting me to teach there as a faculty member. We decided to go.

In Saudi Arabia, we encountered many things for the first time. One particularly interesting phenomenon for a Westerner like me was to see the fervor and devotion of Muslims in their daily prayers. The prayers sometime begin as early as 4:30 in the morning. The prayers would boom from the loud speakers of the four mosques near our home. It was a nightmare to wake up in the middle of a night and hear loud chanting from our neighbors. During the daytime prayers, we soon learned that the majority of businesses are closed, with a few exceptions such as hospitals. Many times we were forced to wait outside of the stores until prayer was over. I was also quite shocked to see the commitment of Muslims to proselytize. Individual Muslims made diligent efforts to win converts; also many private and public institutions, including colleges and universities, acted as mission organizations. When a non-Muslim foreigner was hired, their Muslim coworkers would form a support group to convert him or her to Islam. In Saudi Arabia, if one becomes a Muslim, there is $5,000 reward for the convert.

I also learned that in Saudi Arabia anyone who tries to proselytize a Muslim away from Islam faces the death penalty. To avoid this problem, I would often ask those people who were trying to convert me to Islam if they knew what I believed as a Christian. Many of them could articulate the gospel of Jesus Christ; for although Muslims do not accept Jesus as the divine Son of God (he is considered a prophet like Mohammed), they do believe in the Bible (as Mohammed did), including the virgin birth of Jesus. While the Muslims I encountered in Saudi Arabia knew the Gospel, they were not Christians, of course. Muslims are followers of the false prophet Mohammed, who has corrupted the gospel message of Jesus Christ.

This brings us back to Galatians 1 and Paul's warning against perverting the true gospel message. One way to determine true from false teaching is by looking at the moral conduct of the teacher himself. In this case, we know that Mohammed (and Joseph Smith, the founder of the Mormon church) could not be a true man of God, as he was known for many interesting scandals with women. One case was with Aisha, who was a nine-year-old child when she married Mohammed who was in his mid-fifties. Another major scandal of Mohammed was with Zainab, his daughter-in-law. His adopted son Zaid divorced his wife so that she could be Mohammed's wife. This marriage raised two major moral, legal, and doctrinal problems among the Muslim community. First, a Muslim was not to take more than four wives. Second, one was not to marry one's daughter-in-law. However, Mohammed claimed to have received two divine messages from Allah, who sanctioned these problems. First, Mohammed was allowed to have more than four wives. Second, the adoption system and all the adoptions made in the past were to be abolished and nullified. This is what Muslims accept according to their Quran and Hadith (the historical recording of the words and deeds of Mohammed).

Thus, one way that I attempted to subtly share the Gospel with Muslims was to turn the tables on them: I would remind them of these stories about Mohammed from their own scripture and tradition. I would ask them how anyone in good conscience could trust someone like Mohammed as a prophet of God. Surely, an immoral man like Mohammed was a false teacher. When I would bring up these stories I could often see the dismay on their faces, and they hardly ever had an answer for me. These Muslims were beginning to hear and understand the truth by themselves, as the Holy Spirit actively worked in their hearts concerning sin, righteousness, and judgment.

For me, then, Galatians 1:6–9 is a passage that I keep at the forefront of my mind: I want to be a minister who proclaims, with Paul, the one true gospel of the Lord Jesus Christ. That tiny chill is still there, warning me not to follow false teachings or to promote a perverted gospel.

Richard K. Min (Ph.D., M.S., MBA, M.Div., and STM) is an ordained pastor and chaplain; he is currently a Visiting Professor at Taylor University in Indiana, United States.

MALE CIRCUMCISION AND HIV/AIDS IN SUB-SAHARAN AFRICA

David J. Downs, Lucas D. Fuunay, Mary L. Fuunay, Mary Mbago,
Agrey Mwakisole, and Jennifer A. Downs (Tanzania)

If one thing is clear about Galatians, it is that its author, the apostle Paul, passionately and uncompromisingly opposes the adoption of male circumcision among non-Jews in Galatia who had come to believe in the gospel of God's grace through Jesus the Messiah. Paul penned the letter in response to the arrival in Galatia of certain Jewish-Christian teachers who had a very different understanding of the gospel than Paul—or who preached a completely different gospel, as Paul angrily puts it (1:6). These teachers were advocating Torah-observance as a means of Gentile inclusion in the community of God's people, the descendants of Abraham (3:29). And while Paul's opponents probably encouraged Gentile believers in Jesus to follow the entire law of Moses (cf. 4:10), it is the requirement of male circumcision as a sign of identity among the people of Abraham that particularly provokes Paul's ire (cf. 3:1; 5:2–4, 10–12; 6:12–13). So strident is Paul in his opposition to circumcision for Gentile believers that he caustically wishes that those advocating male circumcision would castrate themselves (5:12)!

Today in sub-Saharan Africa, however, male circumcision has the potential to save hundreds of thousands, if not millions, of lives due to its effectiveness as an HIV/AIDS prevention measure. Approximately 2.7 million people were newly infected with HIV in 2010, with 1.9 million (70 percent) of them living in sub-Saharan Africa (unaids. org). Although this represents a decline, both globally and regionally, in new infections per year from a peak in 1997, we should not by any means underestimate the enormous impact that the epidemic continues to have on families, communities, and nations in sub-Saharan Africa. There were approximately 1.2 million AIDS-related deaths in the region in 2010 alone.

In the past several years, three large randomized, controlled trials of male circumcision (MC) conducted in South Africa, Kenya, and Uganda have each shown an approximately 60 percent reduction in HIV incidence among circumcised heterosexual men. The protective effect is thought to occur because of high concentrations of cells that are susceptible to HIV infection in the foreskin. Based on these results, the World Health Organization now recommends that MC "should be considered an efficacious intervention for HIV prevention in countries and regions with heterosexual epidemics, high HIV and low MC prevalence" (http://libdoc.who.int/publications/2007/9789241595988_eng.pdf).

In many parts of sub-Saharan Africa, however, MC does not receive widespread implementation. In our context, the Mwanza region of Northwest Tanzania, a recent study of over 4,000 late-adolescent boys found that only 17.3 percent had been circumcised. There are a variety of cultural, economic, and religious factors that contribute to this low rate. First, the dominant tribe in the regions of Mwanza and Shinyanga, the Sukuma, is traditionally noncircumcising, has no rituals of circumcision, and, in the past, has often espoused pejorative views of the practice. Second, the procedure is not widely available at regional hospitals and health-care centers, and it is frequently prohibitively expensive (approximately $20–25 USD) when it is offered. Third, the practice of MC in this region is deeply influenced by religious identity. Among Muslim adolescent males, 61 percent undergo circumcision, compared with 18 percent of Christians. One of the significant findings of focus group interviews conducted by our team among Christians in the region in 2011 is that, while Christians believe that their views and practices should be shaped by scriptural teaching, there is a great deal of confusion regarding what the Bible teaches about the topic of MC. Physical circumcision—as opposed to "spiritual circumcision" or "circumcision of the heart" (cf. Romans 2:27–29) as metaphors for spiritual and ethical purity—is almost never discussed in churches.

What might it mean, then, to read Paul's letter to the Galatians in such a context? Is it possible to offer a reading of this epistle—a letter in which the apostle Paul mounts a vigorous and uncompromising polemic against the practice of male circumcision—that could be employed by Tanzanian church leaders and theological educators to promote the very practice that Paul so strongly opposes?

Our reading of Galatians contextualized in light of MC as an effective HIV/AIDS intervention in East Africa is rooted in the apocalyptic nature of the epistle. Paul's opponents (and perhaps Paul himself at an earlier point in his life; see Galatians 5:11) were advocating circumcision as a means of Gentile entry into the family of Abraham, a religious position indicative of a worldview in which Torah is central and the cosmos is defined and divided according to the antinomy of circumcision and noncircumcision, Jew and Gentile.

Paul's letter to the Galatians is an attempt to explode that particular binary cosmology. Following Paul's experience of the revelation of God's son (1:16), the old world—with its antinomies between Jew/Gentile, circumcision/uncircumcision, Law/not-Law—was obliterated by the cross of Jesus Christ. This leads Paul to declare twice in Galatians that the antinomy of circumcision and uncircumcision has ceased its world-defining role: In 6:14, for example, Paul explains that in light of the cross of Christ, the old way of structuring the cosmos, and human social relations within it, through the governing binary of circumcision/uncircumcision has been crucified to Paul—and Paul to this cosmos. In Paul's apocalyptic perspective, therefore, Christ-believers in Galatia must not submit to the rite of circumcision because the practice, in that particular context, denies the invasive, world-shattering power of the gospel and reflects a cosmology characteristic of "the present evil age" (1:4) rather than the new creation effected in the cross of Jesus Christ.

Given this apocalyptic reading of Galatians, an appropriate Christian embodiment of Paul's message in Tanzania in light of the realities of the HIV/AIDS crisis would, it seems to us, encourage the very practice that Paul discourages, while also standing with Paul in his apocalyptic view of the world. Apocalyptic eschatology has fundamentally to do with the conviction that *in the present time* God has inaugurated a liberating war against the powers that have enslaved humanity and set the world in opposition to God—powers that Paul elsewhere identifies as Sin and Death (see esp. Romans 5–7). In the context of the Galatian controversy, Paul presents circumcision as problematic in part because the Law that prescribed the practice was itself involved in the enslavement of humanity (3:23–25; 4:3–5, 21; 5:18). Since "neither circumcision nor uncircumcision" is anything, an insistence that *uncircumcision* is mandated for Christians as a faithful interpretation of Paul falls victim to the same cosmological binary that Paul works so hard to challenge in Galatians.

Thus, we suggest that, from a theological perspective informed by Paul, circumcision as an identity marker for God's people or a means of defining the world is not a viable option for those who read Galatians as Christian Scripture. Yet that conclusion paves the way for a consideration of the role that advocacy of the practice of MC might play in a robust theology of embodied existence. We would insist that God's care for the health and wholeness of the physical body is an integral part of the New Testament's witness (see, e.g., Jesus' ministry in the Gospels of healing the sick, lame, blind, etc.). Therefore, to the extent that male circumcision offers numerous health benefits to Tanzanian Christians (not limited to HIV/AIDS reduction, but also including the prevention of urinary tract infections and some types of cancer, as well as the reduction of other sexually transmitted infections), the practice can be supported, not as a badge of identity for male inclusion within the local church, but as a public health intervention that has the potential to diminish significantly the loss of life, dignity, and power associated with the HIV/AIDS epidemic.

We would suggest that Galatians is an apocalyptic text of *life* that has an important role to play in the battle against the *death* brought by HIV/AIDS. We ought to do all we can to restore dignity to those living with HIV/AIDS and also to prevent the spread of the disease to more people in sub-Saharan Africa, all of whom are created in God's image. As the apostle Paul himself says at the conclusion of his letter to the Galatians, "So then, whenever we have an opportunity, let us work for the good of all, and especially for those of the family of faith" (6:10).

David J. Downs is Associate Professor of New Testament Studies at Fuller Theological Seminary in Pasadena, California, United States. Jennifer A. Downs is Assistant Professor of Medicine at Weill Cornell Medical College in New York, New York, United States. Lucas D. Fuunay, Mary L. Fuunay, Mary Mbago are instructors at P.A.G. Bible College in Mwanza, Tanzania. Agrey Mwakisole is a Pastor and Regional Bible School Coordinator for the Pentecostal Assemblies of God Tanzania in Mwanza, Tanzania.

QUESTIONS

1. What do you think Paul would say about Yeo's notion that the *Analects* provide a valuable complement to Paul's letter?

2. Is there inevitably a "dominant group," as Berger discusses, in every culture which forces its religious views on others? Is there one in your culture? If so, are you part of it?

3. What is your assessment of Min's contention that Mohammed is a false prophet? How, if at all, would your application of Galatians 1:6–9 differ from Min's?

4. Explain in your own words what Downs and his associates mean when they write: "The old way of structuring the cosmos, and human social relations within it, through the governing binary of circumcision/uncircumcision has been crucified to Paul—and Paul to this cosmos."

CHAPTER 17

EPHESIANS

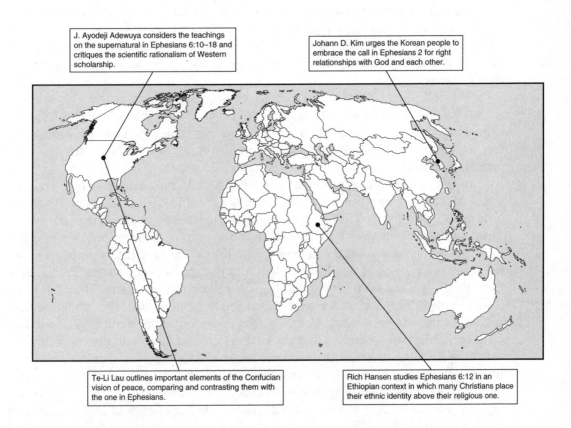

J. Ayodeji Adewuya considers the teachings on the supernatural in Ephesians 6:10–18 and critiques the scientific rationalism of Western scholarship.

Johann D. Kim urges the Korean people to embrace the call in Ephesians 2 for right relationships with God and each other.

Te-Li Lau outlines important elements of the Confucian vision of peace, comparing and contrasting them with the one in Ephesians.

Rich Hansen studies Ephesians 6:12 in an Ethiopian context in which many Christians place their ethnic identity above their religious one.

READINGS

A Call for Koreans to Practice Right Relationships with God and Each Other
Johann D. Kim

Ephesians 6:12 in an Ethiopian Context
Rich Hansen

The Supernatural in Ephesians and a Critique of Scientific Rationalism
J. Ayodeji Adewuya

Comparing Ephesians and the Confucian Vision of Peace
Te-Li Lau

A Call for Koreans to Practice Right Relationships with God and Each Other

Johann D. Kim (Korea)

Since 1945, the tiny nation of Korea has been divided into two nations because of ideological differences. South Korea is a capitalist nation, while the North is communist. There are also major religious differences. North Korea follows the path of Juche (translated "self-reliance"), while the South has become increasingly Christianized. Into this context of division, strife, and tension between North and South Korea, we can turn to Paul's call in Ephesians 2 for unity in Christ as a source of hope for the future of Korea.

The first major Christian revival in Korea occurred with the arrival of missionaries in 1907 in, ironically enough, the current capital city of what is now North Korea, Pyongyang. The revival swept the whole country, with some reports showing that more than a quarter of a million conversions occurred within a year. Indeed, after the 1907 revival, the city of Pyongyang began to be called "Jerusalem of the East."

In 1945 things changed dramatically when Kim Il-Sung established the separate nation of North Korea when it was liberated from the colonial rule of Japan. He developed an ideology that took its root in Marx-Leninism but soon became a personality cult called Juche. Since his death in 1994, Kim Il-Sung has been worshiped as a god and Juche has become the national religion in North Korea. The idea that the Juche ideology functions as a religion in North Korea becomes undeniable when we realize that they have places of liturgical functions just like the church in Christianity. They call these places "Kim Il-Sung Revolutionary Thought Study Centers" and there are more than 450,000 of them in the country. Here is where, according to the North Korean political dictionary, "the party members and the laborers are equipped with the comrade Kim Il-Sung's immortal revolutionary thought, Juche ideology and the glorious history of revolution in order to advance the revolution." There are such centers at every factory, office, or government building as well as every high school and college. These buildings are built according to standardized designs: three stories with lecture halls and various rooms for discussion and study. In the cities, any work unit with more than 100 workers has its own center. In rural parts of the country, at least every other village has a center. These centers are maintained with utmost care in order to keep them spotlessly clean. Inside the center, the portraits of Kim Il-Sung and Kim Jong Il (his son and successor) are prominently displayed. People are expected to enter the centers without wearing coats and shoes.

In stark contrast, in South Korea Christianity has grown to be one of the largest religions in the nation (Buddhism being the other major one), with close to 10 million followers, nearly 30 percent of the population. However, the numerical growth of Christianity in Korea does not tell the whole story. Numerous reports of corruptions and scandals in the Korean churches have seriously undermined its credibility among the public, where the church ranks dead last in trustworthiness in opinions polls. The essential problem is Mammonism: money, greed, and power. Indeed, the rapid economic growth in the last quarter-century swallowed the gospel of Jesus and spit out a new type of religion mixed with the powerful and sweet gospel of prosperity, which has, unfortunately, mesmerized many. The church is in crisis. If in the north, Juche replaced Christianity, then in the south, Mammonism has replaced it.

In Ephesians, Paul argues that it is God who unifies the universe under the lordship of Jesus Christ, his Son. Paul declares that "you were dead through the trespasses and sins" (2:1). But Jesus defeated "the ruler of the power of the air" on the cross and we were made alive together with Him in resurrection because of God's abundant mercy and love toward us. Paul argues that we have been saved by the grace of God so that no one can boast—it is the gift of God (2:8–9). Not only did God save us by His grace, but also He prepared beforehand "good works" for us to carry on with our lives. In 2:11–22, Paul delineates the nature of the good work that God prepared for us: It is none other than to work to be "one new humanity" (2:15) in Christ who broke down the dividing wall of the hostility and became our peace (2:14). Paul uses Temple imagery to explain this process: "In him the whole structure is joined together and grows into a holy temple in the Lord; in whom you also are built together spiritually into a dwelling place for God" (2:21–22). The vertical restoration of humanity's relationship with God results in the horizontal restoration of relationship between people.

This is the message that the Korean people must embrace. This is the good news of God that is being spoken to them. Both in North and South Korea, people are still following their passions of the flesh, its desires and senses (2:3). It appears that very few Christians have survived the long period of persecution in the North. Likewise, it seems that very few faithful and renewed Christians have survived in the tainted churches in the South. However, if we know the power of God who raised Jesus from the dead, we also believe that it is possible for us to see another revival in Korea, not just in the South, but also in the North, and the Korean people will become one again in the Lord. With Paul, we confess, "there is one body and one Spirit, just as you were called to the one hope of your calling, one Lord, one faith, one baptism, one God and Father of all, who is above all and through all and in all" (4:4–6). Amen.

Johann D. Kim is Associate Professor of New Testament at Colorado Christian University, United States.

EPHESIANS 6:12 IN AN ETHIOPIAN CONTEXT

Rich Hansen (Ethiopia)

Human life flows through various "structures of existence" that give coherence to our lives—government, family, religion, social expectations and traditions, and so forth. One's clan, tribe, or ethnic group is a prime example of these structures that bring order and cohesion to life for many of the world's people. In Ephesians 6:12, Paul warns that these structures of existence can be invaded by and even taken over by evil powers. When he speaks of the "principalities and powers," he is referring to the fact that good structures God created for the benefit of the world (Colossians 1:16) have been warped from their good purpose and now stand in opposition to God and Christ (Colossians 2:8).

Human government is a perfect example. Paul speaks of the positive role of the "governing authority" as God's servant in Romans 13; yet in the book of Revelation we see this same Roman government vilified as the "beast"—the instrument Satan uses to bring horrible persecution to the early Christians. An even better example is the Old Testament law, which the Bible repeatedly tells us was God's gift to his people. Yet Paul is just as clear in Galatians that this law has mutated into an enslaving legalistic power, keeping people from Christ. Theologian Stanley Grenz offers this helpful summary:

> Despite God's good intention for the structures, however, they can be manipulated for evil purposes. In this manner, what God intends as a means to promoting community can actually weaken it. Rather than aiding people in building community, the powers enslave them. Structures become a channel for evil, whenever they are pressed into the service of evil ends (Theology for the Community of God [Grand Rapids: Eerdmans, 1994], 233).

So the structures God intends for good, to bring meaning and stability to human life, can (and often *do*) become warped and evil.

Here in Ethiopia, as in much of the global south, ethnic identity is *the* primary structure that not only tells people "who they are" but makes life both meaningful and livable day-to-day. Ethnic diversity—Ethiopia has more than 80 distinct people groups—enriches the society in the same way biological diversity enriches our natural world. But exactly because ethnic identity is such a primal structure of existence, it is always susceptible to be co-opted by the "principalities and powers" to spawn great evil. The Hutu versus Tutsi ethnic cleansing in Rwanda in which more than 800,000 died was a dramatic demonstration of what continues to happen under the radar of worldwide attention. About two years ago, deadly conflict erupted between two tribal groups in western Ethiopia, tragically including Christians taking up arms to fight one another, sometimes even members of the *same congregation*. Ethnic identity trumped Christian identity.

However, when Christians consider their ethnic identity, we encounter a paradox. Unlike Islam, which forces Muslims worldwide to worship in the Arabic language, Christianity promotes exactly the opposite—planting faith and worship as deeply as possible in every indigenous language and culture. In Ethiopia, vast resources are being expended translating the Bible into many tribal languages because we Christians believe so strongly (especially after the mistakes of the nineteenth-century mission colonialism) that every human being has the right to grow as a disciple of Jesus Christ without having to reject his or her own ethnic/cultural identity.

But *tribalism*—giving ultimate loyalty to one's own ethnic group—is idolatry. Tribalism is always lurking around churches here, ready to snatch what God intends for good and turn it toward evil. Particular tribal groups, who jealously guard the leadership positions for their own tribe and are unwilling to share power with those from other tribes, dominate most Protestant denominations in Ethiopia. Minorities are made to feel "second class" by those in the majority. Churches split and withdraw from one another over which language to use in worship.

Ethiopian Christian leaders struggle mightily against ethnic identity being co-opted by the "principalities and powers" and turned into the false god of tribalism. However, they are not alone. The Apostle Paul engaged in the same struggle throughout his ministry. Listen to his own confession in Philippians 3:4–7: "If anyone else thinks he has reasons to put confidence in the flesh, I have more: circumcised on the eighth day, of the people of Israel, of the tribe of Benjamin, a Hebrew of Hebrews; in regard to the law, a Pharisee; as for zeal, persecuting the church; as for legalistic righteousness, faultless. But whatever was to my profit I now consider loss for the sake of Christ." Eugene Peterson in his modern English paraphrase, *The Message Bible*, translates the last verse with extra punch: "Compared to the high privilege of knowing Christ Jesus as my Master, firsthand, everything I once thought I had going for me is insignificant—dog dung."

In his words we can recognize Paul's subtle pride in his own ethnic heritage. Paul is *not* saying everything about being a Jew is "dog dung." He is not criticizing his Jewishness in and of itself anymore than in other places he criticizes the Old Testament law in and of itself. No, it is *to what purpose* that ethnic identity (or the law) is used. Whenever Paul's ethnic heritage gets in the way of following Christ...whenever people assume they are part of "God's people" simply because they are Jewish, or Amhara, or Oromo...whenever, in short, ethnicity is overrun and bent toward evil by the principalities and powers...*then* Paul will set aside his heritage and be sure everyone in his church knows it. In relative terms, his new identity in Christ is far *more* important to him than his ethnic identity.

Paul's radical Magna Charta of human identity is this: "There is neither Jew nor Greek, slave or free, male or female, for you are all one in Christ Jesus" (Galatians 3:28). This is the challenge for church leaders here in Ethiopia—where ethnic identity is still "everything people have going for them" to get ahead, to belong, to survive. Church leaders here are challenged to walk in the Apostle Paul's sandals, let his mind-set shape their own personal agenda, and then declare that Christian identity always trumps ethnic identity as passionately and as courageously as Paul does. Will outsiders look at the church and see the same ethnic rivalry, nepotism, and even violence they are accustomed to seeing between tribal groups in every other sector of society? Or will they look at the church and see Christians not denigrating their ethnic heritage but setting it aside whenever necessary in favor of their far greater identity as *"one in Christ Jesus"*?

Rich Hansen is Professor of Systematic Theology at Ethiopian Graduate School of Theology, Addis Ababa, Ethiopia.

THE SUPERNATURAL IN EPHESIANS AND A CRITIQUE OF SCIENTIFIC RATIONALISM

J. Ayodeji Adewuya (United States)

Ephesians 6:10–18 is perhaps one of the clearest descriptions in the New Testament of the nature of the spiritual warfare that believers face. Yet its interpretation is less than clear due to cultural influences. Paul does not call the believer to enter into spiritual warfare. He simply announces it as a fact. The fact that our real battle is not against flesh and blood is lost on many Christians, who put all their efforts in that direction. This passage informs us of the nature of our divine weapons, which imply the nature of the struggle that we are in.

Proper preparations are the key to executing a successful war. One aspect of preparation is to know the enemy's capabilities and limitations. C. S. Lewis makes the perceptive observation: "There are two equal and opposite errors into which our race can fall about the devils. One is to disbelieve in their existence. The other is to believe, and to feel an excessive and unhealthy interest in them. They themselves are equally pleased by both errors, and hail a materialist and a magician with the same delight" (*The Screwtape Letters* [New York: Macmillan, 1961], ix). Perhaps at no other time is C. S. Lewis' observation more important than in the twenty-first century. Western scholarship is dominated by antisupernaturalistic rationalism in which the mention of evil powers in the New Testament is as a myth that needs to be removed in order to make the message suited to a postmodern scientific age. Such understanding not only refuses to share the first-century Mediterranean worldview concerning the spirit world but also argues that supernatural powers are incapable of interfering with, or interrupting, the natural realms of cause and effect. Other scholars, although recognizing and accepting the presence and reality of the supernatural forces as described by Paul, nonetheless diminish their primary malevolent influence. As such, the powers are considered to refer to good angelic powers rather than to hostile demonic forces. These interpreters also suggest that the powers refer to social, economic, and political structures that affect people's everyday lives. Thus, these powers constitute "a collective symbolization of evil" and the "collective weight of human existence." These interpretations are different from Africa, where there is a deeply rooted belief in a mystical power or force in the universe. As such, there is no difficulty in accepting the existence and reality of the influence of evil spirits. Without doubt, the African and the first-century Mediterranean share similar beliefs about the spirit world. Thus, the African understanding of Ephesians 6:10–18 is closer to Paul's than that which prevails in the Western hemisphere.

Paul describes the enemy in rather vivid terms. It is completely irrelevant if the particular opponent we face is a "principality," a "power," or a "ruler of the darkness of this age." Collectively, they are all members of spiritual hosts of wickedness in the heavenly places. They are all part of a spiritual army that is organized and established into ranks and under the headship of Satan, the devil, who comes against us with his wiles. These are not just "the world of axioms and principles of politics and religion, of economics and society, of morals and biology, of history and culture." Such a view is reflective of people in the Western hemisphere who downplay the existence of real evil forces that wreak havoc in the world. Paul believed in the personal character of the powers of evil in the universe.

Paul lists several items of the believer's armor in the order in which they would be put on. Together they comprise the *panoplia* worn before taking the field. First is the belt of truth to deflect the lies and tricks of the devil. The "breastplate of righteousness" stands for uprightness and integrity of character. But this moral rectitude and reputation for fair dealing results directly from the appropriation of Christ's righteousness. Christians are not to seek their protection in any works of their own but only in what Christ has done for them and in them.

Once the breastplate has been fitted into position, the soldier puts on his strong army boots. The Christian soldier must have the protection and mobility that come with one's feet "shod with the preparation of the gospel of peace." The Christian soldier is then to "take up the shield of faith." For the Christian this protective shield is faith, both in action and in its objective content. With such a shield, the believer can extinguish all the incendiary devices flung by the devil (v. 11). The Christian's shield effectively counteracts the danger of such diabolical missiles not merely by arresting or deflecting them, but by actually quenching the flames to prevent them from spreading.

The Christian's only weapon of offence is "the sword of the Spirit." "The word of God" is the divine utterance or speech, the powerful spoken word. Finally, Christians are to "pray in the Spirit on all occasions." By doing so, they can stand firm and true, successfully resisting all enemies and spiritual foes only as they remain in the spirit of prayer, ready always to cry unto the Lord and lay all their needs before him.

In brief, in Ephesians 6:10–18, Paul not only assures us that there is a spiritual war but also warns us that apart from utilizing the weapons which God has provided for us, we are hopelessly underpowered. If we plan to win the battle, we must rely on provisions and resources beyond human capabilities.

J. Ayodeji Adewuya is Professor of New Testament at Pentecostal Theological Seminary, Cleveland, Tennessee, United States, and a Fellow at Manchester Wesley Research Centre, Didsbury, Manchester, United Kingdom.

COMPARING EPHESIANS AND THE CONFUCIAN VISION OF PEACE

Te-Li Lau (United States)

Ephesians and the Confucian *Four Books* (a collection of four key Confucian texts) both share a grand vision of peace. The Ephesian vision of peace encompasses the household, the local church, the heavenly church, and the cosmos; the Confucian vision of peace likewise encompasses the household, the state, the empire, the world, and the cosmos. Moreover, both demonstrate a complex relationship between ethics, politics, and metaphysics. Putting both texts in conversation may therefore provide insights for a fresh perspective of Ephesians. Here I will briefly outline important elements of the Confucian vision of peace, compare and contrast them with Ephesians, and conclude with some implications for reading Ephesians.

The Confucian *Four Books* is traditionally ascribed to Confucius and his school. Confucius lived during the Eastern Zhou period (770–256 B.C.E.), a time of great political upheaval that saw the dissolution of old feudal structures. Framed within the chaos and anarchy of this period, Confucius and his disciples created a vision of peace that attempted to recapture the stability of the glorious past as witnessed in the Western Zhou Dynasty (1100?–771 B.C.E.). This vision encompasses several elements:

1. The Confucian vision of peace is dominated by the concept of harmony. Harmony is not static uniformity; it is the dynamic unity and tensive balance that forms when one pole constantly adapts to the push and pull of other poles. Such a harmony or perfect balance is brought about by proper practice of the rites that reflect the underlying pattern or principle of all things in the universe. Although originally developed within a religious context, the concept of rites gradually expanded into a complex system whose scope includes norms of acceptable behavior in all aspects of human life: from liturgies in various ceremonies, such as weddings and sacrifices, to norms regulating social conventions, such as receiving a guest, and to rules of conduct in the minute details of life, such as sweeping the floor.

2. Confucianism envisions peace in multiple concentric circles of focus: individual, household, kingdom, and the cosmos. At the individual level, peace is the full realization of one's innate good moral nature, the maintenance of perfect balance in all aspects of life, and the uniting of one's feelings, thought, will, and action. At the household and the kingdom level, peace results from the acceptance of one's preordained social station in life and the fulfillment of one's moral and social obligations within the social and political hierarchy. At the cosmic level, peace ensues when all beings realize their innate principle, proceeding according to their nature and the Way of Heaven.

3. The means of attaining peace within the multiple concentric circles of focus starts with the moral cultivation of the individual. Only individuals who have fully realized their nature and become a sage are able to develop the nature of others through a ripple-like effect, thus bringing harmony first to their immediate household, then their kingdom, and then the entire world. The moral influence of the sage does not, however, stop at the human social world; it also encompasses the cosmic and natural order. Sages who manifest absolute integrity form a trinity with Heaven and Earth, participating in their transformative and generative processes which ultimately bring balance and peace to the cosmos. The sequence for implementing the vision of peace is thus laid out as follows: Individual ➔ Household ➔ Kingdom ➔ World ➔ Cosmos.

4. Given the political context in which Confucius lived, the primary frame of reference for his vision of peace is the state, and the intended audience includes the intellectual elite, political advisers, and rulers. If the Confucian vision of peace begins with the moral cultivation of the individual, then the primary individual in focus is undoubtedly the king. When the king acts virtuously, he will effect the ethical transformation and renewal of the people as they imitate his example.

We turn now to a comparison with the Ephesian vision of peace. Ephesians was written to various Christian communities in Asia Minor who were familiar with the Jewish Scriptures, not least of which is the creation account in Genesis (Eph. 3:9). The Ephesian vision of peace is therefore located within a context of initial cosmic order followed by a rupture and chaos that necessitates a reconciliation and uniting of all things under Christ. This larger context differs from Confucian thought as it does not seek to recover the past but to forge a new cosmic order, a new creation (2:10, 15; 3:9; 4:24). Further comparison with the Confucian vision of peace can be laid out as follows:

1. While Confucianism is dominated by the concept of harmony and balance, the Ephesian vision of peace is communicated by a cluster of terms including "peace" (2:14, 15, 17; 4:3; 6:15), "reconciliation" (2:16), "unity" (4:3), "submission" (1:22; 5:21, 24), and "oneness" (4:4–6). Moreover, while Confucian harmony is brought about by meticulously following the prescribed rites at every social level, the Ephesian vision of peace is brought about by means of Christ's death on the cross. Christ plays such a vital role in the Ephesian vision of peace that not only is he the *basis* for peace, he is also the *locus* (1:10; 2:13; 3:6) and the *personification* (2:14) of peace.
2. As in Confucian thought, Ephesian peace operates at multiple levels. In the human sphere, peace is the elimination of ethnic enmity between Jews and Gentiles, the use of individual gifts for building up the ecclesial body, and the maintenance of household codes within a framework that presents God in Christ as the true *pater familias*. In the spiritual sphere, peace is the reconciliation of believers to God and their incorporation into the body of Christ. In the cosmic sphere, peace is the summing up and uniting of all things under the headship of Christ (1:10).
3. In contrast to Confucian thought, Ephesians considers the basis for attaining peace not to rest on human effort but on the prior work of Christ. Due to Christ's sacrificial death, believers are reconciled to God and consequently to one another; due to Christ's subjugation of the cosmic powers, cosmic peace is inevitable. Ephesians nevertheless stands in the tension of the "already" and "not yet." The Ephesian vision of peace has been decisively inaugurated, but its full realization will only occur in the coming age (1:21; 2:7). Standing in this tension, the church must embrace the unity brought about by the Spirit (4:3) so that it can function as the proleptic symbol of the future perfect unity under Christ. The existence of a united church then proclaims to the evil spiritual powers that their authority has been broken and that their demise is certain.

4. The primary frame of reference for the Ephesian vision of peace is the church, and the intended audience is not the leaders of the church but its members. As an intentional community or voluntary organization, the church seeks to transform members with different worldviews and backgrounds into a unified body politic. Central to this goal is the formation of a common pool of values (4:4–6); a common communal history that recalls their election before the foundation of the world (1:4) and their formation through the death of Christ (2:16); and a common understanding that they are no longer strangers and aliens, but fellow citizens and familial members within God's household (2:19).

Finally, we can consider some of the implications for reading Ephesians. The ability to compare meaningfully Ephesians with the overtly political Confucian texts confirms the presence of political elements in Ephesians. Nevertheless, one must not ignore its theological character. It is therefore best to understand Ephesians as a politico-religious letter on peace that lays the framework for constructing a new communal identity within the reality of Christ's supreme rule. Ephesians lays out the foundational narrative of the community, explaining that believers were predestined before the foundation of the world. It also guides the church to embrace the certain hope of a fully restored cosmos in the coming age (1:10, 21; 2:7). Ephesians, however, does not only present past and future aspects of the ecclesial community in relationship to God's decisive act in Christ; it also stresses the present mission of the church. By setting ethical standards for the community and presenting their present life as a conflict with malevolent spiritual forces that threaten ecclesial unity, Ephesians urges the church toward peace so that she can function as a testimony to the power of God's plan of reconciliation in Christ. In a time where the church is still divided by cultural, ethnic, geographical, and socioeconomic factors, the message of Ephesians is still powerfully relevant today.

Te-Li Lau, originally from Singapore, is Assistant Professor of New Testament at Trinity Evangelical Divinity School, Deerfield, Illinois, United States; he is the author of The Politics of Peace: Ephesians, Dio Chrysostom, and the Confucian Four Books, *from which this essay is taken.*

QUESTIONS

1. How are Juche and "Mammonism" alike? How are they different?
2. How, if at all, is Paul's "ethnic heritage" different from the context in Ethiopia?
3. How do your own views about the existence of evil spirits compare to Adewuya's? What arguments would you make in support of your position?
4. Which vision of peace do you find more appealing, the Confucian or Ephesian one?

CHAPTER 18

PHILIPPIANS

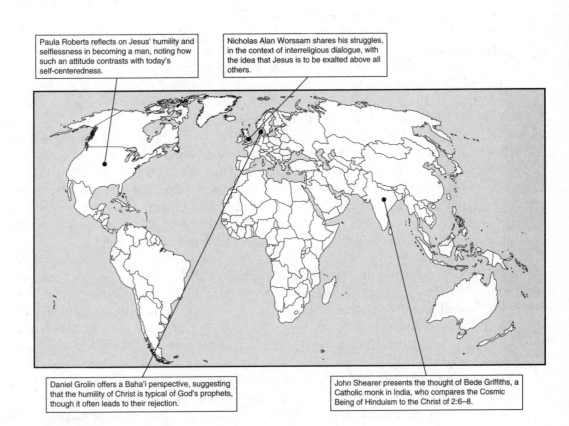

Paula Roberts reflects on Jesus' humility and selflessness in becoming a man, noting how such an attitude contrasts with today's self-centeredness.

Nicholas Alan Worssam shares his struggles, in the context of interreligious dialogue, with the idea that Jesus is to be exalted above all others.

Daniel Grolin offers a Baha'i perspective, suggesting that the humility of Christ is typical of God's prophets, though it often leads to their rejection.

John Shearer presents the thought of Bede Griffiths, a Catholic monk in India, who compares the Cosmic Being of Hinduism to the Christ of 2:6–8.

READINGS

"Jesus Exalted above All Others" and Interreligious Dialogue
Nicholas Alan Worssam

The Cosmic Being of Hinduism and the Christ of 2:6–8
John Shearer

A Baha'i Perspective on the Humility of Christ
Daniel Grolin

Jesus' Humility in Contrast to Today's Self-Centeredness
Paula Roberts

"JESUS EXALTED ABOVE ALL OTHERS" AND INTERRELIGIOUS DIALOGUE

Nicholas Alan Worssam (United Kingdom)

One passage that I have inhabited for many years comes from Philippians 2:5–11. It is a beautiful passage, probably in its original form a hymn that Paul has adapted for his letter, filling out the earlier statements with explanatory phrases. As such it is one of the earliest statements of Christian belief, one of the hymns to Christ that the first Christians sang in the catacombs or in their own homes in the gray light of their early morning meetings. It is a hymn that glorifies Jesus for his role in the salvation of humankind, showing his descent from heaven as Son of God, his saving death and resurrection, and exaltation in glory. It is a kind of creed, a forerunner of the more formal and fully developed Christian doctrinal statements (e.g., Nicea).

But it is also a problematic passage, particularly for those of us who have been involved in interfaith dialogue or who have drawn deeply from the wells of wisdom in other religious traditions, such as Buddhism. Is it true that Jesus is exalted above all others, and that every knee will bend at the name of Jesus, submitting to him as Master and Lord? To the ears of a Buddhist, this passage can sound triumphalistic and overbearing. As such, it requires careful examination if it is to be understood in a way that makes sense of our contemporary experience of the encounters of different faiths.

In fact, however, there are many ways of understanding this passage from Philippians, rooted in the text itself, yet open to a wider embrace of other religious traditions. First, Paul exhorts his readers to have "the mind of Christ," which is in itself a bridge to the Buddhist emphasis on the mind as the focus of the spiritual path. It is a mind of love, compassion, sympathy, and joy (three of the Buddha's "Divine Abidings"). For Paul, as for the Buddha, it is a mind that moves radically beyond self.

Second, this passage is not necessarily about a divine redeemer descending from above. There are many New Testament scholars who see this rather as a meditation on the role of Adam, and of Christ as the new archetypal "everyman." Philippians 2:6 speaks of Christ as being "in the form of God," but this is an echo of Genesis 1:27, where it says that "God created humankind in his image." Likewise, in Colossians 1:15 Paul says that Christ is "the image of the invisible God." Christ, then, is to be understood as the new Adam.

Paul then goes on to say that Christ "did not regard equality with God as something to be exploited" (or grasped). As with the Buddha, it is attachment, particularly to self, that is the root cause of suffering. A truer response is that of self-emptying (*kenosis*), though a Buddhist would nuance this by encouraging the realization that there is in fact no self to grasp. For the Christian, this grasping of equality with God is the sin of Adam, which Christ rectifies by his relinquishment of all grasping at self. Adam and Eve literally grasp the fruit of disobedience, thinking to gain the knowledge of good and evil, and so fall into the primordial dualism of self and other, gain and loss, life and now-inescapable death. Christ, however, humbles himself, accepting death, not holding on to one side of the life–death continuum. His divinity is expressed by his letting go of divinity—his life lived by nonattachment to life or death.

Just as the Buddha teaches that the path to enlightenment is open to all, so the new Adam, Christ, shows us the way to a new humanity, revealing a death to self in which we are all encouraged to share (Phil. 3:10). The death of Christ is an inclusive event, in which everyone who dies to themselves and lives by the power of the Spirit of God may participate. Christ's death is ours, just as we share in the power of his resurrection. All are linked to the Adam recapitulated in Christ: "For as in Adam all die, so in Christ will all be made alive" (1 Corinthians 15:22).

But then we get to the tricky part of Philippians 2: "Therefore God also highly exalted him and gave him the name that is above every name, so that at the name of Jesus every knee should bend." Does this mean that the particular name "Jesus" is above every name, and that at the name "Jesus" every knee shall bow? That is the traditional understanding and what I had always, despite my interfaith embarrassment, felt to be the unavoidable interpretation. But to really understand this passage I think we need to ask again: What is the name that is given to Jesus? I suggest that it is the unspeakable name YHWH, first revealed to Moses at the burning bush (Exodus 3:14). YHWH means something like, "I am who I am" or simply "I AM." With added vowels for pronunciation, "Yahweh" is really a breath, a sound of sheer silence.

When this concept is translated into Greek, we get further clues to this divine name carried by Jesus. YHWH in the Greek becomes ὁ ὼν, pronounced *Ho Ōn*, and translated The One Who Is. This is the name often found inscribed in the nimbus (halo) around the head of Jesus in Orthodox icons. The name given to Jesus, then, when pronounced in Greek is merely an exhalation of breath, rather than a name per se. (Is it just a wild flight of fancy in my mind that connects this with the Sanskrit divine name of *Aum* or *Om*?)

So, in the Philippians passage, the name given to Jesus is YHWH, otherwise known as The One Who Is, Being Itself, the Eternal. So while the name "Jesus" is still profoundly precious to Christians, it need not be understood as a name truly beyond all names. Thus we are able to move toward a more universal, inclusive understanding of this text, one that fits more comfortably in interfaith conversations.

In sum, this enigmatic passage from St. Paul's letter to the Philippians is full of surprises. It takes us back to Christ the new Adam, the truly Human One, who, by his humility and self-emptying, is given the name beyond all names. It shows that there is nothing to grasp and everything to receive, that God speaks God's name within us, and we are set free. And Paul wishes that the joy of this discovery, the compassion and sympathy that it evokes, be the ever-present experience of those "who have the mind of Christ."

Nicholas Alan Worssam is a member of the Anglican (Episcopalian) religious community, the Society of Saint Francis; he is based at Glasshampton Monastery in Worcestershire, England.

THE COSMIC BEING OF HINDUISM AND THE CHRIST OF 2:6–8

John Shearer (India)

The Cosmic Being, or the Universal Self (Purusa) as it is called in certain branches of Hinduism, is a concept that is quite difficult to put into words, often evading description and clear understanding. The Spirit of the Cosmic Being is everywhere, but we cannot see it. It is not necessarily meant to be seen, but to be experienced in the heart of our very being. It is a notion that can be found at the deepest core of many religious traditions, assuming the same elusive nature in each one, yet ever present within our very selves and in everything around us. It exists within us all, and can be found only when one relinquishes control of that which is material, and looks inward, wherein lies an in-depth wisdom that rejects the ego and selfishness. Still, we are only human, and to our finite minds this concept of a Cosmic Being is difficult to grasp.

Bede Griffiths (1906–1993) was a Catholic monk who lived in India and adopted the practices of Hindu monastic life; he wrote 12 books on Hindu–Christian dialogue. According to Griffiths, the figure of the Primordial Cosmic Being is an archetype that can be found throughout history among many of the world's traditions, thus linking humanity together in a Universal Spirit. In Christianity this all-encompassing figure is the Cosmic Christ that we see in Philippians 2:6–8 and Colossians 1:15, where Jesus Christ is referred to in His original form as the firstborn of all creation and in whom all of creation in heaven and on earth was brought into existence. While many have understood this to be saying that Jesus is God, for Griffiths this passage was specifically saying that He is the manifestation of God, or the Primordial Man in whom God revealed Himself. Griffiths goes on further to state, "What happened was that He emptied Himself of that heavenly state, and took the form of a (universal) man" (Griffiths *A New Vision of Reality: Western Science, Eastern Mysticism and Christian faith* [Springfield, IL: Templegate, 1990], 122). Here Griffiths is referring specifically to the notion expounded on in Philippians 2:6–8, which says that Christ is, "in the form of God...but emptied himself...being born in human likeness," as well as that found in Colossians 1:15, which refers to Christ as the image of the invisible God. This implies that the invisible God's image, or reflection that was created in the beginning, and was the preexistent, all-encompassing Christ, was at once the same as, and yet distinct from, God. As Griffiths points out, all things were made through Him and for Him, but they were not made by Him, again distinguishing between God and Christ (Griffiths, *A New Vision of Reality*, 123).

Griffiths also claimed that the Cosmic Christ, in which the fullness of God dwells, is truly at the center of each and every one of us, within our heart, at the depths of our very being. He elaborates further on this idea, saying, "the one Spirit is present in every moment of love...The Father gives Himself in love to the Son, who is the very form, expression, of his love...This is its [the universe] coming into being, this response to the drawing of Love. At the same time it's [the Cosmic Christ-Universal Soul] being continually drawn to give itself in love...and so the rhythm of the universe is created" (*Return to the Center* [Springfield, IL: Templegate, 2002], 60–61). He went on to say that the Cosmic Christ is also within every religious tradition, including Hinduism, Buddhism, and Islam, even though members of various traditions may not know it. He is even present in the hearts and minds of those who claim not to believe in anything at all. This being the case, we are all united in the Cosmic Christ. As Griffiths asserts, "Our ecumenical task is to cooperate with that mystery of grace, seeking to discover that presence of Christ in every religion and in every human soul" (*Christ in India* [Springfield, IL: Templegate, 1984], 177).

In accord with the claim that the Cosmic Christ is present in every religion, Griffiths expounds on the form He takes in other various traditions, one of those being Hinduism. In this tradition the Cosmic Being is known as the Atman (Self), or Purusa. Throughout the epic tale *The Bhagavad-Gita* the god Krishna elaborates on who the Self is. The first reference to the Self is in 2:17–19 where Lord Krishna tells the warrior Arjuna that this great presence, this Universal Soul, is indestructible, pervading all the eye can see and beyond. Krishna continues to elaborate on the essence of this Cosmic Being, claiming that He is enduring, constant, and primordial. Here Krishna is imparting to the much grieved prince Arjuna who is facing a terrible battle that we are all part of the ever-present Self, which endures beyond all that is.

Krishna then goes on to reveal to Arjuna that it is he (Krishna) who is actually the Cosmic Being, referring to himself as the womb of all creatures and the source of the universe. Krishna explains how humans can fully embrace him, and enter into him, the Cosmic Being upon death: "A man who dies remembering me at the time of death enters my being when he is freed from his body; of this there is no doubt."

Akin to the concept of the Atman (Self) or Universal Soul, the Cosmic Christ belongs to the figure of the Son within the Holy Trinity, but it is Christ in His heavenly, universal form, larger than life, and far more profound than the human mind can even begin to fathom. As such, He is the bridge that connects humanity and the world directly to the Divine. In *The Bhagavad-Gita* Krishna reveals himself as the cosmic, all-encompassing spirit, permeating throughout all of creation, and in which all of creation exists. Likewise the Cosmic Christ, this Cosmic Being, is ever present, and to know it one must be silent, listening deep within to that which speaks to the heart.

This Cosmic Being is the Universal Spirit who connects humanity and all of life back to the source, the Godhead. It can only be perceived in spiritual terms, requiring one to think outside of time, space, and that which is material. That this is a universal notion makes sense, for when one looks at the myriad traditions and religions of the world, and the goals therein, they will see many similarities. Griffiths says the primary goal of all religions is "the absolute, transcendent state, the one Reality, the eternal Truth, which cannot be expressed, cannot be conceived. This is the goal not only of all religion, but of all human existence" (Griffiths, *Return to the Center*, 74). He claims that essentially all religions are the same, and all will ultimately end in the same understanding of the Cosmic Being.

John Shearer is a graduate student of Religious Studies at Florida International University, United States.

A Baha'i Perspective on the Humility of Christ

Daniel Grolin (Denmark)

Baha'u'llah is the prophet founder of the Baha'i Faith. There is, I would propose, a certain way in which God sends his chosen ones, such as Baha'u'llah, which is unchanging like the seasons, and which the keen observer can recognize. This is the underlying assumption of Jesus' Parable of the Fig Tree (Luke 21:29–31) and his condemnation of weather-watching hypocrites (12:54–7) and in Baha'u'llah's many allusions and references to the Bible, calling his readers to consider carefully the lessons of the past. One of the most important lessons is the cautionary tale of rejection of God's emissary.

At the heart of the rejection is how God's emissary appears. In Paul's letter to the Philippians he refers to what one might think of as divine humility. In the hymn of Philippians 2 the image of Adam is used to compare and contrast. Adam too was made in the form (*morfe*) of God (2:6; Genesis 1:26). Unlike Adam, Jesus did not seize divinity to become the same as (*isa*) God (in Genesis 3:22 God says that man had become like God), instead he became like a servant (2:7). Unlike Adam who was cast out of Paradise, Jesus was exalted by God (2:9). Yet, until his crucifixion Jesus appeared to most as nothing but a servant.

Nevertheless we must ask why so many of Jesus' contemporaries reject him. Certainly one reason was a sense of complacency about their religious assumptions. John the Baptist castigated "this generation of vipers" for not showing proper repentance, and relying on the assumed safety of the thought, "We have Abraham as our father" (Luke 3:7–8). I once asked a bishop if he would be willing to discuss the merits of the Baha'i Faith and in answer I was told that as far back as one could remember it was Christianity that had carried them through. Such a response has a striking similarity to the kind of reliance on forefathers that John the Baptist condemned. Surely when one venerates the faith of one's forefathers because it is the faith of one's forefathers, it has become a veneration of one's forefathers.

Yet, forefathers made mistakes. Because when prophets come, it is seldom a comfortable thing. It was easier to kill prophets than to heed them. Heeding them meant changing the status quo. Those who were in a position of power (rulers, priests, and learned) were particularly interested in keeping their positions. People not only failed to accept Jesus because of fear of losing their leadership status, or the status granted by wealth, but sometimes they were also simply caught up in their own expectations. Paul addresses this idea several times in his writings. For instance, 1 Corinthians 1:22–23 reads, "Because Jews require a sign and Greeks want wisdom, but we proclaim Christ crucified, an offense to Jews and foolishness to Greeks." Likewise, in Philippians 2, Christians are urged to have the mind of Christ, who made himself into nothing, took the form of a servant, humbled himself, and willingly died a humiliating death on the cross. This is not the type of person that would naturally be recognized as a divine emissary. A dead man on a cross could hardly be God in the flesh.

Jews required signs that would demonstrate that Jesus was who he said he was, but Jesus failed to live up to almost every expectation that most Jews had for the Messiah. To be sure, Christians referred to scripture that they regarded as fulfilled by Jesus, but none of these were what the Jews wished to see fulfilled. They had no need for a humble Messiah, but wanted one who would stand against Rome. Was that not what had been prophesied? Where was Elijah on the chariot of fire which whorled him into heaven (2 Kings 2:11) who was supposed to return on the great and dreadful day of Yahweh (Malachi 4:5)?

Ironically, the Romans expected something akin to it. The idea of a divine man was not incredible: Caesars were clearly and manifestly divine and visibly powerful since they ruled most of the world. What was incredible was that a poor, humble man from an insignificant village, from an unremarkable family, was divine. Who was this Jesus who had been executed embarrassingly like a common criminal? To believe such a one was divine was utter foolishness. For instance, sometime in the second century, in Rome, someone thought to poke fun at some Christian acquaintance by the name Alexamenos, by depicting him worshipping a crucified man with a donkey's head. Like Jews, Christians were widely believed to be worshipers of donkeys. Such foolishness was obviously worthy of the graffitist's derision.

What was more, Christians were superstitious. The same label was also used of Jews, but unlike Jews, Christianity could not, in a society that venerated all things ancient, call upon great age to garner respect. The Greek word *deisideaimonia* applied to Christians (which stands in place of the Latin *superstitio*) literally means "fearful of demons." The label had the sense of people who were immoderately scrupulous in their observance of religious practice. This behavior, which was offensive to the sensibilities of the educated people of the Graeco-Roman world, was regarded as stemming from an ignorance of how deities behaved, and leading to a fretful following of religious cultic minutia. All of this was, of course, utter foolishness, as absurd as trying to imitate the humility of a crucified criminal.

But today, of course, it is clear that those who labeled Christianity as a superstition failed to heed history. The foolishness of the present may turn out to be the established wisdom of the future; the lowly servant who died on a cross might turn out to be the one whom God exalts (Phil. 2:9). As George Santayana said, "Those who cannot remember the past are condemned to repeat it."

In the opening passage of his *Book of Certitude*, which makes extensive use of the Bible to present its arguments, Baha'u'llah writes that "No man shall attain the shores of the ocean of true understanding except he be detached from all that is in heaven and on earth." He later goes on to state:

> Consider the past. How many, both high and low, have, at all times, yearningly awaited the advent of the Manifestations of God in the sanctified persons of His chosen Ones. How often have they expected His coming, how frequently have they prayed that the breeze of divine mercy might blow, and the promised Beauty step forth from behind the veil of concealment, and be made manifest to all the world. And whensoever the portals of grace did open, and the clouds of divine bounty did rain upon mankind, and the light of the Unseen did shine above the horizon of celestial might, they all denied Him, and turned away from His face—the face of God Himself. Refer ye, to verify this truth, to that which hath been recorded in every sacred Book. (Chapter XIII)

Philippians should remind us that Jesus, despite his divinity, outwardly was only a servant, and that he was crucified on a cross, the final sign of rejection. And yet Jesus was exalted by God. Unfortunately, the same thing has again happened with Baha'u'llah: Too many have rejected God's emissary because he came in an unexpected form. Indeed, Baha'u'llah observed in his own days that many were too taken with their preconceptions to see that Baha'u'llah had come to once more fulfill God's promise of guidance and salvation.

*Daniel Grolin (Masters of Computer Engineering, University of Southern Denmark) is an information technology architect, journal editor (*Baha'i Studies Review*), and author (*Jesus and Early Christianity in the Gospels: A New Dialogue*).*

JESUS' HUMILITY IN CONTRAST TO TODAY'S SELF-CENTEREDNESS

Paula Roberts (United States)

He is obviously maladjusted; the poor soul doesn't think much about himself but focuses on meeting the needs of others regardless of what it costs him personally. He doesn't even demand his rights or what he is entitled to. What a perfect candidate for an "extreme makeover." He needs a good therapist who would reprogram his thinking, shift his values, and teach him to look out for "number one."

Interestingly enough, this individual is joyful, content, fulfilled. His life has meaning and direction. He is at peace, has no worries, and enjoys lasting, loving relationships. So, what's the problem? There is none. He has what we all desire. His example: Jesus Christ.

It begins with the Christmas story—the birth of Jesus, the Son of God. We picture Him sweetly resting in a manger and stand in awe of His miraculous virgin birth. Equally profound and incomprehensible is the fact that this baby boy Jesus was God incarnate, God born in the flesh. In Philippians 2:5–11 the Apostle Paul presents a clear, concise synopsis of this life- and death-changing event. Let's place these verses in context. In verses 1–4 Paul is encouraging the church at Philippi to be one in love, spirit, and purpose. He instructs each believer to do nothing out of selfish ambition or self-glorification, to humbly esteem every person better than himself, and to concentrate more on the welfare of others than his own.

Paul then exhorts the Philippians in verse 5 to adopt the attitude of Christ, which he proceeds to reveal in the subsequent three verses. Although Jesus Christ was in His very essence unalterably God, He did not concern Himself with asserting His right to be equal with God. He did not tenaciously cling to His supreme existence, His omniscience, omnipresence, omnipotence, majesty, glory, privileges, or honor. Instead, in an inconceivably selfless act, Jesus emptied Himself not of His deity, but of all that was rightfully and uniquely His in order to become a man, a mere human being. He abandoned His life in the heavens among the angels, forfeiting his seat at the right hand of His Father God, to take up residence shoulder-to-shoulder with sinful mankind.

It is virtually impossible to grasp the ramifications of Jesus becoming man, clothing Himself with the rags of human nature; it transcends the mind. Reduced to an ordinary life with its mundane routines, countless limitations, and unpleasantries, confined to a physical body susceptible to infirmities, surrounded by flawed man in an imperfect environment is at best an epically inadequate portrayal of what the God–man endured.

Verse 7 captures the depth of Jesus' extraordinary journey on earth. Not only did He condescend to become a man, but also assumed the position of a bondservant, the lowliest of the lowly, a person without status, power, respect, or entitlements of his own—not a role to be coveted or envied.

It would be reasonable and justifiable to expect the Son of God to safeguard His glory by detaching Himself from the masses and joining the upper class with its power, prestige, and comfortable lifestyle. No one would begrudge Him that. In unparalleled contrast, however, He elected to be less than a commoner and to serve rather than be served.

Submission was the hallmark of a servant. The same held true of Jesus with God as His master. In His case, however, perfect obedience ushered Him to death's door. In one stunning final demonstration of love, humility, and obedience, Jesus died on a cross, the most excruciatingly painful and degrading form of execution imposed on a human being. He willingly suffered the punishment for the sins of all mankind, establishing the one and only way to God. Without the sacrifice of Jesus' sinless life, sinful man would forever be alienated from God and condemned to eternity apart from Him.

Paul concludes the passage by recounting in verses 9–11 the exaltation of Jesus. Reflecting on His son's obedience, God bestowed on Him a name which is above every name. That name and all it represents is worthy of worship from every thing and every being, in every place, bowing down and confessing that Jesus is Lord, to the glory of God, the One who willingly relinquished His son to redeem man.

Without a doubt, Jesus Christ in His incarnation epitomized the life Paul outlined for the Philippians to pursue, which could be condensed in two words—"be selfless." Reversing the syllables of *selfless* pinpoints its meaning—less self. Not something we are eager to hear and certainly not an acceptable or popular philosophy in today's world.

Self is a driving factor, a powerful motivator, a relentless priority in our society. Self-actualization, self-esteem, self-worth, self-love—number one sits proudly on the throne. Yet, man remains restless, still searching for meaning, peace, joy, contentment, and love. Perhaps there is another way.

Paula Roberts is a retired English teacher, author, freelance editor, and nonprofit director.

QUESTIONS

1. Assess Worssam's argument that "YHWH" is the name given to Jesus. What implications does this have for an interfaith interpretation beyond those mentioned by Worssam?

2. Is the Cosmic Christ compatible with Philippians 2:6–8? How would Griffiths deal with verses 9–11?

3. How might one who accepts Christ as an emissary of God, but not Baha'u'llah, argue with Grolin?

4. How is the biblical context important for Roberts? Does she offer a compelling reading of verses 5–11 in light of verses 1–4?

CHAPTER 19

1-2 TIMOTHY AND TITUS

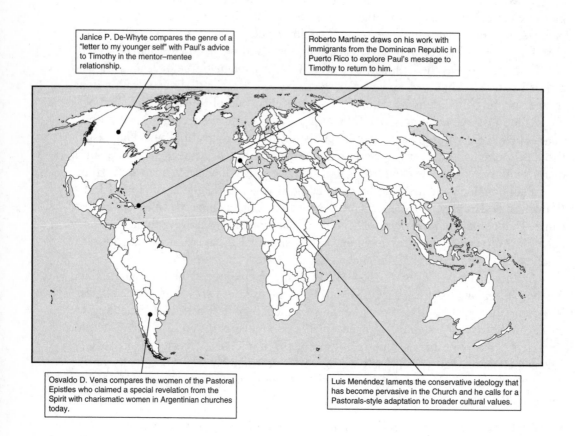

Janice P. De-Whyte compares the genre of a "letter to my younger self" with Paul's advice to Timothy in the mentor–mentee relationship.

Roberto Martínez draws on his work with immigrants from the Dominican Republic in Puerto Rico to explore Paul's message to Timothy to return to him.

Osvaldo D. Vena compares the women of the Pastoral Epistles who claimed a special revelation from the Spirit with charismatic women in Argentinian churches today.

Luis Menéndez laments the conservative ideology that has become pervasive in the Church and he calls for a Pastorals-style adaptation to broader cultural values.

READINGS

The Pastorals and Progressive-Liberalism
Luis Menéndez

Women in the Pastorals and in Evangelical Churches in Argentina
Osvaldo D. Vena

Paul's Relationship with Timothy
Janice P. De-Whyte

"Faith and Family" for Paul and Immigrants in Puerto Rico
Roberto Martínez

THE PASTORALS AND PROGRESSIVE-LIBERALISM

Luis Menéndez (Spain)

Known as the Pastoral Epistles, 1 and 2 Timothy and Titus feature straightforward "administrative" instructions for specific groups in the early church (women, leaders, and elders). This focus on administrative structure is usually seen as a departure from a fresher, more charismatic, "spirit-led" Pauline theology as portrayed in the so-called "authentic corpus" (i.e., books authored by Paul himself, as opposed to the Pastorals which were presumably not written by Paul). Scholars mostly agree that the Pastorals represent an advanced stage in church institutionalization, a more hierarchical mode of authority that replaced the charismatic view of power and looser community structures—where, for example, women would have been leaders—seen in earlier Pauline documents such as 1 and 2 Corinthians or Romans. As time passes by, movements and organizations that may have initially had little structure or organization (thus could be led by anyone who was "spirit-filled") begin to sort out inner and outer conflicts by developing new rules and regulations (which limit the number and types of people who could have power and authority in the church).

I am a 35-year-old Spaniard pursuing Ph.D. studies in New Testament in the USA. To a certain extent I consider myself a "theological exile," someone who decided to abandon his country because of the suffocating theological climate. As a long-standing left-wing activist, there is certain irony in coming to the "belly of the beast" to find intellectual freedom and theological openness. Spain has been a democracy for 36 years now. After a civil war (1936–1939) that lead to a right-wing dictatorship supported and legitimized by the national Catholic Church, my country entered a full-fledged democracy in the late 1970s and, at the religious level, pursued *aggiornamento* (a spirit of change and open-mindedness) inspired by the Vatican II, not without numerous ecclesiastic conflicts. Despite a long tradition (under the dictatorship) that equated Christianity to fascism, in the mid-1980s the fresh breeze coming from an incipient Liberation Theology taught many Christians (including myself) that it was possible to reconcile religious beliefs with leftist activism. To say it differently, Latin American Liberation Theology provided the theoretical, theological, philosophical, and biblical ground for many of us Spaniards not to opt out of religion. Theological creativity thrived, church activism increased, long-held gaps between the religious and the civil collapsed. It was a time and place where, despite serious conflicts, it was possible to explore new paths in biblical theology in an attempt to disentangle religion from its past linkage to an infamous dictatorship.

Nowadays, however, the most conservative ideology has become pervasive in church life, both at the intellectual/theological level and in terms of community-based activism. The material consequences are appalling: Liberationist approaches have been erased from seminary education, and most social transformation movements have been suffocated. Official statements have increasingly aligned with right-wing politics and belligerently opposed any progressive-liberal position (abortion rights, divorce laws, education bills, gay-marriage, and so on), legitimizing such positions on a purportedly orthodox view on "truth" and "tradition."

How is this situation related to the Pastoral Epistles? As noted, the Pastoral Epistles could be interpreted as an attempt to reread the recent Pauline tradition in socially accommodating terms. Take for instance the so-called household codes (Titus 2:1–8; 1 Timothy 2:8–15; 1 Timothy 5) where detailed instructions regarding virtuous behavior (and right doctrine in the text's own words) are addressed to church leaders (Titus or Timothy) and target specific groups (husbands, women, widows, etc.) The strengthening of behavioral rules for congregants is caused by a desire to fight heterodox groups that question the supposedly proper authority of Timothy and Titus and by a willingness to conform to the imperial ethos, that is, the standard cultural norms of the day.

Regarding the first cause, the Pastoral Epistles insist on "sound doctrine" (2 Timothy 2:17) against those who defend *heterodidascalia* (the other teaching) and dismiss them as just interested in vain discussions (1 Timothy 6:4) and as corrupting women's thoughts (2 Timothy 3:6–9). Regarding assimilation, the Pastorals tend to conform to the imperial virtue system at the same time they recommend submission to official authorities (Titus 3:1). So how is this connected to the aforementioned context in contemporary Spain? The enforcement of tighter doctrinal and practical Church rules strikingly resembles that of the Pastoral Letters. The rhetoric deployed to legitimize such strategies is also very similar: terms like "truth," "tradition," and "orthodoxy" are used to dismiss alternative configurations of the Christian ethos. For instance, while the Pastorals emphasize those aspects of the Pauline tradition less favorable to women's roles within the community and stress the authority of the "legitimate" male leaders, the Catholic Church in Spain not only has done away with any attempt to read Vatican II in an emancipatory fashion, but it has also banned any possible *heterodidascalia,* that is, any dissenting view (thus "feminism" and "liberation theology" are seen as false teachings).

A full-blown parallelism between the two contexts might obscure, however, the reasons behind the adoption of such strategies both in the present and in the past. For the Pastorals, the conflict with "deviant" knowledge can be read as an attempt to adjust to the imperial ethos and to pass as normal by appealing to a broader base of believers. In the Spanish case, on the other hand, the struggle to remain in "sound tradition" pits the Church "against culture." As the latest polls indicate, society increasingly views the Church as anchored in the past and out of touch with modern sensibilities. It is interesting to notice that, by pursuing an analogous approach, the ideological outcome of implementing similar strategies turns out to be the opposite: adaption to culture in the past, contestation of society in the present.

The question of whether the Christian message ought to be cultural or counter-cultural depends on the context in which such an issue is raised. In the Spanish case, and reading from a liberationist perspective, the room for optimism is small. While in the past, on the one hand, adaptation resulted in more restrictive roles for women and a strengthening of imperial values, in the present, contestation has had the effect of displacing feminism or any emancipatory movement for that matter from the theological agenda, and censoring those teachings or traditions that threaten to unsettle the *status quo.*

For me, the status quo is precisely what must be up-ended by emancipatory theologies. Thus, a Pastorals-style adaptation sensitive to feminism, liberation theology, and other leftist contributions might help to deepen the national dialogues between the religious and the secular spheres.

Luis Menéndez is a Ph.D. candidate in New Testament and Early Christianity at Vanderbilt University; he previously taught Theology at Loyola College in Maryland in Alcalá de Henares (Madrid) and Hebrew Bible at Saint Louis University in Madrid.

Women in the Pastorals and in Evangelical Churches in Argentina

Osvaldo D. Vena (Argentina)

The main issue in the Pastoral Epistles (PE) seems to be "false" teachers who promote doctrines opposed to the traditional Pauline teachings. The Pastor (the author of Timothy and Titus) attempts to bring his congregation in line with this tradition by invoking the name of the long-gone apostle (Paul). Apparently part of the "false" teacher's doctrine appealed to women because it gave them an opportunity to escape their role in the patriarchal household by avoiding marriage and exercising some type of leadership in the congregation. Legends like those found in the apocryphal work The Acts of Paul and Thecla, which featured Thecla as a celibate and prominent female coworker of the apostle, may have inspired them.

In connection with the work of the "false" teachers, the author addresses the subject of wealth. This idea appears especially in 1 Timothy 6:1–19, where he distinguishes between "those who want to be rich" and "those who in the present age are rich." The PE do not seem to judge people by their social status or their desire to exercise leadership. Rather the opposite seems to be the case, namely, that it was expected that the leaders would have a recognized position in society. This may explain why the Pastor does not criticize "those who in the present age are rich" (6:17) but rather "those who want to be rich." Furthermore, the Pastor is not objecting to some people's aspirations for positions of leadership (cf. 1 Timothy 3:1 where he affirms this "vocation") but rather to the fact that some think that these offices are a means for getting richer. Therefore he advises his audience to be content with the basics of life (6:8). The desire to be rich, the love of money, is something to be shunned, a temptation which leads people into destruction. And he accuses some of doing precisely that.

But who were these people who wanted to be rich? In trying to find out their identity, one has to delve deeper into the broader rhetoric of the PE:

a. In 2 Timothy 3:6 women who follow the false teachers are described as being "swayed by all kinds of desires (*epithumiais*)." In 1 Timothy 6:9 those who want to be rich are said to be "trapped by many senseless and harmful desires (*epithumias*)."

b. In 2 Timothy 2:26 the "opponents" are described as being captive in the "snare (*pagidos)* of the devil." In 1 Timothy 6:9 those who want to be rich fall into temptation and a "snare" (*pagida).* Interestingly enough the Latin Vulgate adds "of the devil" to the verse.

c. In 1 Timothy 1:19 those who rejected conscience have "suffered shipwreck in the faith." In 1 Timothy 6:9–10 those who want to be rich have "wandered away from the faith" (cf. 4:1) and their fate is described in terms that correspond to the shipwreck metaphor: "...foolish and selfish desires that *plunge* people into *ruin* and *destruction*."

All of this strongly suggests that those who wanted to become rich were the false teachers and their followers, among them perhaps were women and young men who aspired to some of the positions of leadership in the church. These people were competing with the existing officers of the congregation for positions of leadership and were probably charging a fee for their instruction, so the author accuses them of doing it out of love for money (6:5, 10). But when the author talks about those who in the present age are rich, he seems to be addressing a different group. He cautions this group to be willing to share their wealth and to put their hope in God but does not say anything about money being the root of all kinds of evil! It is obvious that the author is exercising here a double standard. Some people, adult males, heads of households, which made them wealthy *de facto*, are allowed, even expected, to lead. Others, especially women, even if they were wealthy (1 Timothy 2:9–10), were excluded. The main objection to women's leadership seems to be, then, not their love of money but their gender.

I come from a lower-middle-class family of artisans in Argentina. My father was a cobbler who converted to a conservative, almost fundamentalist, version of Protestantism in a church founded by U.S. missionaries. *Evangélicos* were, and still are, a minority in a predominantly Roman Catholic country. Women in my church did not have an official position but they held considerable power when allowed by the minister who is always male. They were Sunday school superintendents, teachers (the best I had!), presidents of youth groups, deaconesses, and so on. But they never preached in the main worship service. Preaching was the domain of the pastor and only occasionally an elder or a deacon would be given this responsibility. Women had a very important function in the congregation but it was always a supervised, limited role. Nonetheless they managed to develop important ministries that made a difference in people's lives.

But in the late 1960s things started to change. The charismatic movement, imported from the USA, swept through the country and created problems among many conservative churches, mine included. Women were prominent in this charismatic movement. Because charismatic practices were at odds with the practices of my evangelical denomination, when women were influenced by the charismatic movement, their work in my church was disqualified. One of the main objections was to women having the gifts of tongues and interpretation of tongues. Therefore women in churches in my denomination who became charismatic in this regard found themselves excluded from the traditional ministries in which they had always participated (Sunday school teachers, deaconess). They found support only among the charismatic-minded members who slowly but surely separated from the congregation to form their own independent, though marginal, group.

Likewise, the women of the PE claimed a special revelation from the Spirit, independent from the control of the officers of the church, through whom the gifts of the Spirit were mediated (1 Timothy 4:14). Because of that they were demonized, ridiculed (2 Timothy 3:6; 1 Timothy 4:7), and excluded from positions of leadership, especially teaching—although they were allowed to teach young women to be submissive to their husbands (Titus 2:5). The women in my congregation, who also claimed to have received a special anointing of the Spirit that allowed them to speak and interpret tongues and to perform healings through the imposition of hands, were also excluded from leadership in even the traditional ministries. They could no longer teach Sunday school, lest they would infect those young minds with their charismatic doctrine. They were forbidden to speak, not to mention to teach, about their experience.

A surface-level reading of the PE would suggest that the teaching of false doctrines and the love of money that sprang from it were the main problems being confronted by the author. Women who followed these false teachings were then excluded from the traditional ministries of which they had previously been permitted to participate. But the real reason for their exclusion was their gender, as 1 Timothy 2:11–15 clearly shows. Something similar happened in my home church. The limited access women had to the ministries of the church was further hampered when they embraced the teachings of the charismatic movement. And so it is to this very day that the same attitude remains in many of the more conservative denominations of Latin America: Women are an accessory to the male minister, enjoying a limited freedom, thus depriving congregations of alternative styles of leadership that are most needed and that would balance out the usually male-dominated, patriarchal style. The fact that these denominations tend to read the Bible as the literal Word of God does not help, for they find ample justification for their ideas in the PE.

Osvaldo D. Vena is Professor of New Testament Interpretation at Garrett-Evangelical Theological Seminary, and Ordained Minister with the Reformed Churches of Argentina.

PAUL'S RELATIONSHIP WITH TIMOTHY

Janice P. De-Whyte (Canada)

As a theologian and a youth pastor, I read the Bible not only for its theological intentions but also to understand the people and social contexts described. The epistles of Paul have long been esteemed as the doctrinal center of the New Testament. In our mining for theology, however, we risk missing the treasures of the social and relational nature of these epistles, particularly that of 1 and 2 Timothy.

While containing theological teachings, these letters are profoundly relational in nature. Serious doctrinal disputes, controversies, and church management procedures are discussed, yet Paul's heart for the young Timothy is very visible. First and Second Timothy are two letters from a father to his son in the faith, from a mentor to a mentee, and from a more traveled friend to one who is just beginning his life. As such we do a disservice to ourselves when we focus only on the doctrinal details and miss the relational atmosphere.

Paul's letter to Timothy can be helpfully viewed in light of the contemporary genre of "a letter to my younger self," in which an older, seasoned individual, often a celebrity, gives advice to the next generation of leaders. Oprah Winfrey, a talk-show host and philanthropist, and Phylicia Rashad, famously known as Mrs. Claire Huxtable of *The Cosby Show*, are two who have written such books. In writing to their younger selves, they do not attempt to go back in time but rather they attempt to influence younger people with wisdom that they wish they had had at that age. For instance, Rashad reminds her 21-year-old self that everything she does will have consequences and therefore she must be careful with her choices. Likewise, actor Hill Harper's book *Letters to a Young Brother* also endeavors to share nuggets of wisdom with younger men. Stories and advice abound on issues such as money-management, education, career-choice, relationships, and self-esteem. In a certain sense, this is exactly what Paul was doing in his epistle to Timothy.

Timothy's background and personality are of significance and offer insight into why he and Paul developed a good connection. Timothy was a young single man who, after accompanying Paul on missions, had finally been left in charge of the Christian community at Ephesus. The child of a Greek father and Jewish mother, Timothy was a "mixed-race" or "multiracial" child. In our contemporary Western society, freedom and acceptance for all ethnicities is public policy; yet even in this multiethnic context, there is still prejudice against and tension experienced by those born to parents of differing ethnicities. One can only imagine, then, that in Timothy's day being a multiethnic child must have had its own unique challenges. However, by mentioning Timothy's diverse heritage, Paul communicates that what may have been seen as a challenge by society was exactly what God would use to embody the fact that the Gospel was truly for Jew and Gentile alike.

Apart from Timothy's ethnic makeup, the family structure which he grew up in is also of interest. The extent to which Timothy's father was present in his life is unclear. Timothy was raised by his mother, Eunice, and grandmother, Lois. These two ladies are fondly remembered for their sincere faith and are, in Paul's estimation, the reason for Timothy's genuine faith (2 Tim. 1:5). While the faith and dedication of his mother and grandmother stood him in good stead, Paul notes the missing figure of a father in Timothy's life and takes on the responsibility of a mentor. The importance of male-to-male role modeling and mentorship has been noted in developmental psychology research. Paul, an older man in the twilight of his years, and Timothy, a young man at the dawn of his years, engage in a synergistic relationship.

Timothy's vocation as a preacher is taken seriously by his mentor. This shows that one is never too young to employ his or her passions and gifts. Timothy is not addressed as an apprentice who is bumbling his way through his craft, but rather as a young man who is competent and could use the advice from an experienced and wise person. That

Timothy has been entrusted to the important metropolitan of Ephesus speaks volumes about his capability.

There are key things we may learn from Paul, the teacher and mentor. Paul had a vested interest in Timothy which was holistic in nature. He is not only concerned about the evangelistic efforts of the young pastor but also about his physical well-being. It appears that Timothy had a frequent stomach ailment, for which Paul offers a practical remedy (1 Tim. 5:23). An excellent mentor is interested not only in the academic or ministerial pursuits of his mentee but also in the physical toll that these may take.

Another characteristic of a great mentor or teacher is that he or she gives the mentee an opportunity to lead. This was the intention behind giving Timothy the opportunity to pastor people in one of the biggest centers of Christianity. A mentor is not afraid to pass the baton at the appropriate time. The tenor of Paul's second letter to Timothy is one that shows he is anticipating greater things from the next generation of ministry. With instruction and encouragement Paul charges Timothy to "fight the good fight" (1 Tim. 1:18).

Perhaps the most difficult part of mentoring or teaching is the ability to be appropriately transparent to the extent that it provides the opportunity for the growth of the teacher and student. Paul shows both courage and discernment as he is transparent about his dark past so that Timothy can learn from it (1 Tim. 1:12–17). Modeling and mentorship is made more effective through transparency since no one can learn from someone who thinks that they have been, and always will be, perfect.

As an academic and a youth pastor, I learn much from the Pastoral Epistles that are 1 and 2 Timothy. At some point, our hunt for Christian dogma in Paul's writings must not cause us to miss the reality of the Gospel embodied through relationships. Paul not only wrote to instruct but also modeled for Timothy what it meant to be fully devoted to Jesus Christ and the Gospel. As Paul and Timothy were respectively at the dusk and dawn of their ministries, 1 and 2 Timothy allows us a unique insight into their synergistic relationship. Today the worlds of academia, church, and life in general may benefit from such relationships being fostered and nurtured. A reading of Paul's letters to Timothy highlights the positive influence and synergy which can be found in mentor–mentee and teacher–protégé relationships.

Janice P. De-Whyte is a Ph.D. candidate at McMaster Divinity College, Canada; she also serves as a Youth Pastor.

"FAITH AND FAMILY" FOR PAUL AND IMMIGRANTS IN PUERTO RICO

Roberto Martínez (Puerto Rico)

The second letter to Timothy is one of the so-called Pastoral Epistles. These letters are addressed to Timothy and Titus, two prominent coworkers of Paul during his Aegean ministry. In 2 Timothy, Paul encourages Timothy, who is away from his mentor undertaking a challenging mission, to remain steadfast in his vocation and to return to him as soon as possible in order to be by his side during a time of apparent personal suffering and uncertainty. Perhaps nowhere else in the letter is the urgency of this appeal heard more dramatically than in 2 Timothy 4:6–8, a passage that has been interpreted as hinting at Paul's imminent demise and considered by many his final testament or farewell discourse—an epilog to his long and fruitful career. Whether or not 2 Timothy 4:6–8 is Paul hinting at his impending death, the persuasive force of his plea supports the letter's emotional strategy aimed at urging Timothy to return to him (1:4; 4:9, 11, 13, 21). Paul's call invokes two values that he obviously considers important to Timothy: family and faith.

These are two of the same values that many immigrants from the Dominican Republic, with whom I work in an impoverished *barrio* of San Juan, Puerto Rico, hold close to their hearts as they live and work away from their loved ones. Concerns for family and faith shape many of their decisions, justify their sacrifices, and give meaning to the hardships they have to endure as immigrants in a neighboring, yet foreign country.

Like other Hispanics from the Caribbean—such as Cubans and Puerto Ricans—Dominicans have been raised in an environment that treasures the *familia*, a close-knit unit that usually extends beyond the nuclear family. In the *familia*, they have learned not only to be affectionate and caring toward each other but also to be concerned for their relatives' welfare. They have acquired a profound sense of moral responsibility that compels them to aid other members of the family whenever they are experiencing financial or health problems or other life issues; the inability to fulfill such a solemn duty can cause considerable angst. This family-oriented upbringing conditions not only the way immigrants live and work in Puerto Rico but also how they respond to news from their families abroad.

As with immigrants in other countries, Dominicans in Puerto Rico often feel disenfranchised, vulnerable, and helpless. Like Timothy, they struggle. Yet, it is precisely under these difficult circumstances that faith plays an important role. For Dominicans, faith is truly a sacred matter. The beliefs and religious practices they have learned from their parents serve not only as a refuge and comfort in times of difficulties but also help them to cope with the separation from their families and the isolation that their immigrant status often entails. Faith is their source of motivation and encouragement and provides the parameters within which they find spiritual meaning and direction for their lives.

The way in which immigrants from the Dominican Republic, who like Timothy confront difficult challenges and value their families and their faith, respond to the needs of their loved ones gives us an interpretative framework within which to evaluate how Timothy may have responded to Paul's emotional appeal. In 2 Timothy, the kinship language is pervasive and Paul uses it to his rhetorical advantage in urging Timothy to return to him. Paul calls Timothy my "beloved son" (1:2; see 2:1) and demonstrates his paternal concern for him by pointing out how he longs to see him and how he prays for him "day and night" (1:3–4). Paul underscores this familial relationship by reminding Timothy how he "recalls his [Timothy's] tears" (1:4) and the faith of his "grandmother Lois and his mother Eunice" (1:5). Paul points out that he was instrumental in Timothy's vocation (1:6; 2:4) and in instructing him to live a Christian life (1:13; 2:2;

3:10–11, 14). Paul also recalls that he has known Timothy since he was a child and that from an early age he has known the sacred scriptures (3:15).

To compel Timothy to return to him, Paul builds on this close relationship and portrays himself as someone who has suffered because of his faith. For Jesus, Paul has become a prisoner (1:8, 16; 2:9). He lets Timothy know that he has been abandoned by some of his closest allies: Phygelus and Hermogenes (1:15), Demas, Crescens, Titus (4:10), and Alexander the coppersmith (4:14). Paul tells Timothy that nobody has come to his aid (4:16) and that he is suffering even as a criminal for Jesus (2:9). He reminds Timothy of the persecutions and sufferings he endured in Antioch, Iconium, and Lystra (3:11). By contrast, Paul presents Onesiphorus (1:16–17) and Luke (4:11) as the only ones who have not forsaken him, implying at the same time that these are the examples Timothy should emulate.

In 4:6–8 Paul brings this personal experience to bear on his exhortation and, to add urgency to his appeal, intimates that his life is in imminent peril. By portraying himself as the beleaguered mentor and minister of the Gospel, Paul tries to persuade Timothy to remain faithful to his ministry (4:1–5) and expedite his return to him (4:9). Could Timothy turn a deaf ear to his mentor now that he has been abandoned by so many of his closest allies and his life is in apparent danger? Timothy, who owes his faith to Paul and cares for him as family, cannot refuse his request. For immigrants, whom I have had to console when they have received news that a relative is either gravely ill or in need, an appeal for a speedy return is not only a source of angst and anxiety but a compelling call to action. For people whose culture deeply values family and faith, a request from a suffering relative can hardly be ignored.

Hence, within the rhetoric of the letter the strategic function of 2 Timothy 4:6–8 lies in the decisive support it lends to Paul's final appeal to Timothy. Like immigrants from the Dominican Republic who feel compelled to rush to the aid of their relatives in need, Timothy must hastily return to Paul to be by his side upon hearing that his life is being poured out as a libation (4:6). Ultimately, Paul wants Timothy not only to "fight the good fight, finish the race, and keep the faith" (4:7) but also to return to him and be by his side in this time of uncertainty.

Roberto Martínez is an Adjunct Professor of New Testament at the Dominican Graduate School of Theology of the Caribbean and the Evangelical Seminary of Puerto Rico.

QUESTIONS

1. Explain in your own words what Menéndez means by the last sentence of his article.
2. What role do women have in the church (or other arenas) in your context? How does it compare to the experiences described by Vena?
3. Imagine writing a letter to your younger (or older) self. What would you say? How would it compare to the advice given to Timothy, as noted by De-Whyte?
4. How important is the *familia* (which extends beyond the nuclear family) in your cultural context? How does it compare to Martínez's context?

CHAPTER 20

JAMES

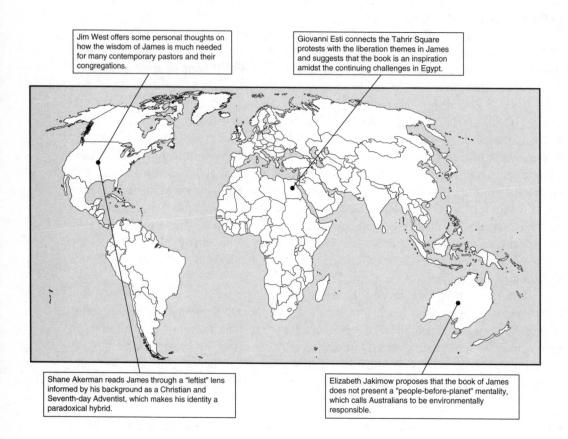

Jim West offers some personal thoughts on how the wisdom of James is much needed for many contemporary pastors and their congregations.

Giovanni Esti connects the Tahrir Square protests with the liberation themes in James and suggests that the book is an inspiration amidst the continuing challenges in Egypt.

Shane Akerman reads James through a "leftist" lens informed by his background as a Christian and Seventh-day Adventist, which makes his identity a paradoxical hybrid.

Elizabeth Jakimow proposes that the book of James does not present a "people-before-planet" mentality, which calls Australians to be environmentally responsible.

READINGS

Pastoral Reflections on the Wisdom of James
Jim West

James as a Manifesto of the Christian Left
Shane Akerman

Australian Ecology and the Book of James
Elizabeth Jakimow

James and the Tahrir Square Protests
Giovanni Esti

PASTORAL REFLECTIONS ON THE WISDOM OF JAMES

Jim West (United States)

My reading of James is from the perspective of a middle-aged, middle-class, white male. I serve the community of faith as both a Pastor and an Adjunct Professor of Biblical Studies. My residence is in the Southern United States (Tennessee to be specific) though my place of origin is California. Theologically I am both conservative (concerning social issues) and thoroughly middle of the road (concerning my rejection of Fundamentalism in its right-wing political garb).

Reading James from that point of view allows me to have a unique perspective, for it allows me to understand James as a text rife with wisdom. To put it another way, though the little letter of James isn't as well known as the Gospels, it contains important spiritual truths that, when applied, will greatly benefit believers. James addresses his readers in a no-nonsense straightforwardness unrivaled in much Christian literature. "Faith without works is dead" and "Brothers, consider it a blessing when various trials befall you" and "Every good and perfect gift comes down from the Father above" are all examples of well-known epigrams from James that challenge our perceptions of God, life, self, and relationship to others. These are exactly the kinds of things which Church members need to embrace, in my estimation, for I have seen many of them over the years act as though faith without works was paramount, think that every good gift comes from the Government, and see various trials as a curse rather than an opportunity for personal and spiritual growth.

Readers of the letter of James are challenged to step outside of themselves and place themselves under the umbrella of faithful, wise living. More challenging still, however, is the insistence of James that we, the "dispersed" tribes of faithful disciples, not show partiality. Indeed, James spends a fair amount of space and time dedicated to precisely that insistence.

He illustrates his point by relating a little story: Suppose someone rich comes to your assembly. And now suppose that you treat that visitor as special, as more important, than anyone else. You give him the best seat and show him the greatest kindness; and meanwhile you tell a poor visitor that he can stand there or kneel here to serve as the footstool of the rich man. James asks if this is right and if this is proper. He further asks if you are unaware that the rich are your oppressors and even more than that, that they persecute the church. No, he continues, it is not proper for believers to exalt some to special status and ignore or even denigrate others—because God himself does not do such a thing.

Many modern Christians, and not a few modern pastors, fall into the trap which James warns against. They pander to the wealthy, ensure that they receive the lion's share of attention, visit them in the hospital, listen to their complaints, and follow their advice. They (these contemporary pastors) curry favor and learn how to navigate the ministry with just the right measure of acquiescence to the powerful and the rich. It is precisely at this point—where ministry and life, where self-interest and self-promotion at the expense of the less well-off—that James's wisdom is most striking and most necessary. However, it seems, amazingly, that many churches want exactly this sort of pastor. But why? To what end? Perhaps the ugly truth (which makes the message of James so crucial to hear) is that the flock is like the shepherd. Many Christians are themselves more interested in "getting ahead" than they are in helping others get to God. The message of James, if heard properly, disabuses us of that mistake.

But the wisdom of James isn't exhausted once he moves beyond the dicey topic of "favoritism." He is also quite adept at calling disciples to discipline, specifically in terms of the tongue. A giant forest is set ablaze by a tiny spark, he remarks. A massive ship is controlled by a small rudder, he observes. Mankind has learned, he opines, to control just about every sort of animal under the sun but he claims that he simply cannot control what he says. Yet, James insists that we can indeed control ourselves—our language, our words, our output—if we are but wise. As Christians are told, and must be told, with numbing regularity by pastors who are doing their job: you can't unring the bell. You can't take back those harmful words. Many have begged forgiveness for a word said in haste; and even when the word is forgiven, the scar remains forever.

Wisdom is the key, then, to both our treatment of others and our control of ourselves. If we are wise, James teaches us, we will know how to treat others fairly. If we are wise, then we will be able to exercise self-control. Our faith, if it is real, manifests itself in wise behavior in word and deed.

Should we, though, abandon wisdom and remain self-seeking, self-promoting self-deceivers, then we should not at all be surprised if our lives are filled with all the unpleasantness that comes with strife and struggle. "Where do wars and fights come from," he asks. And then he answers that they come from within us. We want what we shouldn't want, we crave what we shouldn't crave, and we do whatever we need to do to get whatever we wish to get and all hell breaks loose, literally. We don't have what we really need because we don't ask for it.

So, instead of making our own plans (which is most unwise), James urges that we leave our lives in the hands of God. Helping church people understand this is the crucial task of our day. God is Lord. The modern church has forgotten that. His will is the will we should will. His desires are the desires we should desire. That is to live wisely. By the time James concludes his letter, he has called the wise to gather in prayer for those who are ill and in need. If one is sick, he encourages them to call for the elders and let them pray, and anoint with oil, and says that God will hear and he may even grant their request and heal. He also asks them to confess their sins to one another. In short, wisdom results in community and compassionate caring. The community of believers is summoned to prayer and mutual support.

Wise living, so far as the Letter of James is concerned, centers on authentic fairness, real faith, and compassionate participation in the community of believers in mutual support. Unwise living, on the other hand, manifests itself in favoritism, lack of self-control, and disinterest in the well-being of others. Wisdom lived is life without boundaries either socioeconomic or material. Wisdom lived changes lives from the inside out.

Jim West is Adjunct Professor of Biblical Studies at the Quartz Hill School of Theology and Pastor of Petros Baptist Church, Petros, Tennessee, United States; he has written a number of books and articles.

JAMES AS A MANIFESTO OF THE CHRISTIAN LEFT

Shane Akerman (United States)

Growing up in the United States as a Seventh-day Adventist Christian is a very unique experience. As an American Christian, I am at once included into the mainstream of American civil religion, a realm which is dominated by conservative Protestantism. However, by being a part of the Seventh-day Adventist Church, a group that prides itself on doctrinal distinctiveness, my Christianity is never recognized as being full-fledged. To be Adventist in America is, therefore, to be simultaneously included and excluded.

When it comes to questions of politics, because I am a Christian, the expectation in the United States is that I ought to support capitalist expansion and military intervention. Thankfully, my Seventh-day Adventist background prepares me to proudly accept the role of a minority voice. Faithfulness to a certain reading of Scripture has always separated my views from popular Christianity. Now, as one who engages political and economic theory, my reading of Scripture sets me at odds with mainstream political discourse in the United States.

The Epistle of James is a text with radical political implications for me. Perhaps outside of the teachings of Jesus himself, this text is the most straightforwardly leftist in orientation. Obviously, the term "leftist" is a bit out of place when referring to a first-century religious text but leftism (which includes various forms of socialism, communism, social democracy, and anarchism) is a form of political thought that puts its strongest emphasis on social and economic equality. In this sense, one might say without exaggeration that the Epistle of James is a manifesto of the Christian Left.

Right from the beginning James offers this lyrical wisdom: "Let the believer who is lowly boast in being raised up, and the rich in being brought low, because the rich will disappear like a flower in the field" (1:9–10). The success of the poor is not tied to the furthered success of the rich but is directly related to the "lowering" of the rich, and their eventual disappearance. Certain logic might hold that social hierarchy is beneficial to a community because those most privileged have the resources with which they can assist and empower the lower classes. James, of course, will have none of that. When we give preferential treatment to the rich, especially when it is done out of self-interest, James calls us "evil judges" (2:4).

James is thoroughly unimpressed by the argument that greed and self-interested competition can somehow be harnessed for the good. For the Christian, these actions, even if they do make for an efficient and productive economy, make us enemies of God. This leftist epistle explains that when we desire what we do not have, we will fight and even kill to satisfy our own desires (4:2–3). This is the way of the world, and when we participate in this mode of being—this economy—James tears us out of our place of comfort and calls us God's enemy (4:4).

Many Christians who want to avoid these difficult issues of class conflict altogether will say that the Christian gospel is about spiritual things, not material concerns.

According to this supposedly nonpartisan or apolitical position, the duty of the Christian is to engage strictly in spiritual struggles. James does not leave this position unaddressed. He explains that when a member of the community is in need of food or clothing that anything short of supplying those material needs is a failure on the part of the Christian (2:14–16).

We may be tempted to respond to this call to aid the hungry by talking about mere charity: "This is a private matter. The alleviation of poverty is not a political issue," one might say. But for the early Christians, the notion of any aspect of the gospel being apolitical would certainly have seemed strange. For Jesus and his apostles came heralding the *kingdom* of God and James explains in no uncertain terms that God has "chosen those who are poor in the eyes of the world to… inherit the kingdom" (2:5). The gospel is always political, because it always concerns God's kingdom. And, I would claim, those politics are always leftist because God's kingdom is always a kingdom of those who are "poor in the eyes of the world."The author's impassioned rhetoric reaches a crescendo when he begins to address the rich themselves. "Weep and wail!" he commands. Echoing many of Jesus' polemics against wealth, James warns of the miseries that await the rich as their wealth is rotted, their clothes devoured by moths, and their very flesh consumed as with fire (5:1–3). With words of such scathing rebuke that rival the ferociousness of modern radicals such as Franz Fanon or Che Guevara, James becomes very concrete in his accusations. He calls out the rich for failing to pay proper wages, for living in luxury, and for using violence to impose labor on those below them (5:4–6).

From the perspective of a leftist, the worst aspect of our culture of inequality and cut-throat competition is that we cannot escape it. It's everywhere. Living in the United States means, in most cases, living in relative luxury and benefiting from a system of global markets that flows wealth toward people of privilege. I am the perfect example of such a person: I am a Christian, white, American male. So, when I speak from this context of the evils of imperial domination and of unethical accumulation, am I not a hypocrite? What is the appropriate response for persons of privilege, such as myself? If God is on the side of the poor and the suffering, then I must follow the wisdom of James as he tells twenty-first-century Americans: "Grieve, mourn and wail. Change your laughter to mourning and your joy to gloom. Humble yourselves before the Lord, and he will lift you up" (4:8–10).

My identity is a paradoxical hybrid. As a Christian I am included; as an Adventist, excluded. As a white American male I am privileged; as a leftist I am scorned. But the call of the Epistle of James is to lay down all that I have in order to identify with those whom God has chosen: the poor, who are the inheritors of his kingdom.

Shane Akerman, a Seventh-day Adventist and political leftist, is a graduate from Claremont School of Theology in the disciplines of New Testament Studies and Ethics.

AUSTRALIAN ECOLOGY AND THE BOOK OF JAMES

Elizabeth Jakimow (Australia)

Perhaps surprisingly for a country where approximately three-quarters of the population live in urban areas, Australians tend to have a great appreciation and love for the Australian bush. Undoubtedly, there are exceptions. Australia is a diverse country, containing people of many different nationalities and beliefs. They do not all share the same views about Australia, nor do they all share the same views about the environment. It would be fair to say, though, that many of us want to protect nature, especially those parts of nature that make up our amazing Australian landscape. However, this does not always mean that people are willing to place environmental issues above their own needs, wants, and convenience.

When the carbon pricing legislation was passed in 2011, many Australians were concerned, first and foremost, about whether it would disadvantage them. Liberal senator Gary Humphries seized on the fact that many Canberrans would end up worse off under the carbon legislation since they would receive less compensation than the rest of the country. Despite the fact that this was because Canberrans had a higher average income than other states, it played to the idea that Australians should not have to make even minor sacrifices to avoid environmental destruction. It seems that while Australians do want to protect the environment, they do not want to make even minor changes to their lifestyle in order to do so.

At first glance, James 1:18 appears to be a verse that suits the "people-before-planet" mentality. James calls his readers the "firstfruits" of God's creation or, as one translation puts it, God made us "his most important creatures." The use of the word "firstfruits" may refer to his intended audience being among the first to become Christians. However, we may also surmise from this verse (along with the dominion verses of Genesis 1:27–28) that humans are given a privileged place within Creation. But even on this interpretation of the word, this does not necessarily mean that human concerns are always more important than environmental concerns. Indeed, other verses in the book of James seem to speak against this view.

James 4:1–3 may be discussing people in the first century, but these verses are equally applicable to us today. James speaks of craving and coveting things that we cannot obtain, which leads to quarreling and fighting, and even murder (v.2). Nowadays we have a multi-billion-dollar industry that deliberately tries to create those desires in people. While this may not always result in disputes and conflict (let alone murder), it can (and often does) lead to sin. In fact, if we consider the damage caused to the environment because of our cravings for possessions, perhaps it may not be too far-fetched to say that we *are* guilty of murder. At the very least, we are not truly valuing the lives of other species or future generations. Like those people addressed in James 4:3, our pleasure is our primary concern.

There are, of course, many people today who are focused on "doing business and making money." Australian society often sees this as a good thing. Our highest-paid CEOs earn significantly more money than our prime minister. And those who earn high incomes are generally considered to be successful. However, James does not see things the same way. Rather than praising those who are rich, he gives them some very strong warnings: "Come now, you rich people, weep and wail for the miseries that are coming to you. Your riches have rotted, and your clothes are moth-eaten. Your gold and silver have rusted, and their rust will be evidence against you, and it will eat your flesh like fire" (5:1–3).

If these verses are to be read as a literal account of what *will* happen, then I fear everyone in my home country of Australia is going to face much weeping, wailing, and miseries. While some of us may not feel rich compared to others in our own country, we are all incredibly wealthy compared to people in other parts of the world. I think we may safely presume, though, that this is not a predetermined outcome for everyone who is rich by world standards. However, it is a warning that everyone in first-world countries must pay heed to.

We particularly need to take note of what James says about possessions. Our riches will rot, metaphorically that is. In reality, considering the amount of plastic nonbiodegradable items we own, much of it will not rot; rather it will end up either in landfills or littering our land and oceans. With this in mind, we must seriously consider the importance of James 5:3 concerning our own possessions. Everything we own will not only be meaningless in the end, but may be evidence against us. We must therefore realize that the environmental damage caused by the production, transport, and disposal of our possessions is important.

The warnings to the rich continue in James 5:4–5 and again they have relevance for Australians. The laborers and harvesters may not appear to apply to us, as only a small percentage of Australians would employ such people. However, people are employed to make the goods that we buy and are not always treated justly or paid fair wages. We might also perhaps read these verses as applying to everyone (or everything) that suffers in our quest for possessions. Yet again, we are faced with the realization that the things we buy cause harm, and the harm that we cause matters to God.

It is easy to read James' description of people who live "on the earth in luxury and in pleasure" (5:5) and believe that descriptions does not apply to us. Not all Australians enjoy the same standard of living. As a low-income earner myself, when I see the word "luxury" it seems to refer to people who own yachts and do not worry about bills. However, compared to other areas in the world, just about all of us in Australia live in luxury and pleasure. Furthermore, where they lived "on the earth in luxury and in pleasure," we actually destroy the earth for our luxury and pleasure. We cannot dismiss James' words as not applying to us. Australians fit the description far better than the people James had in mind.

So while we (either as Christians or, more generally, people) may be the firstfruits of all God's creation, this does not give us permission to destroy the earth for our own pleasure. That James mentions God's creatures at all shows that, despite our privileged position, they are still important. The strong warnings James has for the wealthy should cause us to examine our own lives. We must look at how the earth suffers because of our cravings and pursuit of pleasure and try not to let our possessions be evidence against us.

Elizabeth Jakimow is completing a Bachelor of Theology at St Mark's Theological Centre in Canberra, Australia; she has a blog on ecotheology called God and Gum Nuts.

JAMES AND THE TAHRIR SQUARE PROTESTS
Giovanni Esti (Egypt)

On January 25, 2011, people in Egypt, particularly youth, began a protest against the government and its abuses. People marched to Tahrir square and made it a symbol of nonviolent resistance to injustice and oppression. The question of what all this meant transcended the political outcome of these unexpected, uncertain, and yet promising events. This has begun a process of transition within this country and the outcome is still difficult to predict now, two years later.

The protagonists of this uprising were unaffiliated with any particular group. They represented the middle ground between Western and Eastern identities. They sought values like democracy, freedom, and equality in a spirit of nonviolence. They expressed their disapproval of poverty, lack of opportunities, corruption, and discrimination, which deprive people of their God-given right to a dignified life.

The aspiration of liberation is a call that finds profound roots in the Letter of James. Passages such as 2:2–4—an exhortation not to show favor to the wealthy—make a case for distributive justice, that is, the socially equitable allocation of goods, which creates a society that does not privilege the rich and powerful. Here James voices not only a challenge to the Christian community but also a universal aspiration, which, if disrespected, will eventually bring a breakdown of society.

Freedom and justice may be "global" desires, but they take form in very specific and local contexts. Such was the case for me some time ago when several hundred young people passed before the gates of our church, "Cordi Jesu," a short walk from Tahrir Square. They were challenging the incarceration of a militant whose name I could not understand, let alone the reason for his imprisonment. Instead, I know rather well what happens in prisons: brutal and arbitrary torture. We witnessed such when some of our collaborators had been seized.

The event had blocked the street and thrown into a panic those trapped among the rioters. Choirs of loud chanting declared the purpose of the protest. Among the words that were most often repeated was *hurreya,* or freedom. Suddenly a stone-throwing began between the protesters and the police. A little later, the whistle of ambulances trying to squeeze through the traffic brought back a familiar sound of screaming and inhaling of toxic gas. I hastened to close the gates, not without asking politely some young people that if they had to throw the stones to avoid, if possible, the windows of the church. Indeed, the idealism that soaked the streets and squares of Egypt in early 2011 will need time to become reality—change, true change, is slow in coming.

"Freedom" is the cry that has broken the reckless "democratic dictatorship" of Hosni Mubarak. A little more than a year after, however, the same word is confronted with a pile of rubble: freedom struggles to gain a foothold. The elections brought to power Islamic fundamentalist parties, structurally resistant to what we would define a civil rights in the Western world. The economy stagnates due to the crisis caused by social instability. The relations between Egypt and the United States are increasingly tense. Representatives of the future government, at the warnings that American economic aid could suffer cuts unless civil rights are upheld, have threatened to revoke the 1979 peace treaty with Israel, which could bring even more instability to the Middle East. Understandably, there are many who now say that it was better when it was worse (under Mubarak); they desire to trade liberty for the sake of security.

This desire for safety and predictability is natural, whether amidst a violent protest in Egypt or an economic downturn. But here again I turn to the wisdom of James for inspiration and encouragement: "But one who looks intently at the perfect law, the law of liberty, and abides by it, not having become a forgetful hearer but an effectual doer, this one shall be blessed in what he does" (1:25). When the road to freedom becomes narrow and steep and difficult, it is easy to give up. It is easy to give in to the disheartening and unsettling feeling of risking one's safety, even one's very life. The temptation to "save oneself" is the instinctive human reaction—whether for those who want to break walls in the fight for freedom or for those who erect them tall and impenetrable in the name of power and domination. But the pursuit of freedom has a price. Solidarity costs. The determination to dialogue costs. Forgiveness costs. Starting over costs. Not giving up costs. But such costs cannot be paid by force. Rather, people must exercise their inherent God-given freedom to make the sacrifices that are necessary to pursue truth, justice, and equality.

Once more James is instructive: "Even so faith, if it has no works, is dead, being by itself" (2:17). We cannot only say the words; we must live them out. There must be works, actions which give evidence of our faith. Freedom and justice are not simply abstract ideals or beliefs. We must be doers of the word, not hearers only. We must seek diligently and courageously to abide by the perfect law of liberty. The person who does this, James says, will indeed be blessed.

Giovanni Esti (Ph.D., Claremont Graduate University, USA) is a priest working in Cairo; he is in charge of Comboni Mission Center, an organization promoting within churches a spirit of openness, dialogue, and attention to diversity and poverty.

QUESTIONS

1. West observes that "self-interest and self-promotion" are common among today's preachers. What drives this? In what other arenas of your society or culture is such self-promotion apparent?

2. Assess Akerman's reading of James. Is James a "leftist" epistle? Are there texts in James that would undermine Akerman's reading?

3. Jakimow encourages us to think about ways we indirectly impact the environment. Do you participate in any activities that indirectly harm nature or cause suffering for others?

4. Esti notes the natural desire for safety and security. How, if at all, is this desire manifest in your life? What are you sacrificing to obtain such safety and security?

CHAPTER 21

REVELATION (PART I)

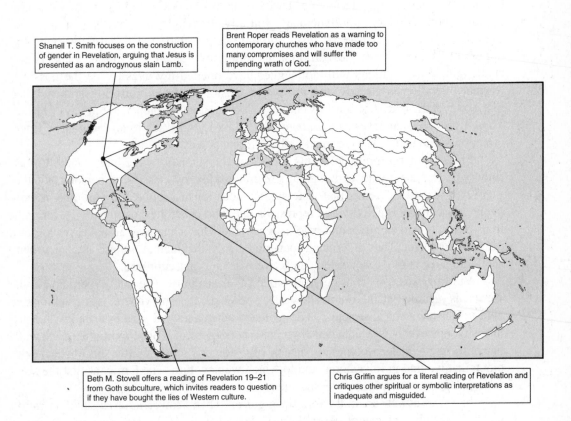

Shanell T. Smith focuses on the construction of gender in Revelation, arguing that Jesus is presented as an androgynous slain Lamb.

Brent Roper reads Revelation as a warning to contemporary churches who have made too many compromises and will suffer the impending wrath of God.

Beth M. Stovell offers a reading of Revelation 19–21 from Goth subculture, which invites readers to question if they have bought the lies of Western culture.

Chris Griffin argues for a literal reading of Revelation and critiques other spiritual or symbolic interpretations as inadequate and misguided.

READINGS

The Construction of Gender in Revelation
Shanell T. Smith

A Goth Reading of Revelation 19–21
Beth M. Stovell

Revelation as a Warning to Contemporary Churches
Brent Roper

A Literal Reading of Revelation
Chris Griffin

THE CONSTRUCTION OF GENDER IN REVELATION

Shanell T. Smith (United States)

As an African American, Christian, female New Testament scholar (representing myself, and not as a spokeswoman for any of these perceived "groups"), I will focus on the construction of gender in the book of Revelation as it pertains to ancient Roman notions of penetration and viewing. I will argue that Jesus in the figure of the Lamb espouses both genders simultaneously. Initially, I thought that by "preserving" the so-called "feminine" aspect of Jesus throughout Revelation, I had finally done the impossible, that is, made Revelation a liberating text. However, further analysis and challenging conversations with colleagues have opened my eyes to see the possibility that liberation is already and always in tension with the suffering and violence that occur in the text. The borders between liberation and violence are always blurred. Thus, I propose that Jesus, the *androgynous* slain Lamb leads to an *ambiguous* interpretation—one that will have to sit well with me, at least for now.

In the Roman Empire, concepts of gender and sexuality were intertwined. Roman authors (elite males) who wrote about sex often did so by classifying persons as either "active" or "passive," terms that were synonymous for masculine and feminine, respectively. Masculinity is activity and represents one who penetrates; contrastingly, femininity is passivity and signifies one who is penetrated. One's anatomical makeup was not a determining factor. Thus, if a male is penetrated, then that male, for these ancient writers, is effeminized; in the same respect, an active woman is masculinized.

Viewing was also considered a mode of masculinity. The active participant, the viewer, is regarded as the dominant subject; whereas, the one viewed is the submissive object. This hierarchical structure is destabilized when a mutual gaze is shared with equal intensity; however, it is maintained anytime this engagement is disproportionate (i.e., when one of the participants becomes a spectacle of the other's scrutiny). It is this unequal exhibition that we find in Revelation, and to which we now turn. The Lamb, at first the spectacle, is later transformed into the spectator.

In 5:6 Jesus appears in the following guise: "Then I saw...a Lamb standing as if it had been slaughtered, having seven horns and seven eyes..." Jesus is not a human in this passage, but he is also not simply an animal. Although one might consider this small lamb as a beast in its own right, with the presence of its seven horns and seven eyes, which are symbolic of power and wisdom, the fact that the Lamb is slain should not be overlooked. The phrase, "as if slain," reflects the sacrificial markings and scars that Jesus has endured on the cross. Penetration in ancient antiquity is not limited to penile function; it pertains to any form of insertion or any penetration of one's flesh. Thus, according to Roman gender ideologies, the *slain* Lamb would be considered feminine.

The image of the slain Lamb lingers in the recesses of one's mind as we proceed through Revelation. However, when we reach Revelation 14, the vision of this itty-bitty Lamb bearing the markings of torture is replaced with an extraordinary Lamb with a strong stomach for witnessing death and destruction. The Lamb displays strength as he watches and oversees the destruction of those who worship the beast and its image: "Those who worship the beast…will be tormented with fire and sulfur in the presence of the holy angels and in the presence of the Lamb. And the smoke of their torment goes up forever and ever" (14:9–11). Thus, the Lamb, although textually regarded as slain, figuratively emerges as a muscular, robust figure, strong enough to open the seven seals of the scroll (which no one else could do, 5:1–5), and digestively durable enough to withstand the sight of his adversaries being tortured. In essence, the Lamb becomes a man. The Lamb's femininity, as indicated by its slaughtered state, is followed by the emergence of masculinity when the Lamb becomes a powerful celestial warrior.

It has been argued that the Lamb, in the larger narrative of Revelation, makes the move from femininity to masculinity. This argument is problematic to me on two fronts: domination of the masculine gender over the feminine, and its implications for those of us who view Jesus as Christ and a Savior for all. At no time should one gender prevail over another, especially in the figure of Christ (even if depicted as a Lamb). This view, in which the masculine gender is the "last one standing," causes problems for womanists such as myself. The term "womanist" reflects a group of African American women committed to the survival and flourishing of an entire people, both male and female. Furthermore, for some African American women who regard Jesus as the divine cosufferer, that is, a God who supports and empowers them in the struggle to overcome their suffering, reading Jesus as one who overcomes femininity with masculinity would render Jesus as a source of comfort for men only, or suggest that a woman must become manly to persevere, which is clearly problematic. Therefore, I contend that the Lamb maintains both genders simultaneously throughout the narrative, an argument to which we now turn—that is, Jesus as the androgynous Lamb.

Coupling Roman imperial ideology with the two-ness of Jesus' nature suggests that Jesus maintains the supposed "feminine" aspect of his character, what I define as victory and strength masked by the *appearance* of weakness: recall the *slain* Lamb's ability to open the seven scrolls. But it also suggests that he maintains the *supposed* "masculine" qualities to master, conquer, and destroy—qualities he possesses as the celestial warrior. In essence, Revelation imparts a word of caution: looks can be deceiving. Specifically, the appearance of the Lamb is deceiving; that is, his femininity is not to be viewed as fragility.

But what are we to make of the presence of these seemingly conflicting characteristics of Jesus, and what implications does it have for African American female readers of Revelation? Although it can be perceived as problematic, it seems to me that it is a description of God that has the potential to give African American women (including myself) a sense of hope. A victim of tri-fold oppression in terms of race, sex, and class, I need Jesus to be a source of strength and comfort, as well as an avenger, protector, and defender of my well-being. For many African American churches, liberation entails violent images of God (such as in Exodus 14) in which God brings about deliverance and freedom from oppression through violent means.

Thus, in light of the androgyny of the Lamb, I posit that the Apocalypse invites an ambivalent interpretation. The borders of liberation and violence (whether or not justified) are always blurred. Liberation, most often, necessitates violence, and violence most often is a prelude to the need for liberation. Violence and liberation, although seemingly two opposed realities, simultaneously coexist like the two-fold gender of Jesus in Revelation. They both exist in strained relation within the figure of the Lamb. To be sure, this tension does not render the Lamb neutral and ineffective, but rather complex, elusive, and even ambiguous.

In conclusion, we must continue to find ways to reveal inclusive and liberating traditions in the early Christian writings, despite the androcentric nature of biblical texts. John's gaze is exclusionary (elevating the masculine and abandoning the feminine), but my understanding of Jesus problematizes his view by directing our attention to Jesus' gendered complexity. My hope is that reading Jesus as an androgynous Lamb will present a new vision of an all-embracing Jesus, instead of a masculine Jesus who conquers femininity. However, the reality of my reading, despite my dissatisfaction, is that as long as violence and liberation exist in tandem, such as in the text of Revelation via the characterization of Jesus, liberation will always already be and not yet be. This is ambiguity at its best.

Shanell T. Smith is a Ph.D. candidate in New Testament and Early Christianity at Drew University, United States; she is also a Candidate for Minister of Word and Sacrament in the Presbyterian Church (USA).

A GOTH READING OF REVELATION 19–21

Beth M. Stovell (United States)

Here I will offer a reading of Revelation 19–21 through the eyes of the Goth subculture. Often traced to the sounds and images of the band Bauhaus, Goths emerged in Britain in the early 1980s as punk, glam rock, and new romantic merged with other elements to form a new and distinctive music and fashion style. The music of the Goth scene was often described as dark, macabre, and sinister. While in many ways, Goths define themselves in terms of these similar musical interests and fashion style, Goths will often point to other more internal elements that form the Goth worldview.

First, Goth is a resistance subculture that reacts against "mainstream" culture. What the "mainstream" culture of America (and other parts of North America and Western Europe) tells us to deny, Goths instead openly embrace. One example of this is the Goth goal of putting the darkness on the outside where everyone can see it (making it innocuous), rather than keeping it hidden (thereby letting it smolder and become truly evil). By embracing this awareness of evil, Goths also point to the darkness that is inside everyone. When hidden, this inner evil can extend to the rest of the world, impacting society, religion, and the environment. Goth music and movies often react against the hypocrisy present in the world and its inherent effects of oppression, marginalization, and alienation. In contrast, Goth subculture aims toward inclusion of people whom mainstream society has rejected, often getting rejected themselves in the process. Goths also reject the mainstream notion of hiding the suffering and pain present in life. Goths will often note that mainstream culture unreasonably expects everyone to put on a happy face. In contrast, Goths argue that the willingness to acknowledge the suffering and evil present in the world and within themselves can actually allow for more happiness in their lives.

The growing movement of Goth Christianity accentuates these central tenets of Goth subculture in light of Christian belief. For example, the awareness of inner darkness is often heightened among Goth Christians, who seek to warn others of the dangers of ignoring or denying sin. Further, Christian Goths point to the system of lies sold by the world and seek to replace them with the truth. Goth Christians point to Jesus Christ as the model for the inclusion of the marginalized and oppressed and as one who rejected the world's lies. Goth Christians identify their persecution in the world with Christ's persecution. Their acknowledgment of suffering and darkness often causes them to emphasize the suffering of Christ in his Passion and revel in the gruesome cannibalistic language of the Eucharist. For example, in the Goth Christian video *The Night of the Living Bread* zombies eat Christ's body and are transformed by this cannibalistic Eucharist act.

Each of these tenets impacts the way Goths read the Bible. In their reinterpretation of the Bride, the New Jerusalem, in Revelation 19–21, they often identify themselves with the Bride of Christ figure, the New Jerusalem herself. Yet this identification combines the somber, the macabre, and the sarcastic tendencies within Goth subculture. The Bride of Christ becomes a gothic bride. Whether one pictures Tim Burton's corpse bride or a Goth female dressed in a black wedding dress with a silver cross, black fingernails, lips, and nails, and, most importantly, black veil (as found on one Christian Goth website), this reinterpretation cannot help but cause a change in the way one visually imagines this figure in the Apocalypse.

This identification of the Bride of Christ with Goth Christianity is pressed further as some Goths connect the robes of white drenched in the blood of the Lamb in Revelation 7 with the Bride of Christ adorned in white for her wedding day in 19:7–9 and 21:1–9. Such an interpretation draws upon the natural connections between the removal of suffering and the springs of living water in 7:17 and 21:3,6 and the imagery of the bride within these contexts. One Goth poet (David Dellman, "Why Black?" on gothicchristianity.com) connects his black clothes of mourning with his anticipation of this coming day of redemption: "I wear black because it is the color of mourning./I mourn for the dying world…I mourn for each senseless act of injustice. I mourn for Him and with Him and I know that He and He alone will comfort me./And I will wear black until the day when He adorns me in white…" Here the choice of black is linked to the mourning of the present world and the hope of the future age to come where this Goth shall be God's bride and all mourning shall cease. Others push this combined vision of Revelation 7 and 21 in macabre directions. In this depiction, the bride may only be dressed in white because she is first bathed in blood. Thus, the bride must have a "blood bath" to be cleansed. This use of the horror genre allows for dramatic and surprising new ways of seeing the true macabre nature of Revelation's apocalyptic vision.

This vision of the Gothic Bride of Christ stands in contrast to the Goth reinterpretation of the figure of Babylon in Revelation 18. In many ways, the ancient depiction of Babylon as the Roman imperial power representing social injustice, exploitation, and oppression finds its parallel in the gothic interpretation of the United States of America as Babylon. For many Goths, the tendency to "rage against the machine" and to question the duplicitous nature of Western society goes hand in hand with interpreting Babylon in terms of the misdeeds of America specifically. One such example (though there are quite a few) is the song "American Babylon" by Saviour Machine. In this song, terms like "fascism" and "tyranny," which have become "highly organized" by Satan himself, are placed beside the language of liberty and light, demonstrating the distinction between appearances and reality that have caused the ultimate fall of America, according to Saviour Machine.

The ultimate picture of inclusion comes in the final vision of the wedding of the Lamb. As the Bride of Christ herself is pictured as a Goth, not surprisingly the guests at the dinner party include Goths and all others who have been marginalized, oppressed, and alienated. Those "scary freaks" whom some mainstream Christians feared would mislead their children are in fact found sitting elbow-to-elbow with them at the Lamb's dinner table. This subverts the usual expectations of this metaphor by extending the table in surprising directions.

Goth interpretations of Revelation press their readers toward seeing with squeamish eyes the vivid, even horrific metaphors employed to depict the reversal of mainstream expectations. Using the conventions of horror, Goth readings challenge their readers to question whether they, like the merchants wailing at Babylon's fall, have bought the lies offered by today's society—wealth, empty happiness, and false righteousness so prevalent in much of Western culture. Through parody and irony, Goth readings subvert the expectations of their readers, surprising them and moving them toward deeper questions of inclusion and exclusion, of center and margin. The use of inversion of symbolic frameworks of imperialism and the dualism inherent in apocalyptic literature and within Goth subculture leads to a radical and dangerous choice; for choosing to align oneself with those on the "inside" means standing in solidarity with the oppressed and potentially becoming the oppressed. The value of Goth readings of Revelation is the new configuration of this symbolism as culturally relevant to today's world. If America is truly Babylon, how might one "come out of [her]," while still living in her? Perhaps Goth Christians provide at least one way to reside in this tension.

Beth M. Stovell is Assistant Professor in Biblical Studies in the School of Theology and Ministry at St. Thomas University, Miami Gardens, Florida, United States.

REVELATION AS A WARNING TO CONTEMPORARY CHURCHES

Brent Roper (United States)

Did you *really* think no one was watching and you collectively could kill hundreds of millions of innocent babies worldwide through "abortion" and get away with it? The standard is "Thou shalt not kill." Did you *really* think you could start wars and murder at will worldwide with no accountability? There were zero weapons of mass destruction in Iraq—remember? Did you *really* think you could slip mass adultery (remarriage after divorce; Mark 10:11), fornication, sodomy, marrying homosexuals, and the like under the radar past God and He wouldn't notice?

When Christ returns to earth it's going to be as the days of Noah and the days of Lot. That is, mass sin and sodomy will flourish, and all the commandments of God will be cast aside. Christ is coming in judgment. That is the basic plotline of the book of Revelation. The Revelation of Jesus Christ is holy payback time! All mankind will cry for the mountains and rocks to fall on them to hide them from Him and His wrath (6:16). He's coming for you; He's gonna find you!

When the effeminate preachers of this evil, adulterous, and sinful generation speak of a limp-wristed, sissy, apologetic, soft-on-sin, hippy Christ, it is laughable. It's the blind leading the blind. Revelation 1 opens with Christ having eyes as a flame of fire and a sharp double-edged sword coming out of His mouth (vv. 14–16). All peoples of the earth will wail when they see Him (v. 7). And for good reason, the sword is to strike down the nations and to rule them with a rod of iron, and to trod them on the winepress of the wrath of God (19:15–16).

Interestingly, though, before Christ unfolds widespread destruction and mayhem on man, beast, and everything on the whole earth, He turns his full attention to His seven churches (Rev. 2–3). If the pusillanimous Christ of the modern churches were on the throne He would look on them lovingly and accept all their filthy sinful behavior as perfect. Not the true Christ of the Bible! He is interested in one thing: the spiritual state of His churches. He gives a failing grade to five of the seven churches and threatens them! Yes, you read right, He threatens them. He tells them that if they don't immediately repent, He will take their candlestick and leave them to die! It's obedience to the commandments or He's out of there. So, what were these five failing churches doing to anger Him? Answer: Having no zeal for God, fornication, idol worship, woman preachers, adultery, being lukewarm, being rich and arrogant.

In other words, nearly 100 percent of the so-called churches in America have some or all of the same characteristics of these five churches that had enraged their God. Here is what He is going to do to these lukewarm, apologetic, disobedient churches: "I will spew thee out of my mouth" (3:15–16). Spewing time cometh!

With the spiritual state of the churches out of the way, Christ ascends to the throne and now judgment is on (Rev. 4)! Christ steps forward as the Redeemer to pay for the sins of His people and to rid the purchased possession (earth) of the dynasties of wickedness, to cast out the rulers of the darkness of the world and prince of the power of the air, to restore the earth to its proper fertility and peace, and to bring the empire of righteousness and salvation into being. A holy eviction notice is being served on nearly all of humanity as Revelation 6 opens. The time of Satan's rule on earth with gross sin, filthiness, and abomination is over! At Christ's coming He sends forth His angels to gather the wicked tares, and casts them into a furnace of fire, and then the righteous shall shine forth as the sun. Christ is taking possession of the earth by force and moving forward His administration and assuming power. The kingdoms of this world become the kingdoms of our Lord, and of his Christ; and He shall reign forever and ever (11:15).

Once Christ ascends to the throne, He immediately starts opening the seals of the book of judgment and, bang, the four horses of the apocalypse are loosed! Christ on the white horse is loosed to conquer; the red horse, great war and all peace from the earth is taken (there will be no regard for life); the black horse, great famine; and the pale green horse, great disease will reign. These horses will devastate the people of the earth. One-fourth of the inhabitants of the world will be slain by these four horses! That means 1.7 billion corpses will litter the landscape—more than can possibly be buried! And, that's just the opener!

Then, great commotions in the fabric of nature take place: earthquakes, the sun becomes black, and so on. Then it's time for the seven angels with seven trumpets to sound. The de-creation of the earth begins to take place. One-third of the trees and grass are incinerated, one-third of the oceans and life in the sea are killed, one-third of the freshwater is poisoned, and one-third of the sun, moon, and stars are darkened. Then it really gets bad!

Creatures from hell are loosed (Rev. 9) to torment men; angels are loosed, and more earthquakes occur, and another one-third of mankind are killed. After all this, do men repent of their murders, sorceries, fornication, and thefts? No! Then seven bowls and plagues are poured into the earth and more de-creation! Satan, the false prophet, and the beast do not go quietly; instead they assemble to fight God. How stupid is that? The end of the book depicts the King of Kings and Lord of Lords on His white horse hunting down His enemies with their blood on his garments in total and complete victory over Satan and the wicked people that inhabit earth (Rev. 19). Who are the wicked? They are clearly identified: "But the fearful, and unbelieving, and the abominable, and murderers, and whoremongers, and sorcerers, and idolaters, and all liars, shall have their part in the lake which burneth with fire and brimstone: which is the second death" (21:8). Are there any who are the righteous? Yes, "Blessed are they that do his commandments, that they may have right to the tree of life, and may enter in through the gates into the city" (22:14).

The Lord is coming in judgment. Destruction is imminent. Fear God and Keep his commandments while you still can!

Brent Roper is a servant of God and member of Westboro Baptist Church, United States.

A Literal Reading of Revelation

Chris Griffin (United States)

The Revelation of John written in exile on Patmos is a fascinating prophetic work that draws the reader into future cataclysmic events that are the judgments of God, the culmination of this age, and the ushering in of the eternal state. Here, I offer a literal reading of Revelation and an identification and explanation of some pitfalls associated with other nonliteral readings.

An investigation of literal interpretation must precede a look at Revelation in particular. A literal approach to Scripture takes the text at face value, understanding that the writers used different writing styles while under the inspiration of the Holy Spirit; yet the entirety of Scripture is to be understood on a literal level—this approach must be practiced for the whole content of the Bible. For example, it is not acceptable to switch gears from a literal view to a symbolic view when focusing on a different genre of writing. In fact, to interpret it in a spiritual sense is dangerous and inconsistent at best. There are several reasons. First, it is inconsistent because other prophetic writings have come to pass in a literal, physical way. One may read the account of God's dealing with the serpent in Genesis 3 as allegorical, but the fact is that both the punishment to the serpent (crawling on his belly) and his ultimate destruction ("He shall bruise your head, and you shall bruise your heel," 3:15b) have been actualized in a literal, physical way. The same must be said about Messianic prophecy. Isaiah 53:5 uses language such as "But He was wounded for our transgressions; He was crushed for our iniquities; upon Him was the chastisement that brought us peace, and with His stripes we are healed." We can very clearly see that this prophecy came true in a literal way with the death of Jesus.

Another pitfall is that a spiritual, nonliteral interpretation allows all kinds of readings. It would be very difficult to verify or prove false any particular interpretation of Scripture. That is, without any standard of truth to measure interpretation, there would be no grounds for arguing any claim made about the meaning of a passage of Scripture.

It must be noted that John did use allegorical language when writing Revelation, as he attempted to describe what he saw; but there is no reason to think that what he saw will not come to pass in a tangible fashion. For example, there is no reason to conclude that the beast in Revelation 13 cannot or will not come to fruition in a literal way. The "beast rising up out of the sea" that John saw is no different from Daniel 7 where the "four beasts" represented real people and actual earthly kingdoms, such as Nebuchadnezzar and the Babylonians. Indeed, the beast of Revelation 13 is a man, as is evident at the end of the chapter, who is most likely the antichrist. Likewise, why is it difficult to conclude that the many types of judgments (natural disaster, etc.) outlined in Revelation will literally take place? If one believes wholeheartedly in a literal worldwide flood as the judgment of God (Genesis 6–8), why would one not read literally the final verdict of the Lord on an unrighteous world in Revelation?

The book of Revelation is often associated with the rapture of the church (1 Thessalonians 4:13–18) in which Christ comes back to take the church to be with Him.

We will be translated from here to there. It is a literal event that we hope for and should "comfort one another" with these words. This concept is not foreign. In the Old Testament, we read that the translation of Enoch was a literal event as was that of Elijah. There is no reason to debate then, whether or not God could orchestrate a global translation of the church as He did with these individuals. If a spiritualist holds that the future events are of a spiritual nature, then why the physical, bodily resurrection of Jesus? The answer is simple. The prophecies and promises of God are not spiritual, but literal. The fact is that God is consistent in His purpose and writing of Scripture. It does not make logical sense that in the first 65 books of the Bible all prophecy would come to literal fulfillment (as it did), and then in the Bible's final book, prophecy would suddenly change to a spiritual fulfillment. Thus, the reader of Revelation should come to the conclusion that the events of the book will come to a literal completion in some way, shape, or form, even if the reader does not understand precisely how they will happen.

Finally, there are many spiritual truths contained within the Bible, and the writers use many methods to express those truths, including the use of symbolic, allegorical language. But I believe that even this type of language results, more often than not, in a physical fulfillment. There is no doubt that God used the unique abilities of each writer to accomplish His Word, including different writing styles. But my view is that a literal reading of Scripture should be the norm, and any secondary approach should not precede, but rather follow it.

Chris Griffin (B.A., MRE) is a Second Lieutenant and Chaplain Candidate in the National Guard, United States.

QUESTIONS

1. Why is it important for Smith to argue for the androgyny of the Lamb? Are there unintended negative consequences of this reading?
2. Compare the countercultural aspects of Goths with the countercultural aspects of the biblical text. What is your reaction to the association of the United States with Babylon?
3. Assess Roper's reading approach and rhetoric. What critiques might be offered?
4. How might one challenge Griffin's arguments for a literal reading of Revelation?

CHAPTER 22

REVELATION (PART II)

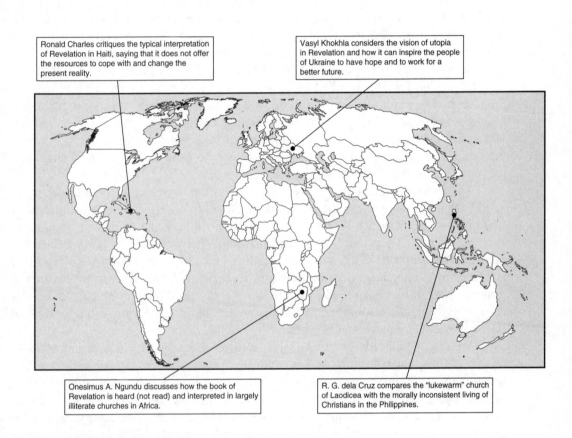

Ronald Charles critiques the typical interpretation of Revelation in Haiti, saying that it does not offer the resources to cope with and change the present reality.

Vasyl Khokhla considers the vision of utopia in Revelation and how it can inspire the people of Ukraine to have hope and to work for a better future.

Onesimus A. Ngundu discusses how the book of Revelation is heard (not read) and interpreted in largely illiterate churches in Africa.

R. G. dela Cruz compares the "lukewarm" church of Laodicea with the morally inconsistent living of Christians in the Philippines.

READINGS

Interpreting Revelation in Illiterate Churches in Africa
Onesimus A. Ngundu

Ukraine and the Vision of Utopia in Revelation
Vasyl Khokhla

A Critique of the Interpretation of Revelation in Haiti
Ronald Charles

The "Lukewarm" Church and Christians in the Philippines
R. G. dela Cruz

INTERPRETING REVELATION IN ILLITERATE
CHURCHES IN AFRICA

Onesimus A. Ngundu (Zimbabwe)

Reading and studying the book of Revelation is a privilege that the original audience did not have. They had to take it all in aurally, probably in more than one hearing (1:3). The book of Revelation was designed to be read aloud in a congregational setting since it was sent to seven churches (1:11). *The one who reads* reflects the early form of worship where a reader would read the Scriptures aloud on the Lord's Day. At that time, only the reader had a copy of the letter or of a particular Old Testament book.

Revelation 1:3 declares the blessedness of the one who reads the book or letter of Revelation to a congregation and of those who *hear* it and take its message to heart. We assume that the original recipients understood the message of the book of Revelation that was read to them because they were encouraged to "*keep* what is written in it." Logically, they could only rightly keep or obey what they would have understood read aloud and interpreted to them at their Christian gatherings.

As someone involved in theological education and church ministry in the Majority World (a much more appropriate term than "Third World"), I can testify that most Christians in the Majority World do not possess a Bible, Bible commentaries, or any Bible study tools. They simply cannot afford them. As I was growing up in a Christian home in rural Zimbabwe, the only Bible reading I ever heard and listened to was either at school or at church services on Sundays. Even when I later became a Christian at a mission boarding high school, I could not afford one. Thus, most Africans totally depend on the public reading and preaching of the Bible at places of worship for biblical instruction and spiritual encouragement.

An African Initiated Church (AIC) is one started independently in Africa by Africans and not by missionaries from another continent. There are thousands of such churches (more than 10,000 in South Africa alone) and each one has its own characteristics. At a typical open-air AIC worship service (AICs prefer open-air gatherings instead of church buildings), the designated Scripture reader stands in front of the congregation next to the leader or preacher. After reading each verse, the reader pauses to allow the leader to interpret the text. Ordinary members, most of them illiterate, totally depend on biblical instruction from what they hear at such worship gatherings.

Indeed, illiteracy continues to plague Africa. In sub-Saharan Africa, primary school enrollment has declined from 58 percent to 50 percent because members of the AICs deny their children school education. They also deny them any hospital treatment or immunization. There are two basic reasons for this. First, AICs have always been suspicious of white missionaries, their teachings, and their motives for establishing institutions in Africa. It was Western mission organizations which introduced school education, hospitals, and clinics in the European colonies in Africa. Second, AICs, as "Spirit Churches," believe that the Holy Spirit is the only teacher of all people. They strongly believe that they and their children only need God (or the Holy Spirit) as their teacher. They try to pattern their lifestyle after that of the children of Israel: no schools, no hospitals, and so forth. Men in AICs mostly wear sandals or sometimes walk barefoot. Their religious practices are based on Old Testament laws and practices. Remarkably, they are the fastest growing church group in Africa today.

Members of AICs unquestionably look up to their spiritual leaders as prophets or messengers of God. They believe that just as the children of Israel heard from God through Moses and the prophets, they too can hear from God through their leaders as they listen to them read and interpret the Word of God.

The character of God who initially revealed the message of Revelation to Jesus Christ who communicated that message to the seven churches in Asia Minor through John should lead us to believe that the message was intended to be understood especially by its original recipients who were apparently quite familiar with apocalyptic literature. It is always good to keep in mind that the literary genre of any literature is determined by its intended recipients. In other words, the original recipients, unlike us today, were familiar with the apocalyptic language and symbols that characterize the book of Revelation. The frustration and confusion we all experience in trying to figure out the meaning of Revelation's symbolism and imagery results from the fact that we are far removed from the time and place when the use of apocalyptic genre was a common practice.

Apocalypses typically contain curious visions whose meaning is not clear until they are explained, usually by an angelic personage. Often the whole apocalypse depends on the contribution made by the heavenly guide. It is not unusual to have God himself pictured as contributing to the apocalyptic message. In the book of Revelation this kind of explanation appears occasionally. For example, in 17:7 an angel explains the mystery of the scarlet woman and the beast on which she rides. But the general practice is simply to narrate the vision and to allow the hearer or reader to work out the meaning. This is where the challenge for any modern reader of Revelation lies.

It is here that AICs leaders and preachers would benefit from some form of theological education and sound Bible commentaries if they are to correctly interpret the symbolism that characterizes the book of Revelation and other apocalyptic sections of the bible. Instead, the leaders believe that their insight is instantaneously God-given as they confidently assign some weird meaning to symbols and images of Revelation. Unfortunately, such imaginative interpretation of apocalyptic literature results in wrong views of the end-times (eschatology).

The purpose of Revelation is stated in 22:6–20. It is to encourage Christians to remain faithful until the end, even if it means martyrdom, since they will also be raised from the dead at the second coming of Christ and live with him in the eternal new kingdom. The focus on Jesus Christ's triumph over death through his glorious resurrection means that Revelation is a book that has far more to say about the exercise of power than about the manifestation of divine love. Divine power is demonstrated throughout the book, even in the vindication of the Lamb who was a victim. It is that power of unmasking everything that runs like a thread throughout the vision of the book.

Indeed, although AIC leaders may offer for their (mostly illiterate) congregations interpretations of Revelation that are uninformed, they nonetheless certainly find encouragement in God's ultimate victory over suffering, sickness, and death. It is quite common to hear them sing in their Sunday worship services choruses and hymns that exalt the all-powerful and almighty God as portrayed in the book of Revelation.

Onesimus A. Ngundu (Ph.D., University of Cambridge; Th.D., Dallas Theological Seminary) is currently a Research Assistant at the University of Cambridge, England.

UKRAINE AND THE VISION OF UTOPIA IN REVELATION
Vasyl Khokhla (Ukraine)

Throughout the ages, people have nurtured the hopes for the ideal, for the perfect, for the high and exalted. Concepts such as democracy, rule of law, peace, and prosperity have been considered as worthwhile aims for the evolvement of steady and prosperous societies. The current climate of "globalization" embodies the ideas of universal peace and harmony. Although such concepts and ideals are unattainable in their pure forms, it does not, and should not, stop people from hoping, believing, and aspiring toward these praiseworthy goals.

A similar idea can be found in the apocalyptic book of Revelation, particularly in its final chapters which describe the ultimate victory of God and the coming of God's new kingdom. It is a dramatic vision in which God "will wipe away every tear" where there will be "no more death or mourning or crying or pain" because the "old order of things has passed away" and God is "making all things new" (21:3–5). Life in the "new Jerusalem" will indeed be one where there is no thirst (21:6), no evil (21:8; 22:15), no darkness (21:25; 22:5), and no death (22:5, 17). This is utopia—a perfect place. And isn't this a picture of what people are aspiring to today? Scientists are revolutionizing their methods of study and research to invent the cure for every kind of disease and ailment; ultimately, they desire to reverse the aging process so that we can conquer death. People are weary of war; they want peace and security. They fight crime, corruption, and other forms of evil. The United Nations, for example, has put forth Millennium Development Goals, one of the aims of which is to eradicate abject poverty by 2015.

But yet for many countries, including my native Ukraine, such a vision remains far from reality. One of the declared goals of Ukraine is to join the European Union (EU), which the people believe will help to alleviate the ills of the notorious era of Soviet rule. Yet, Ukraine has been unable to meet these objectives. Numerous problems continue to exist within Ukraine, preventing its acceptance into the EU. Political corruption is rampant. Politicians are dishonest, constantly scheming to increase their own power and wealth at the expense of the people. The legal system is equally bad, with its fraudulent law enforcement and unfair court system. Many social problems are prevalent—including widespread alcoholism as people try to escape the dreary reality. In fact, according to the

Corruption Perception Index by the renowned Transparency International, Ukraine is rated 2.4 (on a scale from 1 to 10, with 1 being most corrupt); it shares its place with such countries as Nigeria, Sierra Leone, and Togo.

When we read Revelation, we find that there are certain types of people who are left out of God's kingdom—they must be expelled if the utopian vision is to become a reality. These are the cowards, the immoral, the murders, idolaters, liars, and all those who love and practice falsehood (21:8; 22:15). Might we say that it is these types of people in Ukraine—our corrupt leaders—who are preventing the amelioration of our government, of our nation, who are disabling our move toward a better society?

We can also ask if it's worthwhile for the Ukrainian citizenry to keep on hoping, or should all such goals and aspirations simply be abandoned as unattainable? Though the forces of evil are significant, the book of Revelation offers hope that one day Goodness and Truth will prevail. God wins. God destroys his wicked enemies (Rev. 19–20) and institutes an idyllic world for those who are on God's side. This can inspire and motivate the people of Ukraine not only to maintain hope for the future but to work diligently to "make everything new" (21:5), to follow the Rider on the White Horse (19:11) in the fight for political, economic, and social reforms.

Indeed, human striving for the ideal should not be abandoned since it is that compelling force which inspires people to constant improvement. Plato said that our ideas have the capacity to transcend the outside reality. He also advocated the idea that people can achieve their goals and live up to the high standards if they try to understand the things beyond the limits of the human mind. Even if we cannot achieve the ideal, our aim should be to approach it as closely as possible. In a similar vein, Albert Einstein is reported to have said, "Some people do not believe in miracles. I would rather be the one who does, for otherwise life would be very boring."

From my perspective as a Ukrainian now living in the United States, the United States became the land of opportunity because people did not lose their belief in success. They, we might say, pursued their vision of utopia in which each individual has a favorable opportunity at life, liberty, and happiness. Of course, the United States still faces many social problems, but it has attained a level of success that I hope my native Ukraine can also reach. The biggest difference between the two countries remains governmental structures. The United States has managed to make democracy work. It may not be perfect—as Winston Churchill once said, "Democracy is not the best form of government, but so far nothing better has been invented"—but it has brought a relatively high quality of life. The United States, I suspect, has done so in part because of their religious, specifically Christian, heritage. The United States has perceived themselves to be a place reminiscent of Revelation 21:3: "Now the dwelling of God is with men, and he will live with them. They will be his people, and God himself will be with them and be their God." As it says on American currency, "In God we trust." Perhaps this is at least part of the reason why America is much closer to the utopia of Revelation than Ukraine.

As someone who desires peace and prosperity in Ukraine, we should not abandon the hope we find in Revelation, even if true utopia will never be realized. To believe and pursue the vision of Revelation does not guarantee that it will become a reality, but it can inspire, motivate, and give the hope that is so much needed in Ukraine and many other places around the globe where murderers, liars, idolaters, and those who love and practice falsehood thwart the vision of utopia.

Vasyl Khokhla was born in Kalush in Western Ukraine; he is currently working on a law degree in Ukraine and a finance degree in the United States.

A Critique of the Interpretation of Revelation in Haiti

Ronald Charles (Haiti)

The mention of "Apocalypse" has a certain resonance in people's imagination. For those of us from the Third World it brings disturbing images of dictators, bloodshed, coups d'état, ecological disaster, boat people, and abject poverty. For many in Haiti, the Apocalypse is now. Famine, hurricanes, looting, violence, corruption, rioting, and prostitution characterize the daily nightmare of many poor in this small and impoverished country. Thus the question becomes, As a Haitian and as a Christian how can *I* read the book of Revelation *today*? I grew up in Haiti in a Baptist church and then, in my teenage years, moved to a Pentecostal church until I left the country in my late 20s to undertake graduate work, which I am now doing in biblical studies in Canada. The usual reading of the book of Revelation in Haiti that I am about to describe is what I grew up with, and it is this common, debilitating reading that is still the main—or the sole—reading of the book in the Haitian context.

The book of Revelation is written out of the experience of a minority in the colonized Roman Empire. It speaks of sufferings and of struggles with which people from the Third World are too familiar because their communities share with Revelation's addressees a longing for justice, for peace, and for the well-being of humanity. Although the text of Revelation is close at heart to Third World Christian communities, it is also interpreted in ways that are devastating in some Third World contexts. Haiti is a case in point.

Even as a "son of Haiti" myself, I regard it a strange place. It is difficult to comprehend its realities. Many people there live as if they were in a fantastic world where demons and angels, God and Satan, the living and the dead are not so far apart. This extraordinary existential condition makes the whole Haitian social reality fascinating and puzzling at the same time. The Apocalypse is now, but that does not stop Haitians from partying, laughing, dancing, and living with the reality of the supernatural, and to hope for a *demen miyò* (a tomorrow that is going to be better than today) because *Bondye bon* (God is good).

Reading the book of Revelation is an odd exercise for a Haitian. According to many of them, it's about God and Satan, angels and demons, battles and victories; all of which they have some familiarity with in real life. The typical interpretation of Revelation in Haiti is that we are living at the brink of time, that the end is beginning to dawn on our island of 9 million souls. As Christians we need to live a life pleasing to God and not miss the call of the last trumpets in order to ensure that we are caught up in the rapture of the church. There is usually a certain fancy about the idea of leaving the mess behind, of going to glory to live a life of security and of plenty. The usual thinking is that life is extremely difficult and the best way out is to project oneself into a blissful kind of future. The Lord will come to take his own in a sudden rapture, and the rest who did not live up to the biblical standards will be left behind. For those who did not make it to heaven at the rapture, they are to endure the great tribulation and wait until the battle of Armageddon for the final victory of God. Then, those who resisted the Antichrist during the terrible years will be rescued by God and be saved. Afterwards, a thousand years of worldwide peace and security will be ushered in under the Lordship and authority of Christ before the final release of Satan and the ultimate victory of God.

But there is also a second way in which the book of Revelation intersects with life in Haiti. In Protestant churches certain ambivalence has always existed within the in-groups as they see themselves and as they relate to the society at large. The typical social dynamic of internal class divisions based on income, culture, and race spills over in some large Protestant churches in Haiti that are situated mostly in Port-au-Prince (the capital city) to serve middle-class clienteles. Thus, just as Haitian society is greatly divided by political, economical, and even racial factions, so the church in Haiti is greatly divided by denominational divisions and rivalries.

Unfortunately this kind of "combat myth" mentality and horizontal violence as portrayed in Revelation is not far from the minds of many evangelical Christians in Haiti. The predominant mentality of many Protestant churches is that of *Pa m pi bon* (mine is better). The rejection of Christian groups perceived to be different and the diabolizing of other religions is a common and accepted phenomenon in most Christian churches in Haiti.

Many evangelical pastors have used violent language against the religion of Vodou and its practitioners. Many Vodou priests or *ougan* have been lynched, stoned, or burned alive and those horrible acts were perpetuated with the blessings of the church at large in Haiti. Many Haitian Christians (the so-called evangelicals with whom I am more familiar) take a certain pleasure in pointing to the cataclysmic destruction that will befall unbelievers. They divide the world between good and evil, between those anointed to act as agents of God battling the Antichrist, attacking hypocrites and castigating the corrupt, and those who act as agents of Satan. They have a clear agenda to send to hell all who do not share their readings of some particular texts. Usually, the language they use is one not only of exclusion, hatred, and fear, but also a call for apocalyptic violence, in short, the language of war reminiscent of Revelation.

Unfortunately, this common reading of Revelation in Haiti offers nothing empowering to change the present. This uninformed reading has the potential to keep Haiti in its apocalypse forever, while doing two kinds of damage. First, by insisting on a futuristic rapture, it can pacify a population that is otherwise known for its resistance. Second, the combat myth attitude directed against other groups with different religious sentiments can be fatal in a land that has experienced too much violence in its history. It is unfortunate that many in the Christian church in Haiti are caught up in endless debates about the end-times, and about identifying who the Antichrist might be, and are looking at world events to figure out if the time of the rapture is close or not. What is important in this kind of reading is not to worry about global warming, ecological disaster, or any urgent matter that is menacing our lives today, but to hide in a spiritual cocoon in order not to face the overwhelming present realities.

The overall message of the book of Revelation offers an alternative in terms of imagination and faith for the purpose of facing the practical problems of marginalized groups in the here and now (not the hereafter). By renewing his audience's imagination, the writer of Revelation aims to create a new reality to help his communities cope with the uncertainties of the present. Revelation is, in this sense, a call to resistance, to perseverance in the time of persecution, and to faithfulness to God and to Jesus Christ. Revelation can speak comfort to the people of faith in Haiti so that they can imagine, as the text had aimed to produce for the first recipients, a new reality in opposition to the world of the present in its crisis. Indeed, a different reading offers hope for the apocalyptic situation in Haiti, not just for tomorrow, but for today also. We can take this reading/hearing and be empowered by it for social, political, and economic changes now.

Ronald Charles is a Ph.D. candidate in the Department and Centre for the Study of Religion at University of Toronto, Ontario, Canada; he spent most of his early life in Haiti.

The "Lukewarm" Church and Christians in the Philippines

R. G. dela Cruz (Philippines)

The Philippines is a predominately Christian nation, with more than 90 percent of its population belonging to the Christian faith. But there is a fracture between what we say and what we do. The phrase "split-level Christianity" as it applies to Filipino Christian spirituality and values was first articulated by Jesuit priest Jaime Bulatao in the mid-1960s. The "split" is between what is expected and required of Christians and what is commonly accepted in Filipino culture and politics. This so-called "split-level" Christian value of the Filipinos is reminiscent of Revelation 3:14–22 where the Church of Laodicea is judged for being neither hot nor cold. Split-level Christianity results in a country that, like the Laodiceans, is "lukewarm": We do not live like a people who are Christians.

Filipinos have gone through many difficulties as a people. During the Spanish, American, and Japanese colonizations, the Filipinos were oppressed. After gaining independence immediately after World War II, the new state struggled to survive. There was great effort exerted by the people to preserve democracy when the Martial Law was declared. Then the People Power of the EDSA Revolution was successful in a peaceful revolt to bring back democracy. Today, the Philippines are seen by many as the "ill person" of the region. Many Filipinos see themselves as people in need of healing. The nation is disadvantaged in globalization. The impoverished population struggles to survive daily; there is displacement of various ethnicities. One of the ways to survive is for Filipinos to migrate and become OFWs (Overseas Filipino Workers) in different parts of the world. For many, migration is not a luxury; it is a necessity to survive. Thus, it is common to hear about Filipinos being exploited. To witness suffering is common to Filipino eyes. There is a big gap between the wealthy and the underprivileged.

Filipino religiosity is formed by these national encounters of domination and change. Naturally, religion, culture, and politics are intertwined. But there are far too many problems that exist in the Philippines—problems that could be overcome if Christian principles and ethics were followed, instead of allowing "lukewarm" values and morality to continue. For example, when Filipino politicians claim in their campaigns that they are *makadios*, *makabayan*, *makatao* (godly or pious, patriotic or nationalistic, humane or humanitarian), they are sincere. And yet they do not commonly see graft (abuse of power for personal gain) and corruption as wrong; rather, politicians and voters tend to see graft and corruption as unavoidable ingredients of politics. No administration in the Philippine government has solved this problem. But since we are a Christian nation—again, over 90 percent of the population claims they are Catholic or Protestant—something must be done.

The problem for Filipino Christianity is that their lukewarmness, their inconsistency, has become so ingrained in them that they are no longer conscious of it. They have for so long accepted so much that flies in the face of their Christian ideals and values that they fail to perceive the tension. It's part of the culture. It's taken for granted, accepted as the norm.

In light of this tension, Revelation 3:14–22 can be appropriated and read to challenge Filipinos in general to clear up the split and contribute positively to Filipino values. It is well recognized by Filipinos that confronting the split-level attitude is necessary to bring positive orderliness in the Philippine society. Revelation 3:22 is confrontational: "He who has an ear, let him hear what the Spirit says to the churches." There is no mincing of words. It is a straight rebuke of their lukewarm attitude. There is nothing positive said about the Laodiceans. The heavenly Christ says, "I know your works: you are neither cold nor hot. Would that you were either cold or hot! So, because you are lukewarm, and neither hot nor cold, I will spit you out of my mouth" (3:15–16). Repentance and discipline are necessary to deal with the problem: "Those whom I love, I reprove and discipline, so be zealous and repent" (v. 19).

The split-level value system must be addressed head-on. Filipinos must deal with the issue by separating cultural tradition from religious convictions. Establishing a firm separation is the key step toward a solution. When this happens, there is a deliverance from sickness and corruption in society by allowing the values of the heavenly Christ to take over: "Behold, I stand at the door and knock. If anyone hears my voice and opens the door, I will come in to him and eat with him, and he with me" (v. 20). The supper echoes the idea of the Lord's Supper where the continuing and conscious presence of Christ is both symbolized and remembered. There is a promise of harmony and victory (v. 21) for the Filipino who would dine with the heavenly Christ and allow him to take control based on his principles and values.

R. G. dela Cruz is Lecturer at Asia Pacific Theological Seminary in Baguio City, Philippines; he is an ordained minister of the South Central Cordillera District Council of the Philippines General Council of the Assemblies of God.

QUESTIONS

1. Try listening to a few chapters of Revelation. How is the listening experience different from reading the text?

2. Compare the peace and utopia described in Revelation to that desired by Khokhla for Ukraine.

3. Does the biblical text support the use of violence against practitioners of other religions? Does it offer hope for coping with present realities of suffering and evil?

4. What is the "firm separation" dela Cruz envisions as the solution to "split-level Christianity"?

CREDITS

Chapter 1: pp. 2, 3; Translated by Abdullah Yusaf Ali *The Koran* [Wordsworth, 2001]; p. 5; Reprinted by permission from The Taoist Experience by Livia Kohn, the State University of New York Press ©1993, State University of New York. All rights reserved; p. 10; Frederick Buechner, *Wishful Thinking*.

Chapter 2: pp. 14, 15; Accra Confession. *World Alliance of Reformed Churches* [2004].

Chapter 4: p. 34 [Bangalore: TPI, 2007], 488; pp. 37, 38; *New Revised Standard Version Bible*, copyright 1989, Division of Christian Education of the National Council of the Churches of Christ in the United States of America. Used by permission. All rights reserved.

Chapter 5: p. 43; *New Revised Standard Version Bible*, copyright 1989, Division of Christian Education of the National Council of the Churches of Christ in the United States of America. Used by permission. All rights reserved.

Chapter 7: pp. 63, 64; Abdullah Yusuf Ali. *The Koran* [Wordsworth, 2001]; p. 66; *New Revised Standard Version Bible*, copyright 1989, Division of Christian Education of the National Council of the Churches of Christ in the United States of America. Used by permission. All rights reserved.

Chapter 8: pp. 70, 78, 79; *New Revised Standard Version Bible*, copyright 1989, Division of Christian Education of the National Council of the Churches of Christ in the United States of America. Used by permission. All rights reserved; p. 71; Muhammed Ibn Ismaiel Al-Bukhari. *The Sahih of Imam Bukhari*. Translated by Muhammad M. Khan [Houston: Dar-us-Salam, 1997]; p. 72; *Chinese Proverb*. Translated by the author; p. 78; Edwards, Jonathan. *Sinners in the Hands of an Angry God*, 1741.

Chapter 9: p. 87; *Kitab-i-Iqan: The Book of Certitude*, Translated by Shoghi Effendi [Wilmette, Illinois: USA Baha'i Publishing Trust, 1989]; p. 89; *New Revised Standard Version Bible*, copyright 1989, Division of Christian Education of the National Council of the Churches of Christ in the United States of America. Used by permission. All rights reserved.

Chapter 11: p. 111 ; *The Political Dictionary* [Pyongyang: Social Science Publishing, 1973].

Chapter 12: pp. 120, 121; *New Revised Standard Version Bible*, copyright 1989, Division of Christian Education of the National Council of the Churches of Christ in the United States of America. Used by permission. All rights reserved.

Chapter 14: p. 134; *Re-reading Paul: A Guidelines for Christian Clergy and Teachers*. Edited by Council of Christians and Jews [Victoria, Australia, 1995]. Published by www.jcrelations.net; p. 142; *New Revised Standard Version Bible*, copyright 1989, Division of Christian Education of the National Council of the Churches of Christ in the United States of America. Used by permission. All rights reserved.

Chapter 17: p. 166; The Social Science Publisher, *The Political Dictionary* [Pyongyang: The Social Science Publisher, 1973]; pp. 167, 169; *New Revised Standard Version Bible*, copyright 1989, Division of Christian Education of the National Council of the Churches of Christ in the United States of America. Used by permission. All rights reserved; p. 168; *Theology for the Community of God* [Grand Rapids: Eerdmans, 1994]. 233; p. 169; Eugene Peterson. *The Message Bible*; p. 170; C. S. Lewis. *The Screwtape Letters* [New York: Macmillan, 1961].

Chapter 18: p. 178; *Griffiths A New Vision of Reality: Western Science, Eastern Mysticism and Christian faith* [Springfield, IL: Templegate, 1990], 122; p. 179; *Return to the Center* [Springfield, IL: Templegate, 2002], 60–61; p. 179; Barbara Stoler Miller, *The Bhagavad-Gita*;(New York Bantam, 2004) p. 179; Griffiths, *Return to the Center*, 74; p. 180; *New Revised Standard Version Bible*, copyright 1989, Division of Christian Education of the National Council of the Churches of Christ in the United States of America. Used by permission. All rights reserved ; p. 181. *Kitab-i-Iqan: The Book of Certitude*, Translated by Shoghi Effendi [Wilmette, Illinois: USA Baha'i Publishing Trust, 1989]

Chapter 21: pp. 204, 205, 210, and 211; *New Revised Standard Version Bible*, copyright 1989, Division of Christian Education of the National Council of the Churches of Christ in the United States of America. Used by permission. All rights reserved.

Chapter 22: p. 217; Albert Einstein; p. 217; Winston Churchill.